WRITERS IN CONVERSATION

Page	Author
7	NAOMI ALDERMAN AND ANDREW COWAN
27	DAVID ALMOND AND CHARLIE HIGSON
45	TASH AW
65	VINCE CABLE
91	AMIT CHAUDHURI
109	TRACY CHEVALIER AND GLENN PATTERSON
129	BERNARD CORNWELL
145	RICHARD DAWKINS
161	MARGARET DRABBLE AND EIMEAR MCBRIDE
183	STEPHEN FRY
205	DAVID HARE
225	IAN MCEWAN
243	DAVID MITCHELL
261	PAUL NURSE AND IAN MCEWAN
279	JANE SMILEY
295	ROSE TREMAIN
313	DAVID VANN AND LAWRENCE NORFOLK
335	VENDELA VIDA AND EMMA HEALEY

Published in association with
THE ARTHUR MILLER CENTRE
FOR AMERICAN STUDIES

WRITERS IN CONVERSATION
WITH CHRISTOPHER BIGSBY
VOLUME VI

NAOMI ALDERMAN   ANDREW COWAN

Naomi Alderman was born in London in 1974. She read Politics, Philosophy and Economics at Oxford University, subsequently completing an MA in Creative Writing at the University of East Anglia (UEA). Her first novel, *Disobedience* (2006) won the Orange Award for New Writers and has been translated into ten languages. Her second novel, *The Lessons*, was published in 2010, followed two years later by *The Liars' Gospel*. She has also written online games and in 2013 was named one of Granta's Best of Young British Novelists.

Andrew Cowan was born in Corby, Northamptonshire, in 1960. He is a graduate of UEA and a product of UEA's Creative Writing programme. He later became Director of that same programme where he is currently a Professor. His first novel, *Pig* (1994), won a Betty Trask Award, the *Sunday Times* Young Writer of the Year Award, the Author's Club First Novel Award, a Scottish Arts Council Book Award and the Ruth Madden Memorial Award. Subsequent novels include *Common Ground* (1996), *Crustaceans* (2000), *What I Know* (2005) and *Worthless Men* (2013). He is also the author of *The Art of Writing Fiction* (2011).

This interview was conducted on October 9, 2013.

BIGSBY Naomi, you were born into an Orthodox Jewish family, an area of life about which I know nothing, as evidenced by the fact that I had no idea that apparently on the Sabbath you are not allowed to tear toilet paper. Is there such a thing as un-perforated Jewish toilet paper?

ALDERMAN All things have been thought of in the universe of the Orthodox Jews. There is always a way to deal with things. You will have seen the unperforated toilet paper you can get in supermarkets. It comes in boxes with a little slot and you pull it out. I don't know who it is supposed to be for apart from Orthodox Jews, but I know they sell it. Maybe its also for people who have toilet-paper-tearing phobia, but you can get it. When we were at university, the other Orthodox Jews and I, it was hard to come by this cut toilet paper so before the Sabbath we used to rip up toilet paper for ourselves. It's the kind of religion that takes dedication. There is none of this going to church once a week for an hour, singing some songs. The word I am looking for is 'stark', which means really serious. It is stark! I should say I am not an Orthodox Jew any more but after years of therapy I realised that although I can decide now not to be an Orthodox Jew, I could never decide not to have been one. So that will always be a part of my life. The thing that really annoyed me, one of the many things that really annoyed me about it, was that it is misogynist, racist and homophobic.

BIGSBY And I learned from your first novel that there is even a prayer that men say that begins, 'thank God I wasn't born a woman.'

ALDERMAN The rabbis say that if a man teaches his daughter Talmud it is as if he taught her a word that means something like whorishness. The reason for this is that we are taught that the punishment for being an adulteress can be fended off by the merit of having learnt Talmud. So one rabbi says, 'if you teach them all Talmud then they are just going to go and have sex with everybody because they will know there will be no punishment,' though there are people who are teaching women Talmud these days because that is clearly not the meaning of it.

BIGSBY   And the prayer?

ALDERMAN   My brother and I grew up saying prayers every morning. Men say, 'Thank you God for not making me a woman.' Women say, 'Thank you God for making me according to your will.' When I wrote this in my novel, I had grown up saying this so I thought it was just normal, in the way that you think whatever is in your childhood is just normal. I put it in a piece I handed to my workshop here at UEA and they had these really extreme reactions, which was really interesting to me. One person had circled it in red and written across the whole page, 'This makes me want to punch someone in the face.' I stopped being an Orthodox Jew after I finished this novel so I suspect that was part of my process.

BIGSBY   You began writing a novel when you were in your teens.

ALDERMAN   Yes, at fourteen or fifteen. I got about three chapters in. It was a young adult fantasy about a girl who discovers she can manipulate probability, which was not a terrible idea but I had no idea where to go with it.

BIGSBY   You came from a family where there were many books around. In fact there were writers in your family.

ALDERMAN   My dad is a historian, so he was publishing books when I was growing up, which I definitely think is a help because you see that a book is written by a human and not produced by some miraculous heavenly process. My mother's father had been a children's writer while my mother is herself an artist, so, yes, there was all that creative stuff going around in the family. My auntie had won a competition run by the Young Vic when she was sixteen, which is probably why I started when I was fifteen, thinking this was time to get going. She had won a playwriting award and had a play put on at the Young Vic and then somehow, overawed by this, had never written again. So that is a warning!

BIGSBY   Andrew, in contrast, you came from a working class background.

COWAN My dad was a labourer in Corby steelworks and my mum was the receptionist in Corby Swimming Pool which should have qualified me to become a steel worker and a first rate swimmer. I became neither. Actually, I became quite phobic about swimming pools and the smell of chlorine.

BIGSBY And there were no books in your house.

COWAN No, there were no books in our house, or in the houses of anyone I knew. There were no books in the homes of any of my relatives, so the idea of growing up to become a writer was as unlikely as growing up to be an astronaut. It was never something I thought I might one day be. I grew up in an industrial new town and the expectation was that anyone growing up in Corby in the 1960s, if they were male, would follow their dads into the works. So the expectation, that I adopted from my parents and everyone around me, was that, being a bright boy, I would ultimately do an apprenticeship and become a fitter or something.

BIGSBY But you also wrote a story when you were young.

COWAN I was good at English and was adopted by concerned English teachers who wanted me not to waste my potential. I was definitely encouraged by my English teachers to write but I certainly wouldn't do it in my spare time. I came onto the MA at UEA somewhat earlier than Naomi, possibly two decades before Naomi, in 1984/85. The only reason I applied to do the Creative Writing MA was because I had done an undergraduate degree here and loved UEA and Norwich. I went back to Corby after graduation just as the steelworks was closed and Corby had become a ghost town so I was just terribly nostalgic for being a student. I wanted to come back to university and at that time the easiest programme to get onto was creative writing. There were just ten students in my year and I think they had had just eleven applications, so that is how I got onto that programme. Having achieved that, and got onto the programme, I barely wrote anything. I didn't very often come onto the campus and it seemed to confirm for me that I wasn't a writer and never would be. So I didn't then write anything for the following two years.

BIGSBY Coming from that background, did you feel a sense of insecurity?

COWAN Yes, I did, and I think I haven't shaken it off. There's a sense in which the language precedes me, that it is owned by the people who have, through the generations, come to university and become writers and gone into the professions, and so on. When I arrived as an eighteen-year-old to do my undergraduate degree I did feel a bit overawed and very insecure. I felt that what I was doing in completing my BA was acquiring a language which wasn't mine. I was learning a second language and always felt that in a way I was trespassing. It was almost as though the canon that preceded me belonged to someone else and that I would get chased off. I would get found out. Ever since I have had this feeling of inauthenticity when writing, as if I shouldn't be doing it and sooner or later someone is going to point out that fact to me and I will be found out.

BIGSBY So you were a reluctant writer on your MA course, not even bothering to turn up when the literary agents and publishers visited.

COWAN No. I have a little game that I play with myself when I am writing which is that I continue to pretend nobody is going to read it. That is the only way for me. I adopt a slightly naive mindset. That seems to be the only way, just to write it for myself, though that wasn't what I did when I was on the MA.

BIGSBY Before your MA, Naomi, you went to Oxford?
ALDERMAN I did.

BIGSBY But not to read literature.
ALDERMAN No, unlike you, Andrew, I had very off-putting English teachers. I asked my English teacher if she thought I would be able to go to Oxford to do English and she said, 'Oh, no, you wouldn't get in.' So I applied to do philosophy and got in for that!

BIGSBY Philosophy, Politics and Economics: PPE?

ALDERMAN Yes, PPE. I ended up doing philosophy. It is sort of ridiculous to me now that I have got a degree with economics in the title. All I basically know is that when demand goes up the price also goes up, that's right isn't it, and when demand goes down the price goes down.

BIGSBY But you did write a novel at the end of your first year at Oxford.

ALDERMAN I did. I wrote a novel. It is still in a drawer in my parents' house, all printed out. It wasn't very good but I was pleased to have it finished. I remember exactly how I did it. We had a long vacation and I calculated that I had seventy or eighty days. I wrote a thousand words every day except for Saturdays, which was the Sabbath.

BIGSBY Toilet paper!

ALDERMAN Toilet paper. Exactly. No writing, nothing electrical! But then on Saturday I would read over what I had done over the course of the week and then edit on Saturday night.

BIGSBY So you walked away from that novel?

ALDERMAN Yes. I went into a law firm for six years because I thought I should do something sensible.

BIGSBY But something very disturbing and transforming happened because you were in New York at the time of 9/11.

ALDERMAN I worked for four years at this law firm in London and then I tried to leave but they said 'Where would you like to go?' These big law firms have lots of things to offer to keep you around and I wanted to go to New York so they seconded me to the New York office which was very interesting, nice. I was in the office at eight o'clock in the morning, as I always was to catch the people in London, to be able to talk to them, and, yes, I was there on the morning of 9/11. I remember one of the secretaries coming into my office sometime just before nine o'clock saying a plane has gone into the World Trade Center. I thought it was a small plane or something and it was briefly very exciting. I was thinking, 'Oh, this won't be a normal work day.' Then we looked out of the conference room window. We had the television on and we could see the towers burning out of the conference room window but where it was enlarged on the TV it was small out of the window.

For a time it seemed as though everything would be all right until they actually fell. You just thought that it might take months to repair. A guy on the radio called into the TV station saying, 'I am on the hundredth floor but the firemen are coming up and they are going to get us.' But as he was on the phone, the towers went! So I thought to myself, not immediately, not that day but in the weeks that followed – people don't really know that it went on for months, the fire smouldering underneath the towers for about five months and the plastic smell every time the wind blew – and I bet there were people in that building who were thinking the same thing, that 'I will just do this job for another few years and then I will go and write the novel that I always meant to write.' So I gave up my job and came to UEA like a refugee, a refugee from the law, turning up at the gates of literature going 'Will you have me?'

BIGSBY What do you remember of your time here at UEA working on your Creative Writing MA?

ALDERMAN I had a great time when I was here in the last couple of months when I was working on my novel, in that period where you get to work on it and nobody else is reading it. I used to go into the library every day, sign myself out a carrel and write for however long it was and then go home. Now I find whenever I go into that library, whatever else is going on, I just start writing. It is amazing. It makes me want to come back and live in Norwich just for the library because how else do you make yourself write?

BIGSBY Andrew, though you didn't write a novel while you were on the MA, and it would be ten years before your first appeared, in fact you had been working on it for six years.

COWAN I was writing it for a while, wasn't I? What

happened immediately afterwards is that I just continued this process of drift, post-adolescent drift. I thought, what do I do now? I don't have a job in the steelworks. I have a qualification but I don't seem to have any inclination to do a proper job. So I did temporary, crap, jobs. I did cleaning. I actually cleaned the lavatories in the Ziggurats at UEA (university residences), and showers, picking pubic hairs out of the shower stalls, and I was signing on for benefits. I had to go to City Hall to sign some forms to get my housing benefit and I was on a bicycle. It was as I was chaining my bicycle up outside City Hall – this is about six months after graduation – that I met a little old man who was chaining up his bike too. We got into a conversation about bikes. The little old man was called Snowy and he told me that he was eighty years old and had just completed a Lands End to John O'Groats charity cycle ride, which then led him to reminisce about being in a cycle club in Norwich in the twenties and that took him back to being in a boxing club in Norwich during the First World War. As a fourteen year old he was boxing in the back room of a pub on Magdalene Street and was full of these stories.

We stood there, opposite City Hall, chatting. I had to go in and sign my forms and he had business too but he invited me round to his house on Sunday to hear more. I went, and he kind of adopted me as a surrogate grandson. I would go every Sunday. He had a part-time job crushing boxes in a small supermarket on Magdalen Street and was allowed to take home the crushed cans of soup and beans and so on, so every week I would go and see him on Sunday, hear more of his life story, and he would give me some cans of baked beans to take back to my home, which I shared with a bunch of hippies. So we lived off Snowy's beans and soup but I was thinking, as I was listening to Snowy, that this shouldn't be lost, it shouldn't only be me who hears this and knows this stuff. So I applied to charities in Norwich for funds to buy a tape-recorder, cassette tapes, a typewriter and paper and eventually acquired enough money to buy these and I became an amateur oral historian. Snowy then put me onto another person who put me onto another and this became something I did. It was like writing. I went out and I did this research in the field, spoke to old people about their life histories and then brought the tapes home and transcribed them.

Each side of C90 took five hours to transcribe and this typing business felt so like writing I was finally able to convince myself I was actually a writer. I was just typing out other people's words but out of that I was able to persuade a project on King Street, called the Community Workshop, which offered facilities for the unemployed to make things and fix things, to sponsor me. I became a Community Programme scheme all on my own. They put me in a semi-derelict building and for two years I was typing up people's life stories. Then the government pulled the plug on that, so suddenly I was unemployed. I moved to Glasgow just for a change of scene. It was there I trained to be a librarian and became a school librarian.

BIGSBY You did, however, write your first novel, though it wasn't a case of sending it off to an agent followed by instant success.

COWAN No. I began it towards the end of this oral history project because I suddenly had an idea. Three things came together: the loss of a relationship, a grandfather, the loss of my home town – it was a ghost town – and this sense of loss in the sense of suddenly having no moorings. I was encouraged to start writing as a way of retrieving a sense of self and wholeness, so it was very fraught. There was a lot riding on this novel, which made it impossibly hard for me to put any word on the page and to feel secure or satisfied with it, or about it, and so I made really painfully slow progress. It took me a year to write the first twelve pages and that went on for two or three years Then I did that Diploma in Librarianship, which took nine months, so I didn't write a word of this for nine months. When I went back to it, rather than pick up where I left off I started typing it all out, word for word, from the beginning, to convince myself again that I was a writer. So all the time I am self-sabotaging and delaying the day when it will finally be finished and presented to publishers and agents and risk rejection.

Actually what happened was nothing but rejection. For almost a year I was sending it out from our flat in

Glasgow to London literary agents and publishers and waiting three or four months for the rejection to arrive. But in the course of that year I sent it, as a manuscript, to the Betty Trask Awards and forgot about it completely. Then, one morning, an envelope came through our letterbox in Glasgow saying, 'Come down to London. You have won a £7,000 Betty Trask Award.' I went down with a holdall of printouts of my novel and at the award ceremony collected business cards from various agents and publishers who all said they wanted to see my novel, that they would be so delighted to read it. The agents hoped they would be able to represent me; the publishers hoped they would be able to publish me, and of course these were all the people who had previously rejected me. I did go around London the next day dropping off copies of my book and eventually I went with an agent who hadn't had the opportunity previously to reject me and when she finally sorted out the candidates for publishing *Pig* there were three who had previously rejected me and one that hadn't, so I went with the one that hadn't.

BIGSBY And *Pig* then received a cascade of awards. Naomi, your experience was rather different because you produced *Disobedience* fairly soon after leaving?

ALDERMAN Yes, I finished the MA in September 2003, and the book was finished in May 2005, so not too long. There was a bit of a gap after finishing the MA when I couldn't make myself write at all for a few months and became a bit desperate. Then, I said to myself 'Right, this is it. What we are going to do is write every day.' That seems to be always the way it is with me. Either I am writing every day or I am not writing and I think you just have to accept that sort of thing about yourself. It's like you know you need a particular kind of exercise, or that grapes always give you indigestion. You just get to know yourself. I was working part-time for a children's charity and my publication story is really jammy. I am sorry. Writing the book was really hard, though. There was a lot of crying, but I never think a book is really done until I have wept bitter tears over it and gone, 'This is the worst thing that has ever been written in the world.' So! I reached the stage, at the end of May 2005, when I just thought it was the worst book that has ever been written in the history of the world.

I had won the David Higham Award at UEA, which was very exciting and amazing, and my agent, who is still my agent, took me out for lunch, which was a new thing, and said, 'We would love to represent you.' At that point I had four chapters done so I went 'yes please' and sent her the book thinking, well she can read it, she can tell me that it's terrible and then I will be free. I can just let it go like I had with my first book, which was terrible. She took it away on holiday and came back and said, 'It is great. We are sending it out to publishers across London on Friday,' and then she said, 'but you should expect to wait three months to hear anything.' So I had a great weekend. It was the last episode of that current season of *Doctor Who*, which, to me, was an important life marker, and my friends got married. Then I woke up on Monday morning thinking, 'now I have to wait three months,' but at 9.30 on Monday morning, Penguin called with an offer for it and that morning there were another two or three offers.

BIGSBY That first novel was well named *Disobedience* because, while funny, it was also a challenge to Orthodox Jews. How well did it go down with your family?

ALDERMAN Actually, my family were amazing. They are still Orthodox, and would much rather that I were still, but they are also intellectual.

BIGSBY So the lesbian part was all right with them?

ALDERMAN Everybody in my community already thought I was gay, which I am mostly not, a little bit – but mostly not. One might as well be honest about these things! But yes, the *Hendon Times* published a piece about me entitled 'Lesbian Author Speaks Out' and I phoned up and went, 'You didn't ask me that question, did you?' and the woman went, 'Oh, no. I am so sorry, but the editor insisted that you must be!' He has now gone to work for the *Daily Mail*.

BIGSBY This is a book which is not only funny about the Jewish community but is also about love.

ALDERMAN Just after the towers fell the man I was very much in love with told me that he was gay. It was a time a lot of people came out. They decided that they had to live more authentically. So you had people breaking up, or deciding to propose, or deciding that now is the right time to have a baby, or they must move out of the city. A lot of people changed their lives afterwards, I think, in exactly that instant way: 'Right, got to do something.' So quite a number of people that I knew in the Orthodox community came out within a few months of each other and I heard a lot of really painful stories, terrible things. Somebody that I knew had broken up with a partner who then became more religious and accused my friend of rape because he couldn't believe that he had slept with my friend or would have done so willingly because, obviously, being gay is evil. Somebody else I knew had been expelled from a woman's seminary because there was a suspicion she was sleeping with another girl. At the same time that I was thinking that I wanted to write something – all these stories were going on and it weighed heavily with me. I began to feel that I was somehow culpable because I was a part of this community and was supporting it with my membership and hadn't said anything or done anything about any of this. So, yes, there are funny bits in it, and I hope it's got a light touch, but it also seemed very serious to me. To be honest I started writing that book an Orthodox Jew and wasn't when I finished it.

BIGSBY You followed it with a book which might have come first in some ways because it was set in Oxford and is about the world you had encountered there. At its heart is a group of friends and it is very much concerned with the contamination of relationships by money and power.

ALDERMAN I think I was trying to explain myself to myself. Maybe this is what I do when I write. I had not had a good time at Oxford at all and I wanted to understand what had gone wrong. It seemed to me that there is something about the wealth and the beauty, and the way a place can communicate something to you so that you can't even realise your own unhappiness because you are in such a beautiful place and everyone is telling you that everything is brilliant and you are so lucky to be there. You become opaque, completely opaque to yourself. I wanted to write about that so the main character, James, becomes involved with this group of friends who seem on the surface extremely attractive and end up, in one case, literally punching him in the face, and in many cases metaphorically doing so. I suppose it's a metaphor for Oxford, if I am going to analyse my own work. It looks lovely but it turns out to divide you from yourself in certain important ways. I went back to my old college for a dinner recently because I thought, well, it has been getting on for twenty years so let's just see who I was at college. Someone involved with the college made a speech asking for money, as they do, and saying, 'We want this so that the college can continue to accept only the students it wants without government interference,' which means not the plebs because the government increasingly are saying we want you to be taking students from state schools. Phew!!

BIGSBY There couldn't be a greater contrast, Andrew, between that world and the world from which you came, Corby, and yet you said of *Pig* that there is an element of nostalgia in that book. It is the place you came from. But there is also a brutal context to it and your second novel, *Common Ground*, is very bleak. It opens with a group of kids aimlessly smashing up a car and the characters really don't have much common ground, do they?

COWAN No, because it is a book about becoming a parent. It follows the journey into domesticity of a couple. Ashley is a geography teacher while Jay, his partner, is a community artist. She is a kind of a hippie and he has a proper job. They are going to have a child and the child is what gives purpose to their relationship. I think if you take the child out they might actually spin off in separate orbits. The child is what creates the common ground that allows their partnership to work, but meanwhile she is attempting to stop the bulldozing of her protected forest to make way for a motorway. I was writing this at the time that Twyford Down was being bulldozed to make way for a motorway and that is the common ground, in a literal sense, which is being papered or Tarmacked over. Ashley, the geography teacher, gets drawn into that campaign.

Pig took so long because I didn't trust myself, didn't trust the idea of myself as a writer, but when it was so successful it made me believe I could almost do no wrong so I wrote *Common Ground* far too quickly and I let go of it too soon. To my mind it is a third too long. One of the reviews said, 'There is so much going on. Given it is about a protected woodland, you can't see the forest for the trees.' And I think this is quite true and at a certain point, when I was writing my third book and getting stuck again I thought, I know what I can do: I can rewrite *Common Ground* and my publisher will be delighted to have a second version of it which they can publish and get better reviews the second time around, but they wouldn't have it. Each of the books is like a child. Mine is a family of five novels and *Common Ground* is the one which I feel slightly ashamed of!

ALDERMAN In my case, of the three novels to date the middle one is my weakest. *The Liars' Gospel*. It is fine. It works. There are no egregious plot holes, but though I took ages over it, I didn't quite get whatever it was that I was wanting to get winkled out somehow.

BIGSBY Andrew, your next novel was *Crustaceans*. In it there is a man who appears to be trying to hold his life together through a monologue with an unseen character. It is written, as are your earlier novels, largely in Hemingwayesque short, declarative sentences of the kind you used in your first novel.

COWAN *Crustaceans* is the favourite of my books and the one which received the least welcome because it deals with a fairly traumatic subject, which is the loss of a child, a fact established in the first couple of pages. The narrator is driving out to the coast on what would have been his son's sixth birthday and he is going to retrace, through that day, the journey to the holiday caravan where they used to go each summer and the beach where the boy died. He is narrating the boy's life back to him as he drives and then as he is walking along. So he is telling the entire story to the son who isn't there and in the process of giving back to the son the story of his life he is drawn into recounting his own, the story of his own childhood. He also tells the son about how he met the son's mother. Then there is the story of the present day. So there are four stories coming together in a way which I was thinking about as a kind of multi-dimensional puzzle, and I am really proud of the way I slotted those four elements together.

Part of the reason the sentences are so short is because I was conscious that this might not be a very powerful book for most readers. They might not want to read about such a distressing story, so I tried to compensate my reader by making it flawless, I wanted it to be beautifully written and to be satisfying aesthetically. Of course it couldn't be flawless so I became completely bogged down and blocked. It took me a very long time to finish that book but the sentences are not so much short as very, very carefully crafted and that made the Hemingwayesque aspect of them. I did feel I had achieved a voice, in this novel, which was appropriate to the subject matter. The sentences are clipped, economical, because the man narrating it is trying to hold everything together . There is a lot he can't say but also a danger of mawkishness in writing about that subject and I wanted it to be somewhat restrained so that it isn't obviously a tear jerker. It is not supposed to be like that, so that is another explanation for the style, but in the end I felt I had imprisoned myself in a style, in a voice, to achieve a sort of literary voice which I was very proud of but was a prison cell. So subsequently what I have written in other novels is a kind of reaction against *Crustaceans*, a movement away from that in an attempt to write longer sentences. This was my ambition in my latest book, to write page-length sentences.

BIGSBY   Naomi, in *The Lairs' Gospel* you move from the contemporary world back to the time of Jesus.

ALDERMAN   This is a novel in four alternate gospels about characters who don't get a gospel in the original. There is Mary, Jesus's mother, Judas the Betrayer, Caiaphas, who was the High Priest of the temple in Jerusalem at the time that Jesus was tried and executed, and Barabbas, who is the murderer who is released when

Jesus was crucified. I had this idea for this book when I was about sixteen actually so I had been sitting with it for a while. When my Hebrew teacher told me that there were passages in the Jewish scriptures about Jesus I said, 'somebody should write a novel about Jesus but as the Jews would tell the story' and she said, 'Oh no, nobody should do that. It seems dangerous.' So maybe I like to go where it seems dangerous, or maybe it is just that interesting things are where things seem dangerous. There are people who believe that the resurrection happened and that Jesus was indeed the only son of God, sent to earth to free us from sin. I am not going to tell them they are wrong but for those of us who don't believe that then we look around at the world that we see ourselves in and go, 'How did all this come to be, all these centuries of persecution and so on?'

BIGSBY You, too, Andrew, have turned back to the past in your latest novel, *Worthless Men*, but in your case a mere century. Is this the payoff for your time as an oral historian?

COWAN Yes, when they pulled the plug on that government job creation scheme I left copies with Norwich Library and the originals with the community workshop in that semi-derelict outbuilding. When we returned from Glasgow seven years later our return coincided with Norwich Library burning down and when I went to retrieve the originals, or at least to see if they were still there, I found that the semi-derelict outbuilding had been demolished so both the originals and the copies are presumed lost, but I had actually taken some copies of my favourite bits from the achieve and I had been sitting on them for all this time. Actually, my fourth novel was meant to be this novel but I just couldn't see a way of writing a story out of that material because that material is all backdrop. It is not actually the stuff of a story. It is the texture of a novel, it is the detail, but it is not the story. So I came around to starting a novel without quite knowing what the story was but at least I had a theme and the theme was worthless men. This was the time when eugenics seemed respectable. There were those who looked upon the First World War as potentially beneficial to the gene pool in that the social residuum would be removed by the war and that the A1 types, the courageous and the patriotic, the upstanding types, would in some way be tempered by the war and emerge from it stronger and their progeny, their offspring, would be an improvement of the race. So it was that theme of eugenics that gave me my title, gave me my theme, and eventually gave me the story. It took a long time to write, six years, written in the margins of my academic existence!

DAVID ALMOND   CHARLIE HIGSON

David Almond was born in Felling, Gateshead, Tyne and Wear, in 1951. He graduated from UEA with a degree in English and American Literature, subsequently becoming a school teacher, publishing a first collection of short stories in 1985, with another following twelve years later. Then came the children's novel *Skellig* (1998), which marked the beginning of his success with a series of novels including *My Name is Mina* (2010), a prequel to *Skellig*. Other books include *Secret Heart* (2001), *The Fire Eaters* (2003) and *Clay* (2005). He is also the author of plays. His awards include the Carnegie Medal, two Whitbread Awards, the Michael L. Printz Award and the Guardian Children's Fiction Award.

Charlie Higson was born in Frome, Somerset, in 1958 and graduated from UEA. While there he formed two bands, one of which survived several years after he left university. He has been a writer, director, and performer, appearing notably in the long-running television comedy series, *The Fast Show*. In the mid-1990s, he wrote four thrillers for adults but subsequently wrote the Young Bond series for young readers. The first, *Silverfin*, appeared in 2005. This was followed by what he characterised as a post-apocalyptic, zombie-horror series, beginning with *The Enemy* (2009). The seventh in this series, *The End*, was published in 2015, the same year that saw his television series *The Strange Case of Dr Jekyll and Mr Hyde*.

This interview took place on October 16, 2013.

BIGSBY David, you were raised in a smallish town on the Tyne. Yours was a Catholic family and my impression is that the town itself was fairly Catholic.

ALMOND Parts of it were. It was the beginning of South Tyneside so it was very Irish – southern Irish. So I grew up with the Kellys and Flynns and the O'Malleys, so, yes, Catholicism was really quite big there.

BIGSBY And those facts – your Catholicism and your northern roots – resonate in your work.

ALMOND I have fought against those things as a writer. I thought, I am not going to be a northern writer. I am not going to use my Catholicism, but I got to a certain age and if you are brought up as a Catholic it is in your bones. It is a physical thing. You can't do anything about it and if you come from Tyneside you talk like me. So there really was nought I could do about it and I really began to write when I said, 'That is what I am.' Then I allowed those things into my work.

BIGSBY What was your reading when you were a child?

ALMOND I was reading the Catechism but also Enid Blyton. My sisters read Enid Blyton, and I used to steal them. I read Roger Lancelyn Green who wrote fantastically, telling us of the Greek myths, and particularly the King Arthur stories. My favourite book when I was a kid was Roger Lancelyn Green's *King Arthur and his Knights of the Round Table*, with some astonishing illustrations by a German artist called Lotte Reiniger. I read John Wyndham when I was about eleven, or twelve, everything by John Wyndham.

BIGSBY And you weren't only reading because you started writing as a child.

ALMOND Yes, I wrote when I was a little boy. I used to write on paper and then stitch the pages into books and put titles on them. I think they were fake Enid Blytons.

BIGSBY Charlie, what was your reading?

HIGSON Quite similar to David's. I was really into Roger Lancelyn Green as well. The *Knights of the Round*

Table was one of my favourite books. I loved any myths and legends: Greek myths and legends, Viking stories, King Arthur, Robin Hood, anything in which the hero had a sword. I just loved escapism, anything that would take me out of my boring, mundane existence.

BIGSBY   And you also began writing early.
HIGSON   Yes, as a ten year old and, like David, I was just copying the things I liked to read. I think my first one was a rip-off of *Winnie the Pooh*, which I made into a little book as well.

BIGSBY   You have something else in common. David, when you were seven, your sister, who was one, died suddenly, and then when you were a teenager your father died. The reason for mentioning that is that in *Skellig* there is a dying baby who is finally kept back from death by a mysterious force. Then, ten years later, you wrote another novel, *My Name Is Mina*, in which the central character's father dies and she says that it was the big bad thing in her life. Am I wrong to hear echoes of your own life or not?
ALMOND   No, I think it is absolutely right. I think as well as allowing a kind of northerness and Catholicism into my work I found a way to be able to deal with things that had been quite traumatic in my childhood. It was also the time when I found myself writing for children and childrens' writers often have had quite a big trauma in their own childhood. When I was writing *Skellig*, which has a boy who had a really poorly baby sister, obviously I was thinking, 'oh gosh, this is about me,' but if you are writing you can't allow that to be at the front of your mind. You can't say, 'this is a book about this thing that happened to me.' You retain an artistic distance from it and then write it through. The same was true when I was writing *Mina*, in which there is a dead father, and grief. Although those things are really massive in my books, though, you can't personalise it too much because art is a way of objectifying things. They may obviously be powered by your own experiences, your own emotions, but you turn them into something that you can give to other people.

BIGSBY Charlie, you were a teenager when your mother died but that didn't work its way into your work. Did you feel it sharply at the time or did it grow over time?

HIGSON I think it probably grew over time. I was eighteen and, I think like most teenagers, was very self-preoccupied. So I didn't let it affect me as much as I probably should have done and I suppose, yes, ever since then you work that through. It is very difficult to say whether my life might have been different if that hadn't happened, because I don't know, but I have not particularly channelled that through any fiction. I think a lot of writers use writing as a way of separating themselves from the world. It's almost like a barrier between you and the world. You write about it. You don't let it affect you. It comes out there on the page.

BIGSBY David, you went on to a Catholic grammar school, which you didn't terribly like because it seemed to combine education with corporal punishment. Is that why a certain bitterness – aversion to – education comes into your work later on?

ALMOND I think so. I hated secondary school. It was just awful. I go into schools now and they are fantastic compared with the schools I went to. People say how great schools were back in the 1960s and I say, come back and meet Miss Arrowsmith, and come and meet Mr Taggart. Then to my amazement I became a teacher and thought, what am I doing? I became a teacher because I felt six weeks' holiday was fantastic but, as all teachers will know, I was so knackered I didn't write anything for a couple of years. Then I became fascinated by teaching. I found a way of thinking about education, about how society should be run, thinking about the education I had had. So that has become a constant thing in my life and in my work as well. Mina is always banging on about education. I am just fascinated by it. It is particularly important at the moment when we have a very narcissistic approach to how education should be run by certain ministers.

BIGSBY You went to UEA partly, as I gather, as a result of reading Hemingway.

ALMOND Yes, I read English and American Literature and Hemingway was massive to me. I remember in the library, which was just down the street from where we lived, pulling out a volume of Hemingway's stories and opening them. There was something about Hemingway's syntax, his way of just describing the world, I really recognised. It was very non-English. It was not to do with class. It was an amazing moment for me and UEA appealed to me because of the nature of the course. The first time I applied I couldn't get in. I got six to eight rejections and I only found out afterwards that that was because the school had given me such a terrible reference. Then I applied again the next year and got in straightaway.

BIGSBY Charlie, you also came to UEA, in your case to read American Literature and Film.

HIGSON It was the American side of the literature that appealed to me and back then, in the 1970s, I think there were only two universities that were offering that course, here and Sussex. I probably came here because I could do film and, like David, I felt that American literature, modern American literature, just spoke to me in a way that other literature didn't. I had originally been going to Oxbridge but when I found that modern literature ended with D.H. Lawrence I thought, well, that isn't modern literature as I see it, as a teenager. I was into Tom Wolfe, and people like that, along with American crime writers. I liked the immediacy of the way they wrote and the way that the characters' voices would carry the narrative. So I did a lot of that, but I also did a lot of gothic literature when I was here, which I very much got into and that married with my love of horror films, which has stayed with me. In fact in this very lecture theatre I and a friend put on an all-night horror film show. This being the 1970s, there were no videos or DVDs. The only way you could watch films was to see them in the cinema or wait until they came on the TV and there were a load of really great, very nasty, 1970s American horror films which you just couldn't see. The only way we could get to see these films was to rent the prints of the films and show them here. That was the first time I saw *Night of the Living Dead*, which was the very first ever cannibal zombie apocalypse film. It was probably about one in the morning by the time that film came on and there were a lot of drunk students in here who were laughing and arseing about.

The film starts slightly cheesy, but by about half an hour into the film it was absolute dead silence everywhere. It is a very, very, effective film, the first zombie film ever made, so nobody had seen a film like this before. It was a very brutal, scary, bleak film and it is amazing to think that, since then, zombies have become the most popular monster in the world. George Romero can't have had any idea what he was letting loose with that film, which I first saw here.

BIGSBY The other thing you did when you were here was get into music, a punk rock band.

HIGSON It was called *The Right-Hand Lovers*. Sorry!

BIGSBY Paul Whitehouse, your subsequent writing partner, was part of that.

HIGSON Yes. Paul and I started the band.

BIGSBY According to the internet, Paul was educated at UEA. That's not an entirely accurate description, is it, because he dropped out?

HIGSON He wasn't educated, no. He was in the School of Development Studies but never really worked out what it was. He wanted to do geography but when he came here it was quite a political course, about ideas of development in the third world. As far as I can tell he never worked it out, mainly because he didn't go to any lectures, so that was why our band was fairly short-lived because he wasn't here for very long. He claims he left but the university claims it threw him out.

BIGSBY You then formed another band, modestly called *The Higsons*.

HIGSON Yes, and when I left here I was a professional

singer for six years. That is how I made my living, such as it was.

BIGSBY   It was not the only way you made your living, because you were doing things on the side, were you not? You worked as a painter and decorator.

HIGSON   The bass player and I started doing a bit of decorating to make a extra money. Everybody now says, oh, it is terrible what is happening in the music business. It is impossible for any bands to make a living. It has always been the same. The Rolling Stones make money but on the level we were on you couldn't make any money. So we started decorating when we weren't on tour and we realised that if we stuck to the decorating and knocked the band on the head we would actually make quite a lot of money. So that was the end of the band.

BIGSBY   And is it true you painted and decorated for Hugh Laurie and Stephen Fry?

HIGSON   Yes, we did. One of the last jobs Paul and I did was decorating the house that Stephen Fry and Hugh Laurie lived in. They were starting to work in TV, making quite a good living. Harry Enfield, who was a friend of ours, was working with them and Paul and I were decorating. We were also starting to write a bit together. Harry said, Charlie and Paul can do your house, so we did and by the time we had finished – it was a big house – Stephen had made enough money to be able to move out and move on so Paul and I bought it.

BIGSBY   David, you have already said that you went into teaching because you assumed there would be time to write, and indeed you did do some writing, some short stories, but then suddenly, in 1982, you did something that strikes me as rather strange. You threw it all up to come to Norfolk and restore a house, thereafter, for a time, living in Suffolk on the dole. Why did you do that and what was it you gained from it?

ALMOND   Yes, it was a massive decision. I had been teaching for five years as a primary school teacher, which I really liked. I had been married, though the marriage split up, and I had a house and I remember sitting in the staff room and reading a small advertisement in *The Guardian*. It said , 'Have you got a talent or gift that you want to develop? Do you want to come and live in a tumbledown mansion in Norfolk and help to restore it?' I went straight to the phone and phoned up and ended up coming to this amazing Hall in Gunthorpe, in North Norfolk. I stayed there for a year. I sold my house and I gave up my teaching job. I had £1,500 and lived on that for a year. It was fantastic. It was really an astonishing thing. When I tell people about it they think what a glorious thing to do, but then they think,'but it must have been really scary.' It didn't feel scary at all. It felt a really natural thing to do. I grew up in the 1960s so to go and live in a commune in Norfolk, well, what could be better? It was fantastic. It reached a very weird end but the house is now restored. It is a marvellous thing but there was a bunch of writers and artists and musicians who were doing things like nailing roofs on. I thought if I was going to get my roof done I wouldn't employ writers to come and do it, so it was a very visionary thing that these people did.

BIGSBY But equally important was that you went back to the North East, because you were talking earlier about there being something almost inhibiting about coming from that area, having that accent and wanting to be a writer but not wanting to be a particular kind of a writer. You did actually spend a long time writing a novel that never got published, didn't you?

ALMOND Yes, I took five years to write a novel that was never published. It was American-influenced. But then I discovered something else. I read Flannery O'Connor and I was a Northern Catholic writer trying to work out what it meant to be a Northern Catholic writer and I read Flannery O'Connor's stories and novels, but also her amazing essays in *Mystery and Manners* . She said, 'I struggle with the nature of the South like Jacob struggling with an angel to extract a blessing,' and I thought that is exactly what I am doing. She also said, 'The imagination is not free. It is bound, and you are bound by a particular language, by a particular sort of bodily structure.' So, yes, I went back to the North

East and accepted that that was what I was going to do. There is a danger if you see yourself as being regional. It becomes very enclosed, very inwards, jokey and nostalgic, but you have to fight against all those things. It was a way of discovering the world, weirdly by going home again.

BIGSBY That brings us almost to *Skellig*, but before talking about that, let me turn back to you, Charlie. It was at this stage in your career that you began writing for Harry Enfield.

HIGSON Yes, the first TV work Paul and I did was with Harry Enfield, a show called *Saturday Live*. We created two characters, first Stavros, who was a Greek kebab shop owner who dispensed words of wisdom, and then Loadsamoney, the working class lad who dispensed complete gibberish and rubbish. They both did very well. Paul and I wrote those characters. It was a live show and a great way to get into TV. Most TV is not live but this was. We would write during the week, then on Saturday night it would go out live and a lot of people would watch it and be commenting on it the next day. That was really exciting and when that Loadsamoney character took off, it being the late 1980s, he was seen as a poster boy for Thatcherism, a critique of that whole thing. The tabloids got into it and picked it up and then Neil Kinnock used the phrase. He accused Margaret Thatcher of running "a Loadsamoney economy." Then she used the phrase. She said "we have been accused of running a Loadsamoney economy. What is wrong with that?" She obviously hadn't seen the programme. So it was one of those things that got much bigger than we were. On the back of that, because it had been so successful, people left, right and centre, were offering us TV commissions to write other stuff. The main thing we went on to was a series with Harry Enfield, a television programme which he didn't particularly want me to act in. He was happy for me just to write.

BIGSBY Then came *The Fast Show*.

HIGSON Yes. It will be twenty years next year since the first series.

BIGSBY David, you once said that *Skellig* almost wrote itself, but did it come to you whole and entire?

ALMOND No, it came sentence by sentence. I was walking along the street and it began to tell itself to me. I just sat down and began to write and I never knew where it was going. I never knew exactly what was going to happen. I remember discovering that Skellig had wings and I only discovered it when I wrote the sentence, 'Michael put his hand across his back and felt something there.' I thought, Oh God, this guy's got wings! Perhaps I should explain. A boy called Michael goes into a garage and finds a creature, a man, in the back of the garage and this guy turns out to have wings. He is pretty filthy and stinks. He is horrible. He eats bugs and spiders. So by the time I discovered he had wings I thought, that's OK, he can have wings. If he is eating bugs as well he is not going to be angelic. So, yes, *Skellig* just happened to me. It was extraordinary but I think that is the thing about writing. I think you have often to be brave enough to write about things you really don't understand and you don't quite know what is happening. You have to work on a cloud of not really quite knowing. With *Skellig* it was like that sentence, that sentence, that sentence, that sentence.

BIGSBY But even when you finished it there was still a cloud of not knowing around the figure of Skellig because it is not entirely clear if this figure is an angel, the embodiment of goodness, or not.

ALMOND It is mysterious even to me and I think I was allowed to do that because I had never planned to write for children. I thought, I am intelligent, educated, I will write for intelligent educated people and then when I began to write *Skellig* I got halfway down the first page and thought, this is a book for young people and, to my amazement, as soon as I realised that I felt liberated and excited. It allowed me to do things like think, oh yes, he has got wings and I didn't have to explain it. I could just continue because kids' brains are a bit more flexible than ours. Kids also know that they don't know everything yet. The thing about Skellig is that he isn't quite defined in the end. Kids are happy to know that things aren't explained because the world is not explained and the world is mysterious. The world is mysterious to me. You are very mysterious to me.

BIGSBY When you finished it, did you know how special it was going to be to you?

ALMOND When I was writing it I knew there was really something happening which I had never done before. I knew it was the best thing I had done but I knew nothing about children's books so when I told a couple of people halfway through that, 'I think I am writing a children's book,' they said 'Have you researched the market?'

BIGSBY As it happens, the market was already waiting for you because *Skellig* has been read in schools ever since and has become a play, an opera, and a film. In a way Skellig is the embodiment of goodness. Later, though, you wrote another book, *Clay*, in which there is a figure who can mould clay into forms which seem to come to life, a figure who seems to be the embodiment of evil.

ALMOND I think *Clay* is in some ways my most Catholic book. Catholicism keeps coming out and the boy who makes the creatures in clay is a boy who has gone to be trained to be a priest and is thrown out because he is seen as being a very dark force in the training place. I think that if you are Catholic you can't get away from darkness and light, the evil and good in creation. You have to explore those things. It just comes with the territory. I think Stephen Rose, who is the creator in the book, is the most evil character I have written. I learned a lot from writing him. I thought he would be all right. He could be managed. He will be integrated into society, but he wasn't. He resisted everything and I couldn't control him at the end. He goes off to wreak havoc somewhere else.

BIGSBY Charlie, David has gone from writing for adults to writing for children. You have had a similar experience. While those television shows we were talking about were on, you were writing fairly hard-boiled fiction.

HIGSON Yes, I wrote four crime books in the early 1990s which grew out of my love of American crime writing I was talking about earlier. I was trying to write in that style but set the books in England. I like crime books about criminals. I am not particularly interested in detective stories, police stories, but I do like criminal stories where you get inside twisted minds. I suppose that is what nearly all the four books are.

BIGSBY They were incredibly violent at times.

HIGSON Yes, they were, but I was a young man. They are a young man's books. I wrote four of them but then the TV side took over. *The Fast Show* was taking up all my time because Paul and I we were producing it, writing it and being in it. It would take us a year to make a series. I had no time to write books until I was approached by the Ian Fleming Estate, about ten years ago now.

BIGSBY Presumably they had gone back to those books rather than to the shows.

HIGSON What happened was that my editor from my days of writing in the early 1990s had left publishing and was now working for the Fleming Estate. She was trying to revamp the literary side of James Bond, to remind people where it came from and what an important figure Ian Fleming himself was. They have done the adult books with Sebastian Faulks and lately William Boyd, but their first step was to get someone to write some kids' books and she felt that my style, which is like that American hard-boiled crime writing style, would work well with children because it was very direct and, well, it is James Bond so it didn't matter if it was violent as well. Their initial idea was they were going to get a different writer to write each book in the series because they wanted to get proper serious writers to do it and they didn't think that anyone would want to commit to more than one book, which is what they have done with the adult books. By this time I had three boys and was looking for something to write for them, some kind of action adventure story, so this was a perfect fit. I wrote the first one and I really enjoyed doing it. It did very well and I thought, yes, I would like to write some more of these because it was fantastic fun being part of the James Bond family. The Fleming Estate is still run by two of Fleming's nieces so it had that direct connection with Ian Fleming. So it was a great thing to do, but having written five of them I thought I should stop.

BIGSBY   Would you like to write for the adult James Bond series?

HIGSON   Yes, I do keep reminding them that I am here. When they first came to talk to me about the job I thought they were wanting someone to write some new adult books and I thought God, how would you ever do that? How could you do anything that hadn't been done in all the over twelve books that Ian Fleming wrote, and all the continuation novels and all the films? I said, 'What more new could you do with James Bond?' But they said 'No, we want you to do kids' books,' and I thought, oh well, we don't know what James Bond did as a kid, so there was room for me to bring something of my own to it. But having spent all those years researching it and immersing myself in that world, I do think I am ready now to write a much better book than Sebastian Faulks.

BIGSBY   And then you started another franchise.

HIGSON   I found that I really liked writing for kids, writing for that age group. I enjoy doing the school visits and the books were doing well and I thought well, let's write some more. I have always been into horror. My boys were really into horror. So I thought I would try and write a horror series and it went right back to that day in here watching *Night of the Living Dead*. I wanted to write zombie stories for kids. I wanted to write a zombie-type story and I came up with the idea that if a disease has hit the planet which only affects people over the age of fourteen they are either killed instantly or they are left so badly infected, their brains and bodies so rotted away by disease, that they behave like classic cannibal zombies. So it is about kids trying to survive in London, trying to look after themselves and scavenge for food while trying to avoid being captured and eaten by adults.

BIGSBY   I said you wrote adult novels and then children's novels as though these were discrete, meaningful categories. Is there a real distinction? Is there a line, or is that just permeable?

ALMOND I think it is permeable. My next novel comes out in March in an adult imprint. Categories are becoming more flexible. They talk of novels for young adults and I think it is not a way of saying, 'actually I am not a children's writer' because there is a real importance in writing for young people. It is something I am really proud to be doing. I am not one of those writers who say I am writing for children but am looking for adults. I don't feel like that at all. I think that writing for children is one of the most important forms of culture in this country. More and more people are recognising that. The standard of writing for young people is amazing now, absolutely extraordinary. In some ways it is still marginalised but I think it is great. I have got a fifteen-year-old daughter and I know how much she has been helped to grow up by reading teenage books, by reading, when she was younger, writers like Jacqueline Wilson, Cathy Cassidy, who writes the Big Pink books. These are really fantastic writers. You know the quality of Charlie's writing. This is really just fine writing.

HIGSON I will second that! There is some fantastic work being done at the moment. My children's books are written with the same intensity as an adult book. The only concessions I make writing for younger people is that I don't write any explicit sex scenes, although there are quite a lot of YA books now which do have that in them, but as a fifty-five-year-old man I don't think it is seemly for me to be writing that for children. You are allowed to use a few of the milder swear words but otherwise I write in the same way and kids like that. They are written for that age of kids where they are wanting to read something that they feel is more grown up, and in fact horror is a fantastic genre for kids and teenagers to read because it deals with a lot of very heavy matters that they will have to deal with in their lives, but it does it on a fantasy level. They are not going to have to deal with zombies but they are going to have to deal with the reality of death and disease and change, whether you can trust people, whether you can trust adults. As David said, they are learning about the world.

BIGSBY Philip Pullman, of course, is read equally by children and adults and enjoyed by both.

ALMOND Absolutely, and I think that is right. More and more adults are recognising that and do read this work. As a society we are probably becoming less stuffy and there is a playfulness in children's books which adults welcome and also adults can learn lots about writing from children's books. I am aware, when I am writing for young people, that I am writing for writers. Young people write. They all write, so they are really interested in the process of writing. When people say to me, 'kids don't read any more,' I am just thinking 'go to the schools we visit, go and see the children we see, go and see what a great reading culture it is and what a great artistic culture it is.' Kids are natural artists.

HIGSON I don't recognise the statistics that are constantly thrown at us. I have just come back from a period on the road doing schools' visits where the kids are really excited about books and reading. It is at the centre of what they do, though they do other things as well. They play computer games because computer games are brilliant fun. I play computer games all the time. I would write two books a year if I didn't. If people say to me, 'Don't you think kids should be reading instead of playing computer games?' I say, 'Of course not. They should be doing both.' There is room in their lives for both. They do read, and when a kid gets into a book, or a writer, or a series, they get obsessed. Kids say to me, 'I read your book in a day and I have read it six times since.' They are fantastic readers.

TASH AW

Tash Aw was born in Taiipei, Taiwan, in 1971. He grew up in Kuala Lumpur. He studied law at Jesus College, Cambridge, and then at the University of Warwick. He spent several years working as a lawyer before enrolling in the Creative Writing MA at the University of East Anglia (UEA). His first novel, *The Harmony Silk Factory* (2005), won the Whitbread First Novel Award and the Commonwealth Prize for Best First Novel. His second novel, *Map of the Invisible World*, appeared in 2009 and was followed in 2013 by *Five Star Billionaire*. He has twice been longlisted for the Man Booker Prize and is also the author of short stories (winning the O'Henry Prize) along with essays.

This interview took place on October 15, 2015.

BIGSBY Can you tell me something about your name, which I thought should be the other way around?

AW Usually Chinese names have the surnames first. My surname is Aw and my given name means 'glorious sunrise', which is not really poetic but has warlike implications. It is a bit like being called Alexander and I have never quite been comfortable with it. Everyone has always called me Tash, including my parents, and I guess over the years that is the name that has stuck. The only person who calls me by my full name is my mother when she is very angry with me.

BIGSBY I think of you as a Malaysian writer but you weren't born in Malaysia.

AW No, that's right. I am a Malaysian writer, but by a quirk of fate I was born in Taiwan. My parents were working there. They moved back to Malaysia when I was two-and-a-half and I identified as Malaysian, but I have only recently started to discover that the place you are born is incredibly important, not so much for you but for other people. As long as I can remember other Malaysians always saw me as being slightly different because every time I filled in a form at school it was remarked upon that I wasn't Malaysian, that I was Taiwanese because I had been born in Taiwan. So although I never really felt Taiwanese in any way, that tiny bit of difference made me feel like an outsider and I think that that semi-outsider status has informed my work all the way through up till now.

BIGSBY Now you live part of the year in London and part of the year in Malaysia, so you are at home in both places but also simultaneously exiled from those places.

AW Yes, you are absolutely right and I think I have become comfortable with that position of someone who is neither really on the inside nor the outside. I don't really know how to be a proper insider. When I go back to Malaysia I slip very quickly into the life I had when I was a teenager. I still have the same friends. We still speak in the same slang, the same dialect and accent, but somehow I feel nowadays, and I suppose always have done, that I am a bit of an imposter. Likewise, I feel very at home in Britain but something will happen, someone will say something, that makes me think maybe I don't really understand Britain after all.

BIGSBY In *Map of the Invisible World* you write, 'In those days he did not yet understand that home was not necessarily where you were born or even where you grew up but something else entirely, something fragile that could exist anywhere in the world.' Is that how you feel?

AW No, I think that is how I hoped to feel. In my idealistic moments I used to think that one could find one's place anywhere in the world so that is essentially what I have tried to do for the last thirty years, but nowadays I question whether or not that is true. I think you and I were talking earlier about how the world seems to be getting less expansive in its mentality, much more protectionist, much more insular, and I noted that that is not just the case in Britain. Malaysia and Singapore always used to have a lot of mutual understanding but are now attempting to erect walls between themselves and to define their national identity in a way that is exclusive of others. That makes it much more difficult for people like me, who identify with several different cultures, to find their place as they move between those cultures because it seems to me that more and more people need you to identify with one and only one. So my dreaded question is always, 'Where is home?' Actually, it is a question I can answer quite easily. Home is in Malaysia and London. The other related question is, 'Where you are from?' and depending on where I am in the world this could be London or Malaysia. But I am ethnically Chinese so who I am is also Chinese, but people don't want those complicated explanations. They want me to say, 'I am Malaysian.'

BIGSBY But isn't Malaysian itself essentially hybrid?
AW Exactly, it is essentially hybrid but the meaning of Malaysian is increasingly narrowing. It certainly feels narrower now than it used to before, now that Malaysia has experienced huge waves of immigration from other Asian countries, other poorer Asian countries

like Bangladesh and Cambodia. What it means to be Malaysian is now much narrower than it was before so these new immigrants are no longer considered Malaysian in the way that immigrants from fifty or a hundred years ago were.

BIGSBY But hasn't that been true in the past? You said you have a Chinese heritage but legally the Chinese have an inferior status within Malaysia.

AW Yes, I think politics in Malaysia is a difficult thing. Like many other countries in Asia it has a lot of sorting out to do in terms of political structures and the way it deals with various minority groups, ethnic groups, immigrant groups.

BIGSBY You started writing, like a lot of people do, in your teens but was that because you wanted to be a writer rather than anything else?

AW I always wanted to be a writer but in Malaysia, in the 1980s, there weren't any writers for us to look to as examples so I wanted to be a writer in the way I wanted to be an astronaut. I had no idea how to achieve it. All I knew was that I liked reading. I was a very solitary child and spent vast amounts of time on my own. I was writing little short stories from the age of about eleven or twelve. They grew longer and longer and more absurd as I got to university but it was still a very distant prospect. I had no idea how one might become a writer.

BIGSBY When you did become a writer, was there an advantage in the fictional territory of Malaysia not having already been mapped?

AW I never thought of that before but after *The Harmony Silk Factory* a lot of people talked about it as being the first of the modern, post-Burgess, books on Malaysia set in Malaysia. I never really thought of it in that way. As anyone writing novels knows, particularly writing one's first novel, it is difficult to think of how that novel fits into a wider historical plan. You have no idea how your background helps or doesn't help. All you are trying to do is finish that novel. But I think there was certainly a novelty value in that book because people were interested in a novel, by a Malaysian, set in Malaysia. There just hadn't been one for a long time. There was Burgess's *Malayan Trilogy* but before that one has to go all the way back to Somerset Maugham to find stories set there. But when I wrote the novel I just wanted to finish it. I knew I had something to say and I just wrote it.

BIGSBY Let's go back a bit. You came to England to university. Was that something Malaysians did then in the way that Australians would go to England?

AW Oh yes, very much so. That was a very long established tradition certainly back then. Malaysians came to Britain to finish their education and attend university. I came over with lots of other Malaysians. We got on to a Czech Air flight, changed planes in Prague, and I remember very clearly all the bags fell out of the overhead lockers when the plane took off. We landed at Heathrow and I spent a couple of nights in a really quite horrible bedsit in Bayswater before embarking on three or four years at university. I never thought I would stay as long as I have done. I always thought that I would stay a couple of years after university and try and write my novel, because by then I knew I wanted to write a novel.

BIGSBY The first three years you were at Cambridge, and not studying literature

AW No, I was studying law.

BIGSBY And then you went from there to Warwick, still studying law. So when did the novel writing begin?

AW I started *The Harmony Silk Factory* when I moved to London after that. I had already written a series of short stories that were getting longer and longer and longer, but I had no idea where they were going. I wanted to write a novel, but had no idea how to do that either. I knew that I didn't have the skills to write a novel, so at least I had that wisdom. I didn't rush. So I messed about with short stories. I was convinced I could write dialogue so I wrote story after story after story consisting of nothing but dialogue until finally I felt, yes, I am ready to start work on a novel.

BIGSBY Did you send those stories off anywhere?

AW No, of course not. They were terminally embarrassing, so embarrassing that even thinking about them now makes me cringe slightly. I think coming to England was important to me because I saw people who arrived at university knowing they wanted to be writers and they knew how they were going to do it. But they had parents who were writers and uncles who were publishers. They were already going to literary parties in London and doing little readings in Islington. I found it so intimidating. I had no idea how one could ever achieve it, but for the first time it didn't seem that writing as a career, as a way of life, was so exotic. It was something attainable for the first time. So I left university and started writing my novel. I went to the Reading Room at the British Library every day and diligently took up my space.

BIGSBY Like Karl Marx.

AW I always wanted to sit in his spot but that was already occupied by someone who would not relinquish it so I never got to sit in that spot. I went diligently every day with a couple of friends who were themselves writing their novels and by this time we had more articulated ideas as to what we wanted to achieve. I was going to write this expansive, sweeping epic because by then I had realised I was not going to be able to do it in a year. I had to pay my rent. I worked as a gardener. I worked in an auction house as a porter. I wasn't able to make ends meet and eventually I was faced with the choice: I would either have to go back to Malaysia, not having written my novel, or get a job that would enable me to save up enough money so that I would one day be able to take time off to write my novel. I had a law degree so I got a job in a law firm for three years and saved up just enough money to apply to do the Creative Writing MA at UEA. I applied after two years but hadn't quite saved up enough money so I had to defer my place for another year. By that time I already had about half of the first novel and I knew that I could survive for twelve months without working and if I didn't finish my novel then I would go back.

BIGSBY That was quite a step, to leave a job that was secure and which your parents would have loved you doing.

AW I really didn't love the job but I loved the travel, the free travel card. I loved the health insurance, and I haven't had health insurance since and I don't think I ever will. All those little benefits, and having the money at the end of the month, those are things that sometimes I still miss.

BIGSBY What did UEA give to you?

AW UEA gave to me lots of things. I felt as if I was thrust into the deep end and was incredibly intimidated by everything, though that is a recurring thing with me. I felt as intimidated at the age of thirty coming to UEA as I felt at the age of eighteen on first arriving in England. I felt everyone else knew much more than me, had read much more than I had, had a much better grasp of the techniques of creative writing. I had no idea how to create something in a formal sense. I just had an instinct. What UEA gave me was the time and space to explore my own capabilities and to realise that there were limits to what I could achieve then but those limits weren't necessarily any lower than those of the people around me. It taught me to be very resilient. I think the workshop form is incredibly bruising, when you have sixteen or eighteen thrusting ambitious young writers who are not necessarily going to hold back. Certainly my group didn't, and no praise is ever good enough. Even when people said, 'love your work,' it always felt to me slightly flat. I didn't feel that they loved it more than anything else they had ever read. It taught me to be resilient in a professional sense.

BIGSBY So it was enabling you to convince yourself that what you were doing was worthwhile?

AW Yes, yes I think so. I think I was able to form external barriers and external filters to be able to filter the wisdom from the noise. In publishing and writing there is an awful lot of noise and when you are hearing this sort of cacophony of opinion what happens, particularly at the start of one's career, is that it is very difficult to discern the nonsense from the kernel of truth.

You take everything on board, and what UEA taught me was that to be a writer one has to learn to be one's own best critic because no one else is going to do it for you. And it doesn't get better when you are published. You get reviewed and often the reviews are not going to be good, so you have to know how to resist that. Often one sends it to one's editor and the feedback isn't necessarily what one wants. So how does one negotiate? That is something I started to explore at UEA, and it's a really important thing.

BIGSBY Were you ever tempted to write in Malay or Chinese? Was that what your family spoke?

AW We spoke Mandarin at home. We were a typical Chinese family so we spoke Mandarin and Hokkien at home, which is a southern Chinese dialect. At school we spoke Malay. I did all my schooling in Malay but while Malaysia, as a multi-racial country, on the surface is very harmonious, there are also very sharp racial divides so often English is the most politically neutral language. Anyone interested in reading and writing would be reading and writing in English as well as their other language. So for me English was always the obvious language to use not only because of its political and racial neutrality but also because most of the people who live in Kuala Lumpur, or any of the other urban centres, will be speaking English as a lingua franca.

BIGSBY Your first novel, *The Harmony Silk Factory*, is set in Malaysia in colonial times. It has a central character who is hard to get a grasp on because we have three discrete narratives offered by his wife, his son – who really didn't know him but who try to construct this figure – and a colonial. Did you find that last voice more difficult to get than the others?

AW Yes, it was more difficult. He is not just culturally different but also generationally. He is the one furthest removed from me. That voice was influenced by Burgess, not the Burgess of *The Malayan Trilogy*, but the Burgess of *Earthly Powers*. It was about finding the right voice for those characters and I spent longer trying to establish the voice of Peter, the colonial figure, but once I got it it felt very natural to me. I really enjoyed that act of mimicry. I liked putting myself in his place. After the first two, who were much closer to my own personal experience, it seemed strangely liberating to be writing in the voice of someone totally different from me in every single respect. By then, too, I was beginning to see the whole shape of the novel. I could see the end.

BIGSBY You didn't know the end before you started?

AW No, I did not know the end but by the time I started Peter's section, the Englishmen's section, all the pieces of the jigsaw were falling neatly into place until I felt as if I was coasting to the end and I was writing with great freedom and great speed. I was writing over a thousand words a day, which for me is really exceptional. I am generally not a fast writer but I think I got the pace because I got the voice. The voice to me seemed very exciting, that act of pure invention. I haven't heard people say that he didn't sound like an Englishman of a certain generation so I think I did an OK job. But I think part of the freedom and the energy of that voice comes from the fact that I knew, finally, that I was going to finish this novel. After three years spent in a law firm, trying to write in the evenings, I could finally see the end and I think that energy is the energy that finds its way into the voice.

BIGSBY Were you drawn to this particular period because Malaysians didn't look back to that time? A line had been drawn across history with de-colonisation and who would want to go back to that which was, after all, a period of potential humiliation?

AW Absolutely. One of the things that always struck me growing up was how little people of my generation knew about the war, and how little they were concerned by anything that happened pre-1960. Whenever I tried to speak to my parents or grandparents about it (my grandparents had lived in the area where *The Harmony Silk Factory* is set and therefore suffered very badly during the war), I was just confronted by this wall of silence, this weird omerta. It really bothered me and so I began to think more deeply about why we had this conflicted mentality regarding the war and anything that happened in our past.

A lot of it, I realised, was to do with shame and a lot of the novel is about shame, the shame of being poor, the shame of being a third world country, the shame of not being in control of one's own destiny, the shame of not being in control of the stories that one tells. This is the whole problem with colonialism and post-colonialism. How does one take back one's story? How does one tell one's own stories? So one of the reasons I wanted to write that novel, which is set in a series of small towns in a little known region of Malaysia, in a very uncertain period of our history, was to try and explore those areas of silence. That is why there is a slightly enigmatic ending because the novel is built on a series of silences that replicates the silences that I was confronted with when I tried to do my research, when I spoke to people who either had no knowledge of the war, of our past, or did have knowledge but didn't want to talk about it. That is why you get this conflicting view of the central character, Johnny, from people who knew him in one way but didn't know him in another. In a way it becomes a measure for how Malaysians know their own country. We might know one aspect of it but we don't know vast amounts of the other parts of the country.

BIGSBY It seems to me that this question of the difficulty of pinning down identity, of knowing someone, runs all the way through your work. There are also a series of betrayals in this book, personal betrayals, public betrayals, so every time you think you are on secure ground the ground shifts beneath your feet.

AW Yes, that is how I experienced the stories I heard when I was growing up. I always got the impression that I was being told one version of the truth and that behind that lurked a huge expanse of grey area that I wasn't being given access to. People would appear as one thing and then years later, after they had died, it would be revealed that they were something else entirely and that they were harbouring these huge secrets. Even in small-town Malaysia, which is where my grandparents lived and where my uncles and aunts still live, there are all these mysterious family stories that remain untold. Before my grandmother died a few years ago – she was always a lovely person but very typically Chinese so always quite distant – I went up to see her. I was told she was on her death bed but she suddenly perked up, just for that one day (she actually died the following day). During the three hours I spent with her she told me so many stories about how she met my grandfather, had been a child bride but hadn't wanted to get married to him. I learnt all these things about her that I had never known. My grandfather had long since passed away and I suddenly saw him in a different light and I think that justified my wanting to write the novel in the way that I did because I always grew up feeling that there were all these stories lurking in my family, as in other Malaysian families, particularly Malaysian Chinese families who had come from somewhere else and who had often left families in China and started new families in Malaysia. There was some presence outside of our sphere of consciousness that somehow affected our own stories and that is why the novel ends in a slightly mysterious way. We have three different views of Johnny. All those views are true.

Some people find the ending slightly unsatisfactory because we live in an era where we want certainty, closure, but the way I experienced a lot of my stories growing up was that closure was impossible. We couldn't ever learn the truth of what went on, particularly in the war, particularly in those times when people of a certain generation were going through very tough times. There was no way they could pass those stories down to us. I was born in an era of relative wealth. We were the first generation of people to be born in middle class families and I think that my parents and grandparents wanted to shield us from what had happened before. They wanted us to grow up unencumbered by those histories. But what happens when you deny someone their history is that they grow up without a fully formed sense of who they are.

BIGSBY You said it took you ten years to learn to write well. At the end of this you suddenly got prizes and were financially rewarded. Did that give you the impetus to write your second novel or did it inhibit you?

AW I am not aware of having been hugely inhibited but on the other hand I didn't have this huge feeling of euphoria, the conviction that I was suddenly this amazing writer who knew how to write and that I was going to write this splendid novel. In fact when I finished the second one I had exactly the same feeling, and it is a feeling I have right now that I am just starting to think about my fourth one. Having now written three novels, I still feel as if I don't really know how to write. I am not sure but I think that will stay with me for the rest of my life. Indeed, it is a feeling I have learnt to appreciate because I think it keeps me on my toes. It keeps me hungry. The way I think about my writing is that every book is completely different. Whether I succeed in that or not is a moot point. Some people would say I have probably written the same book three times over and thematically that is arguable, however I do think it is important to wipe the slate clean and just reset everything to zero, starting again from scratch.

BIGSBY Your second novel, *Map of the Invisible World*, moves on in time. It is set partly in Indonesia and partly in Malaysia. Two boys have been taken from an orphanage and become separated. In a way it continues the debate about identity, personal and public, because just as the boys have been separated so, too, have the countries which were in contention at exactly the same time in the same way.

AW Yes, it is set in Jakarta and Kuala Lumpur, in what has become known as 'the year of living dangerously', 1964, when Indonesia was teetering on the edge of civil war. In fact the following year there was a massacre. It is said that up to a million people in Indonesia were massacred, and this happened as it was trying to shape its identity post-independence. Malaysia, meanwhile, was having a relatively peaceful time. The British had pulled out, leaving institutions – roads, schools – in place, while Indonesia really had nothing. Growing up in Malaysia we were always told that Indonesia was a country that shared huge things in common with us – the same religion, the same language, a very similar culture – but in fact they have an incredibly different history, so I had this idea of writing a novel about two brothers who seemed to be similar but actually had very different paths through adolescence into adulthood. As their two countries attempt to find an identity for themselves, the boys too are trying to find out who they are and where they are from. I guess in a similar fashion to the first novel, they, too, grew up with huge silences. They don't know where they are from and the entire novel is about their quest to discover that, and in fact they do so to two varying degrees.

BIGSBY Your most recent book, *Five Star Billionaire*, moves away from Malaysia and Indonesia to Shanghai, a huge city in which people have come from Malaysia. Being in American Studies as I was reading this book about Shanghai I was thinking of New York. Both America and Shanghai are places people go to reinvent themselves. They are about change and change is a theme in all of your books but especially so here. One character steals an identity card and assumes a new identity. Another writes self-help books while another reads them, in fact the self-help mantras form your chapter headings. That is very American. Isn't Shanghai the America of the 1910s, the 1920s, the 1930s?

AW I absolutely felt that. When I did the research and writing of the novel, I absolutely felt that. One reads about New York a hundred years ago, and Shanghai seemed to me to be the modern incarnation of that. America and China always think of each other as being polar opposites, arch enemies politically, economically and culturally, but anyone who has spent any length of time in China will realise how in many ways China, today, distils the qualities that we think of as American and ramps them up several degrees. For example, self-help books, which in Britain and Europe haven't really taken off, have always been part of life in America and are today in China. When I lived in Shanghai every single person on the tube, on the bus, would be reading self-help books and a lot of them would be translated titles from those that were originally published in America.

China has changed so much over the last few years and

it feels as if people are desperate to reinvent themselves. The country is going through a fundamental change and so a lot of the books that people were reading were how to get rich books, which are everywhere. But there are also more crass self-help books. For example, one of the most popular books when I was there was a book called *Why Men Love Bitches*. It was being sold in bookshops everywhere. It was being sold on pavements by counterfeit book sellers and successful, professional, young women, educated women, were reading it. It just seemed incredibly anachronistic to me. It is almost as if coming out of a long period when freedom was restricted, people were seizing this chance to be free in the most unsavoury ways and that got me thinking about what I wanted to write and the things I wanted to look at in the novel.

But I was also struck by the number of foreigners who were coming to Shanghai. When one isn't in China one has this impression of China as being this huge monolithic country closed off to the outside world, a bigger version of North Korea, but in fact it is really not. It is incredibly vibrant and open and energetic and certainly big cities like Shanghai and Beijing have become magnets for people coming from other parts of the world, but particularly other parts of Asia, the poorer countries of Asia. People are drawn to the bright lights of Shanghai.

BIGSBY The irony, surely, is that the people who once went to Malaysia now go to China looking for the same thing they went to Malaysia for.

AW Absolutely. Economically, they are the new version of economic migrants that their forefathers were, a hundred, a hundred and fifty years ago. During my time there I was constantly running into people from Malaysia and Singapore and seeing how they were totally reinventing themselves in a way that would not have been possible had they stayed in their home countries. China is a huge country and a city like Shanghai has twenty million people, so it is very easy to get lost in the crowd and re-emerge as someone else, and no one asks you questions. China changes so quickly that the need for human resources, for new talent, new skills, labour, is so great that no one really asks you where you are from. No one is really bothered.

BIGSBY These are characters who have abandoned one country for another and as a result feel isolated. Yet they do eventually come to re-value the place they have left.

AW Yes. Again I think it is a question of that missing part in one's story that we talked about earlier. For all these people who are desperately trying to create a new life for themselves, what makes them whole, what makes them complete, what makes them who they are, is actually that missing part of their story that they either don't know or are trying to escape. They can't articulate it but they have to go through all the ups and downs of life in Shanghai in order to realise that where they are from, Malaysia, is what makes them who they are. It is a novel set mainly in Shanghai but at its heart it is a very Malaysian novel because the people are all incredibly rooted to where they are from. They are trying to escape their past, with varying degrees of success, but at the end of the novel there are those who have realised that that missing bit is what makes them whole.

Anyone who goes to China now will witness the rush for material wealth, but what does that material wealth signify? It signifies a search for happiness but people are patently unhappy. My book is not meant as a judgement. It just raises a series of questions about the path that modern Asia has taken over the last ten years, which is the path of material wealth, the path that guides us inexorably towards greater and greater riches but ironically diminishing levels of happiness and contentment.

BIGSBY And there is a kind of hunt here, as in the other novels, for authenticity. This is a society in which so many of the goods are fakes?

AW And the people are fakes, too. The culture of fakery is so developed that people talk of genuine fakes. One of the characters, Phoebe, is a genuine fake. She has totally reinvented herself. She comes from a small town in Malaysia and wants to become a glamorous Shanghai girl, to be like the sexy young women she sees walking the streets, but she never quite gets there and is always going to be identified as a fake. Her journey through the novel is really what guides us through the various ups and downs, the crossing of paths, the self-realisations. The question is whether they will realise who they are by the end of the novel.

BIGSBY And China is another society where a line has been drawn across the past.

AW Yes, and it is a really powerful and seductive narrative. How does a country like China deal with something as huge and cataclysmic in its recent history as the Cultural Revolution? The answer is not to address it. Let's just draw a line and go shopping. But China is not alone in this. All of south east Asia is like this. How do we escape the problems that were created under colonial rule? How do we deal with the problem of racial divisions? How do we deal with the increasing gap between rich and poor? The answer is to make everyone believe that they can be rich. Everyone should just work and buy stuff, that is the answer. Do not look back, do not go back, do not address things that have happened in the past.

There are other middle class, Western-educated people who are concerned with preserving the architectural heritage of Malaysia and China and they soon realise that they are fighting a losing battle because Asia doesn't care about all that. The attitude towards history, towards one's history or one's past, differs between Asia and Europe. In Europe the past tends to be celebrated, in Asia it is not. I don't mean to sound negative or overly pessimistic. My novels are not depressing reading.

BIGSBY No, and they are also lyrical. Is that lyricism is itself a value?

AW Yes, I think so. I like the word lyricism because most people speak of nostalgia, and the books are not nostalgic. I am not a nostalgic person. I like advancement. What I don't like is advancement at all costs, unthinking advancement without some kind of analysis of what it is we are trying to achieve and what it is we are giving up in achieving it. When I was growing up Malaysia had a very lyrical everyday life which is difficult to discern nowadays. One finds this in the rural areas of China but it has largely gone, and that's what troubles me, that's what drives my writing, I think. What it is we are giving up. I am not a nostalgic person, but I do need the questions to be asked.

VINCE CABLE

Sir Vince Cable was born in York in 1943. He studied at Cambridge University and the University of Glasgow, where he taught for six years. He was economic advisor to the government of Kenya and was later Chief Economist for Shell. In politics, he was a Labour councillor in Glasgow. Having been a member of the Labour Party he joined the SDP in 1982, which later merged with the Liberal Party to form the Liberal Democrats. He was elected to parliament in 1997, subsequently becoming the Liberal Democrat Treasury Spokesman and Deputy Leader, and then leader in 2017. He served in the coalition government from 2010 to 2015 in which he was Secretary of State for Business, Innovation and Skills. He was subsequently knighted. He is the author of a number of books, most recently *After the Storm: The World Economy and Britain's Economic Future*.

This interview was recorded on October 14, 2015.

BIGSBY You were born into a working class family, were you not?

CABLE It was an upwardly mobile working class. My mother and father left school at fifteen and worked in chocolate factories in York but they were ambitious and my father worked hard, night school, all of those things, and became a technical college lecturer in building, teaching bricklayers and people of that kind. But the environment at home was ambitious, hardworking. It was the kind of values that we often aspire to but because of the times my dad had some very, very right wing views. This was when we still had an empire.

BIGSBY So it was racism.

CABLE Yes, and that became quite awkward when I married somebody from India.

BIGSBY And your parents didn't speak to you for six years.

CABLE That's right, and this occurred when I was an undergraduate. I did a summer vacation job in a mental hospital and met my late wife there. She was doing the same thing and by one of those remarkable coincidences she lived in the city I was going to work in, which was Nairobi in Kenya. We met up and got married, but it was too much for my family, who had grown up with a very different set of values, and it was too much for her family as well. They had arranged, or wanted, a marriage with somebody of the same religion, the same caste. She was a Goan but although they are Christian, caste and culture matter.

BIGSBY You have said that your mother, before she married, was beaten by her father because she went out with a socialist.

CABLE That's right. Well that was one of the family stories. She was quite independent minded and courted the man who subsequently became the leader of the Labour group on York City Council but was a trade union activist and socialist, while my grandfather was a real working class Conservative. He fought in the First World War, hated Germans, hated socialists, hated trade unions, all those things, and that was the environment in which she grew up.

BIGSBY You hint, too, that, there was some violence in your family. Was it your father?

CABLE It wasn't an enormous problem but I was painfully aware of it and it was one of the factors that contributed to my mother having a breakdown when I was about ten. She went off to a mental hospital and came back after a year or so. My younger brother had been born and I think these days we call it post-natal depression but in those days it wasn't understood and people were simply shipped off to institutions, but it had one very positive outcome because when my mother came back home she went into adult education. This was somebody who had never had a proper education at school and she taught herself about art and history and philosophy, things that were completely new, and it cured her mental health. One of the last things I did in government, and actually one of the things I was proudest of doing, was getting money out of George Osborne, not a vast amount but a certain amount of money, to launch programmes in adult education colleges to help mentally ill people get back into society and that was a product of my earlier experience as a teenager.

BIGSBY You use a curious word when you describe your relationship to your parents – 'indifference.' Is that because you didn't share anything with them anymore and they didn't have any values that you recognised or embraced?

CABLE We did later in life become reconciled. I went off with my wife and we had a family before coming back to the UK and living in Glasgow. We had no connection with my father but eventually, I think out of curiosity as much as anything else, he wanted to see our grandchildren and we met up and the relationship gradually mellowed and it was quite extraordinary. He had these very, very, old-fashioned and certainly politically incorrect views but he developed a considerable respect for my wife who was phenomenally talented, a great musician. He loved music and discovered that he probably had more in common with her than he did with most of the other people he dealt with. Gradually you saw his old prejudices dissolving and in the later part of our lives that was a really heart-warming experience.

BIGSBY You went to grammar school, as did I, and like me, and perhaps that whole generation of people who had benefitted from grammar schools, had the feeling that, at the age of eleven, suddenly all our friends had disappeared because only 19% went to grammar school while 81% went to that 'undiscovered country from whose bourn no traveller returns', that's to say they went to secondary moderns and very rarely did anyone come back. Did that shape your later views about education?

CABLE Yes, it did. In the city that I grew up in, which was York, the issue about grammars versus secondary moderns versus comprehensives was one of the formative debates until it was finally resolved by Anthony Crosland in the 1960s. One date is certainly engraved in my memory, the day when the Eleven Plus results were announced. I was in the top stream and expected to go to a grammar school but I think there were three or four people in the class who had failed, who didn't pass the Eleven Plus, and they all burst into tears. They were friends and in several cases I never saw them again. It was a trapdoor and certainly my own views about education were very significantly influenced by that.

BIGSBY You went to Cambridge, initially to do science. So how did you end up as an economist?

CABLE In the kind of background that I grew up in my father was a very powerful personality and took the view that you have to do something useful in life. Usefulness meant being an engineer or an accountant or a lawyer, I think. He didn't want what he called 'arty farty stuff' like history and English or anything like that, although I happened to be extremely good at those things. So it was just about acceptable for me to do maths, physics and chemistry and if you have done that you become a scientist, but when I got to Cambridge I developed an interest in debating, in politics, in acting, and it wasn't compatible with spending your day in a laboratory, so I switched to economics and it happens that Cambridge has a great tradition in economics – Keynes and all that – so I became very much absorbed in it.

BIGSBY While there you went on to become President of the Union. At that time you were a Liberal but you then changed to be a Labour supporter.

CABLE I had a dilemma, which has remained pretty much to this day, and indeed we are living through it again. I was what you might loosely call centre left, and I always have been, and when I was a student I was attracted by the Liberals, who were led then by a man called Jo Grimond, very radical but enlightened, very pro-European, but I was also attracted by some of the people in the Labour party like Roy Jenkins, Anthony Crosland and Shirley Williams, who was then a young MP. It was very difficult to decide between them actually, so I initially went with the Liberals but then, when Harold Wilson came along in 1964, with his reference to the white hot heat of the technological revolution, I was attracted and I went along with it. I stayed with the Labour Party until the civil war in 1978, 1979, 1980, when I joined the SDP. I see that history now being repeated all over again. It is an extraordinary circular process.

BIGSBY There was a period when you had a respectable job, that is to say you were a university lecturer for six years. What made you give up on that career?

CABLE One of my earlier jobs was teaching economics at Glasgow University and I doubled up as a councillor in Glasgow. It was an extraordinary thing in a way. I was one of the few English people and certainly middle class English people in what was a very strong Labour, very Irish working class, slightly Mafia-like, operation but in some ways quite competent. They were building enormous numbers of houses, for example, the ones that have just been knocked down a couple of days ago. There was an enormous amount of real, quite progressive, activity but by a series of flukes which are too boring to describe I got elected as a councillor for one of the quite tough working class wards in Glasgow. The next I think was the second safest seat, apart from the Gorbals, and I spent several years helping to run Glasgow. So I wasn't really teaching economics. The university paid my salary though I was really running the city but it wasn't leading anywhere and I wanted to do something else. So I came to London and a new stage of life.

BIGSBY You tried to get elected to Parliament and it took you twenty-seven years to get elected. How do you deal with that? It is like somebody who writes novels each one of them trashed. There must come a point when you say, 'Is this a game I should give up?' Why did you not give up?

CABLE Very often young people come and say, 'I want to do politics. I want to be an MP. I want a political career' and I say, 'It isn't like that. It isn't like deciding to be an engineer or an accountant or even a university lecturer. It is about being in the right place at the right time. It is in large part about luck.' I was often in the wrong place at the wrong time. Obviously you have to be intelligent, up to a point, and a communicator, up to a point, but the qualities you need are stamina and energy above all and I think having the stamina to survive repeated frustrations and defeats was actually a key part of my DNA and the people who survive longest and best in politics are the people who have that kind of character. You can't just say, 'I want to be a politician' and go in there and do it. Some people are lucky but by and large it doesn't work like that. You have to be very persistent and show a lot of stamina.

BIGSBY Everyone has to deal at some stage in their life with failure of one kind or another but to stand up repeatedly beside the Returning Officer and have it explained that once again you have not been elected is a very public failure and I would have thought psychologically very difficult to recover from each time.

CABLE It was, but there was an upside, one of which was that I did spend time with my family.

BIGSBY That's a notorious phrase.

CABLE It is a notorious phrase but that was what the electorate decided I should do and it did mean that I was able to spend time with my family which was very close and very loving and psychologically very strong. My late wife was incredibly encouraging. A lot of people would say 'give up' but whenever I asked for support she always gave it to me. That was one advantage. The other advantage was that I was able to do interesting jobs and learn something about life.

BIGSBY Yes, because you are not one of those people who went from Eton, to Oxford, to Parliament or even from Oxford, to public relations to Parliament. You were the Chief Economist for Shell, a huge corporation and a great responsibility. In your book you write with pride about working for that company. But there was another side to Shell, and you mention it. It has to do with the writer and activist Ken Saro-Wiwa, who I knew personally. He spoke up for the Ogoni people and was executed. Shell ended up paying £15.5 million in an out-of-court settlement for the problems in that part of Nigeria.

CABLE I got directly involved in that particular controversy. One of my jobs in the company, apart from doing long-term scenario planning as we called it, a kind of risk assessment, was trying to plan ahead for Shell operating in some of the big emerging markets – Russia, China, and India, notably. But when the Nigeria crisis erupted around Ken Saro-Wiwa I was asked to work with our Nigerian company to help them plan a way forward. There were people saying, 'You have just got to get out of this country. It is so evil,' but others, notably the Nigerians themselves in our company, were absolutely adamant that we should stay put. I had to go out several times and one of the most frightening things I have ever done in my life was to make a presentation of my work to the ruling military council including General Abacha, who was the military dictator. He was ultimately responsible for the execution of Saro-Wiwa and there was one chilling moment when I was trying to be honest. I pointed out the problems in the country – human rights, corruption etc. – and at the end of my presentation the Nigerian Finance Minister stood up saying, 'Who is this white man coming here telling us we have corruption in Nigeria? There is no such thing.' There was a deafening silence for about thirty seconds and Abacha then burst out laughing and the whole audience joined in the laughter because obviously the place was riddled with corruption and the President was at the heart of it. Meeting Abacha, the last dictator of Nigeria, who had blood on his hands, was quite a chilling experience.

BIGSBY You finally got elected in 1997 at the beginning of a long Labour government and, interestingly to me, you say that, Iraq aside, you were quite an admirer of Tony Blair?

CABLE Yes, and one of the things I just don't understand about the present day Labour party and Jeremy Corbyn is the almost venomous attitude towards Blair. OK, the guy got the Iraq war wrong. I was one of the people who voted against it, the Lib Dems did, and I think he has behaved badly in this money-grabbing exercise since he left Parliament but, that apart, this was somebody who was a Prime Minister for a decade who, working jointly with Gordon Brown, did a great deal of good on the economy, much of it very constructive. He was responsible for a lot of progressive reforms, everything from the devolution settlement to the minimum wage. I vividly remember the day he retired as Prime Minister and spontaneously everybody in the House of Commons got up and applauded him. This had never happened in Parliament before and it was a measure of the respect for the man. The Tories did it, Labour and Lib Dems, we all did it and I just don't understand why, five, six, seven years on, he is just regarded as some kind of dreadful pariah. It doesn't actually make sense because if you lived through that period this was somebody who was probably the most successful leader the Labour Party has ever had. He was a great communicator and managed to accomplish a great deal. So maybe at some point I will write a sympathetic biography.

BIGSBY Well you have got time on your hands. We jumped over something you mentioned earlier, which is that you joined the SDP. What made you take that jump because others didn't?

CABLE I think the thing that made me make the jump was the fact that I lived in London. Had I stayed in Glasgow and worked with some of my former Scottish Labour friends – I had been a special advisor to John Smith, later leader of the Labour Party and a wonderful man – I would have stayed in the Labour Party but what happened in London was a Trotskyite revolt. I belonged to a suburban Labour Party and the Labour Party were never ever going to get into power under them. We used to sit round discussing what would happen when the workers' revolution took place, who would seize the town hall and how would we create a workers' committee to run Twickenham. It was just mind-bogglingly silly but there was one event that did make me leave. I wasn't part of the first wave, with Shirley Williams, David Owen and Roy Jenkins, but I had a good friend who was a Labour MP in Islington and Islington was the epicentre of the Trotskyite revolt in the Labour Party. One of the key figures in that group was a man called Mr Corbyn and my friend George Cunningham, a great MP, not ideologically right wing or anything, was deselected by them. They evicted him from the party because he didn't share the extreme views of the local party. I felt that was a very personal thing and I thought, well, if this is the way it's going I will join the SDP and the future Lib Dems. That was the event.

BIGSBY Let me move you on into the present century and the difficulty with the leader of the Liberals, Charles Kennedy. You were the one who had to take the letter to him suggesting that he ought to resign, is that right?

CABLE Yes, it was a very, very difficult personal experience. Charles Kennedy was a lovely man and in many ways outstanding. When he was on form he was one of the best speakers in British public life. He had extraordinarily shrewd political judgement but unfortunately he drank very heavily and we had more and more episodes of things that were happening that shouldn't be happening, not turning up for events and so on. The consensus amongst my parliamentary colleagues was that this couldn't continue and that we had to ask him to step down. I am not sure quite how it happened but I was told to go and read the riot act to him. These things are never very pleasant. I remember Ken Clarke describing how he was the one who had to go and tell Mrs Thatcher to go and I had to do the same with Charles Kennedy and I have always felt bad about it but I think it was inevitable.

BIGSBY There have been various moments when you could have put in a bid to be leader. Why didn't you, in the end?

CABLE The opportunity never arose. When Charles Kennedy's successor Ming Campbell was struggling, and a lot of animosity and ridicule was directed at him exaggerating the fact that he was an old man – he wasn't actually, he was only 65 or something – I was the deputy at the time and the view of all my parliamentary colleagues was that 'we like you and we think you would do a good job, but after we have had one leader who has been shot down for being too old we can hardly have you.' So they polarised between Chris Huhne and Nick Clegg and I was left to do the job of acting leader which got me a few good lines because it was in the middle of the banking crisis. It was just beginning with Northern Rock and I got completely immersed in that. I thought, this is the biggest economic event of our time, as it proved to be, and I just got distracted from this whole leadership issue and I was happy doing what I did. That was the only real opportunity that arose.

BIGSBY But when you were acting leader you did get to cross-question the Prime Minister and you seemed quite relaxed in that role.

CABLE Parliament is a very strange place. It is either dead, completely dead, and you sometimes see this on the television in the evening. There are probably ten people in the chamber and somebody is speaking at length while nobody is listening. It is very strange and totally lacking in life. It is either that or it is complete bedlam and you have this Prime Minister's Questions when you have five hundred people in a room that is designed for two-hundred-and-fifty and people are shouting and screaming and what I discovered was that – and it may be my early training on the stage when I was in my late teens – I could actually cope with that kind of theatrical environment and function in it. That's probably why I did Prime Minister's Questions quite well because it does require quite a strong nerve to do it.

BIGSBY You mention 2008 and the financial crisis. You have denied seeing it coming, saying, 'Who did see it coming?' especially since it started in the United States with subprime mortgages and Lehman Brothers. On the other hand you were saying things in Parliament before then which were about this country and you were issuing certain warnings?

CABLE I didn't predict what would happen because, as you say, it was a global crisis, but there were certain elements which I did feel at quite an early stage were going to lead to disaster. One of those was the bubble in the housing market which we are still living with. It is still there. It is still dangerous. I mean the relationship between people's earnings and the mortgages they take out are insane, certainly in London and many parts of the East and the South East, but it was reaching extreme levels in 2007, 2008 and the banks were continuing to finance it in a way that was, in my view, totally irresponsible and was only going to lead to trouble. I was also becoming increasingly critical of the way the banks were functioning. There was one episode that stuck in my mind. I went to see the Chief Executive, I think it was of the Halifax, an extremely bright guy, and I said, 'Why are you pouring more and more mortgage lending into this market? You are a bank. Surely you have some basic standards of prudence?' He grinned and said, 'You are right. Perhaps I shouldn't be doing this but if I didn't my shareholders would get rid of me and replace me with somebody else.' The banks were becoming hard-wired to extremely irresponsible behaviour. Then I remember going to see the Governor of the Bank of England and his people. I had regular lunch with them because I was a Shadow Chancellor and I said, 'Aren't you worried about this? There is some trouble coming here. There are storm clouds on the horizon.' Their attitude was, 'We don't think there is a problem and anyway if there is it has got nothing to do with us. It is not our responsibility.' That was the attitude in the Establishment. The banks, the regulators, the Bank of England basically just didn't want to know, but as you say I was getting increasingly agitated and concerned about it and warning that there was trouble.

BIGSBY One thing you put your finger on was demutualisation as the cause of a lot of this problem.

CABLE The first campaign I ever ran as an MP when I got into Parliament in 1997, and one of the big campaigns of that first Parliament, was to do with those very good building societies – you may remember some of them, The Woolwich, Halifax, Abbey National – gradually being converted into banks and of course as banks their job was to provide dividends for shareholders whereas as mutuals they were there to serve their members. These building societies were gradually being gobbled up and it had got to a point where effectively members of building societies were being bribed with shares: Northern Rock, Birmingham Midshires and all the rest of them. Some of us organised a campaign to try to stop this and we did eventually do so and that action kept the Nationwide Building Society mutual, but unfortunately most of the others had gone and it is worth reflecting now that not a single one of those demutualised building societies has survived, not one of them. They have all either gone bankrupt, which is what happened with Northern Rock and Bradford and Bingley, or they have been totally subsumed into other institutions. So when people cast around for blame, certainly some of it lay with the government at the time, Gordon Brown and his colleagues, but the deregulation, the demutualisation, started with Nigel Lawson and the Conservative government in the late 1980s and in a way that was the genesis of the problem.

BIGSBY When you have a regulator it implies there is a need for regulation, in other words that you cannot allow the market, as those on the right would suggest, to simply balance itself out in one way or another. It is funny that those people who believe most fiercely in the market spend much of their time trying to rig it. When did you become aware of the extent of the corruption, because it went far beyond sub-prime mortgages? There was mis-selling of just about everything you could name?

CABLE Nobody used the word corruption.

BIGSBY I like the word.

CABLE Of course the Libor scandal has been unearthed subsequently, but there was a lot of completely unacceptable behaviour whether you call it corrupt or not. People were operating on bonuses not just in the investment banks, which encouraged them to take ridiculous risks of a kind that ultimately brought down Lehman Brothers and RBS and the rest of them, but even in your local branch people who were there to serve you as local customers became salesmen for insurance policies. That is how the PPI scandal, for example, erupted. So there was a pervasive decline in the standards of banking, whether you call it corruption or something else I don't know. It was becoming very widespread but I think now we look back on it we know there was a banking crisis so we look for who was to blame, but it was quite extraordinary the way that almost everybody had rationalised what was going on. For example, in the economics profession, which I was part of, there was a very powerful theory called 'the theory of the efficient markets'. This theory essentially said that the market is always right. They have always factored in all the risks so that it doesn't matter if prices go up and down. That is essentially rational behaviour. The whole profession had closed its eyes to the possibility that you could have a catastrophic meltdown in the system. That was the mind-set, not just of the bankers and the regulators and the central bankers, but also the economists and the people in decision-making. They insisted that what was happening was rational and safe.

What we have had since, of course, is the complete destruction of that mental map.

BIGSBY Then came the 2010 election and the Liberals found themselves much to their surprise, I imagine, in a position of some power and they had to decide which way to go. Was it a case of head versus heart, the head having to do with the mathematics of the number of seats in parliament, and the heart which lay with the Labour party, which after all was your own background? You were involved, to some degree, in negotiations with the Labour party, were you not?

CABLE I was informally talking to Gordon Brown; I was one of his lines of communication. He was trying to continue in office, I think partly for personal reasons but partly for honourable reasons. He could see that there was a big financial crisis going on and had ideas about how to resolve it. So I was one of his main lines of communication. I wasn't a part of the formal negotiation. There wasn't a great deal of choice about it. The numbers didn't allow any other option. It wasn't just that the rainbow coalition of Labour, Lib Dems, Nationalists, Greens didn't add up, it was that leading people in the Labour party didn't want to go into coalition. When we had discussions with them the two Milibands and Ed Balls were very clear. They wanted to go into opposition. They had had a long period in government and knew that there was a terrible period of budgetary tightening coming up. They wanted to get out, choose the next leader etc. So there was no way we could have formed a government with them even if we wanted to, and, as you say, my heart was probably in that direction. The other factor which weighed very heavily was that we were in the middle of a very serious financial crisis and throughout the negotiations I was getting telephone calls from the Chief Secretary, from the chief official in the Treasury, from the Head of the Civil Service, messages from the Governor of the Bank of England saying, 'for God's sake you politicians have got to stop messing around. The country is in crisis. We need a government and we need a stable government to deal with it.' Now you could have argued that they exaggerated the problem but at the time there was a palpable sense of crisis and that combined with the numbers propelled us into that coalition.

BIGSBY Two broken promises, the first one made by the Conservatives, the promise by David Cameron that there would be no top-down reorganisation of the National Health Service, which was followed by the largest top-down reorganisation of the National Health Service in its history. What struck me at the time was he was almost a hands-off Prime Minister. He handed over to the Barons and one Baron was Andrew Lansley, who ran that re-organisation through parliament. Were the Liberals caught napping?

CABLE I think we were. I think I am allowed to talk about this. We had a series of Cabinet meetings in the first six months of the government and the Prime Minister asked us all to prepare our programme of work and I did my thing. We were launching apprenticeship schemes and the beginnings of an industrial strategy and I went through all that and everybody nodded and said 'That's fine, just get on with it.' Then it came to Lansley's turn and he must have spent twenty minutes, half an hour, talking about his vision for the Health Service. Nobody understood a word he was saying. It was full of health service gobbledygook. Anybody in the NHS will know what I mean and I think the attitude in the room was, 'Well, you are the only person here who understands it so just get on and do what you have to do.' It was a terrible mistake. You are quite right. Everybody on both sides of the coalition realised that it was a very bad mistake. The Health Service does of course need some very difficult action but it wasn't that. It wasted money. It wasted time. Once the reforms had taken legislative shape my side of the coalition realised that there was something desperately wrong with all of this and we constantly tried to amend the legislation with some success but we didn't stop this enormous diversion of effort and money into the reorganisation. It was actually one of the worst episodes of the government. I don't think any one particular party was responsible. We all were, but it was a very bad episode.

BIGSBY The other Baron is really a Baroness. Theresa May seems to have been given her head because David Cameron goes off to India to say, 'We are open for business' while she slammed the door so loudly that it drove people away, certainly we have driven Indian students away. They have gone to Australia, to America, anywhere but this country. She has also refused to remove students from the immigration figures, students who are manifestly not immigrants being here to study. If I were a Conservative saying I want to reduce immigration, I would just remove them from the statistics. Theresa May won't do that. How does she get this power?

CABLE You are describing one of the more difficult relationships I had in the government because I was responsible for higher and further education and therefore for the whole of that controversy. I think I should preface my remarks by saying that it wasn't really a personality thing. Theresa May is a very civil, charming, softly-spoken, pleasant woman, but she had a mission, and to be fair to her she was given that mission by her party, which was to reduce net immigration from what it was, a quarter of a million, to a hundred thousand. We made it very clear in our side of the coalition we didn't agree with that but nonetheless they kept describing it as 'the government's policy' but certainly from a party point of view that was her job and she wanted to deliver it. It collided with me because I was responsible not just for higher education, but for long term economic growth and business was telling me that they needed highly skilled people from India, China, Brazil, America etc. and what happened was that Theresa May kept coming forward with measures to make immigration even tighter for those categories that could be controlled and this is where this whole immigration debate is so confusing, because there are significant elements of immigration that you cannot control, movements within the European Union, crucially British people emigrating because that is the other side of net immigration. So in order to try to meet her target she concentrated on the categories which could be controlled by the British Government, one of which was so called Tier 2 visas for skilled people and the other of which were overseas students.

In the case of overseas students there was a genuine problem. There was some abuse. I think it was wildly exaggerated but there was some abuse of the system but I took the view, which you obviously take, that overseas students were good for the country. They are not immigrants. Overwhelmingly, they go back home. They contribute to the income of the universities. They enrich universities. Why don't we have more of them not fewer of them? But for the reason you give they are included in the immigration statistics and inconveniently the United Nations classifies them as immigrants. So Theresa with, to some extent, her tunnel vision insisted that we curb overseas students. I resisted it. I had support from some of my Tory ministers on this, like David Willetts, and we managed to get compromises. We didn't actually impose a quota on overseas students but, nonetheless, a signal was sent out that was very negative and it did discourage Indian students. We are getting a lot more from China but certainly some were actively discouraged.

I think the final point to make about this, and I think it is probably what lies behind your question, is that one of the really interesting things about the government which I could never quite fathom was that the Prime Minister never seemed to be able to have any influence on her at all. We would be appealing to her, even Osborne was, saying, 'For God's sake, you know you are doing a lot of harm'. We had examples of Chinese billionaires coming here wanting to invest in Britain and they were turned away at Heathrow because they were thought to be asylum seekers. There was complete chaos in that system but she took the view 'we are going to keep these bastards out' and of course it didn't work because there are so many bits of immigration you can't control. But she was completely resolute. She wouldn't budge and that is where we are now.

BIGSBY I mentioned students, and mentioned broken promises, and you will expect this question.
CABLE Yes, yes.

BIGSBY Because before that election so many Liberal candidates, including Nick Clegg, were photographed beside a pledge to scrap tuition fees. Obviously, when you went into coalition there were certain red lines, to do, for example, with electoral reform, but there was no red line to do with student fees. When you think that 50% of the age group go to university and that they have families, all of whom can vote, this was, even on that pragmatic level, not a good thing, any more than breaking promises appeals to the public.

CABLE It was a terrible mistake to have made that pledge, a very bad mistake, and we paid dearly for it. We weren't the first party to break pledges on tuition fees. The Labour Party originally promised not to introduce them and did. Then they promised not to increase them and they did, but that was no excuse. We shouldn't have done it. I have to say that when this issue was first raised, back in 2001, by David Blunkett I think, I thought the Labour government were absolutely right to do what they were doing and I argued this with my colleagues but I was overridden. I was in a minority of one, as it happened, and the party became very attached to this policy. Because of the way party democracy works we got committed to something which I knew, and Nick Clegg knew, was a very bad idea because universities do need income and they are normally going to get it in that way. So, anyway, when the government was formed we were in a very difficult position. There was absolutely no way we could deliver that promise. I was put in charge of a department with a twenty billion budget, the largest part of which was universities, and the job I was given was to find twenty-five percent savings in that department. These were numbers I had inherited from Alistair Darling and Peter Mandelson. Where do you get twenty-five percent savings when your budget consists of universities, further education and science?

The advice I was getting from the officials was, 'Don't do too much on universities. You will make a lot of enemies and you have made this pledge. Why don't you take all the money from the further education colleges? Nobody will notice because that is the 60% who don't go to university?' I am afraid I was very bloody-minded and said 'no, I am sorry, these are working class kids for the most part. They should get priority. We are desperately short of good vocational training and I am not willing to make drastic cuts in further education.' So the money had to come in significant part from the universities and the only way we could do that without cutting the funding which universities get was by increasing the fees. Of course you don't pay anything to come to university. It is effectively a graduate tax that, as people graduate, and if they get a high earning job, they pay back and that constitutes the stream of income which then funds the universities. It is progressive because if you have an income under £21,000 you don't pay anything. So the policy I introduced I thought was a good one and it has kept making sure that universities are properly financially supported. You don't find cuts in universities today in the way that you do, say, in the police force or local councils, so it worked well. The policy was a good one but the politics was awful and I have sometimes said that we got two out of ten for the politics and eight out of ten for the policy and I think that is actually fair but we certainly have suffered grievously politically. We should never have made the pledge and we have paid the price.

BIGSBY There was a Conservative narrative in 2010, and again in 2015, that the financial crisis was down to the Labour Party. What amazed me was that the Labour Party seemed to accept this narrative and not challenge it. In your book you go a long way to absolving the Labour party.

CABLE Yes, I think these arguments are quite complex but they are very important. I think the Brown Labour government in many ways has a heavy responsibility. They let things happen. The banks got out of control, the housing bubble got out of control, but what they didn't do was let the public finances get out of control before the crisis. Actually the level of government debt, the deficit, was quite respectable by almost any standards but there were two stories about why this financial crisis happened at that time, and they have a bearing on the way we behave today. One of them was the view that I and other people were taking which was that this was a banking crisis and the problems lay in the banks and the housing market; the other view, the Conservative view, was that it was all caused by the Labour government spending too much money and you remember the phrase about 'closing the hole in the roof when the sun shines'. Well I spent quite a lot of time in my book going back over those events and it is fairly clear that that story is simply wrong. The public finances were actually in very good shape in 2008. Maybe they were going in the wrong direction a bit, but it wasn't a big problem, and yet the Conservatives won that historical argument and this is unfortunately what happens in politics. Many see Richard III as a bad king. He wasn't a bad king. He just lost and his successors wrote the history and this is what has happened now. The Conservatives have won. They have re-written history and it is a history which describes the problem in terms of bad management of public finances and hence the pressure that is building the whole time to cut more and more from government spending.

BIGSBY And they make a great deal of Liam Byrne leaving that note saying, 'Sorry, there is no money left.'
CABLE Yes, and that is a stupid thing to have said.

BIGSBY Except that it was a Conservative Chancellor, Reginald Maudling, in 1964, who left an almost identical note. You were Business Secretary so actually the banks came within your purview.
CABLE Partly.

BIGSBY You have been arguing against their behaviour and arguing against the bonus culture which I think almost everyone feels is deeply pervasive and despicable. People can walk away with tens of millions and, apparently, it doesn't matter if they have failed or succeeded. Personally I don't understand the concept of bonus. You pay people a large sum of money to do their job properly so where does the bonus come from? I just don't understand that. Is government powerless in the face of the power of the banks over bonuses and their behaviour?

CABLE A lot happened to put the thing in the right direction. The bonus pool, as it's called, has shrunk from thirteen billion, which is what it was at the height of the crisis when I was in government, to about two billion.

BIGSBY So they give them shares instead.

CABLE Yes, long term shares, so that people had a long term interest in their institutions and I have no problem with that. The other thing which we did, and it came as a result of an agreement that I reached with George Osborne, was to separate the so-called 'casinos', the investment banks, from ordinary retail banking and we did this through something called 'ring-fencing'. This has been legislated for. It has gone through parliament and is being implemented at the moment. So we did actually effect significant reform of the banks, though not completely. Barclays have just appointed an investment manager, a banker, as their head so some of that culture is still there.

I think we have regulated the banks so that they are much less risky than they were before. They are now required to hold more capital. My main problem with the banks, when I was in government, was that after the crisis they lurched from being extraordinarily reckless to being ultra-conservative in the way that they treated small and medium-sized companies. It was virtually impossible to get money and even today, although we did a lot – I set up this British Business Bank which is doing a lot to finance business – if you are a small builder now trying to get credit to build some more homes, you find it very difficult while if you want to buy a house the government is pushing money at you so the banking system in Britain is not geared to supporting productive activity. That is the central structural weakness. We did things to push it back in the right direction but it is still way off what they have, say, in Germany.

BIGSBY One other thing you did, and you will probably expect this question, as Business Secretary was to be in charge of the sell-off of Royal Mail, and as you will know the response was that you sold low because by the end of the year the share price had gone up by 70% but also that certain groups were given privileges with regard to shares on the assumption that they would hold on to them long term and quite a few of them didn't. Do you think you did exactly the right thing or if you could go back would you have done it slightly differently?

CABLE I made a lot of mistakes in government. We all do. But I don't actually think this was one of them. There are particular aspects I would have done differently but in the big picture I think it was right. Let me just explain why. The problem with Royal Mail is that it is a dying industry. Its main business was – is – delivering and collecting letters and this is declining at a rate of 4 or 5% a year because anti-social people like us send emails. We are depriving them of their main business so that the company was dying. It was making very large losses and the only way to turn it around was to get them new business, and the way to do that was to get them into logistics which is parcels and things of that kind which are growing because of Amazon and the rest. In order to do this properly, and to be able to compete, they had to raise money in the markets because the Treasury would not allow them to borrow because of the wider problem with public finances. So they had to go into the private sector in order to raise the money.

One of the first things I did in government was to set this process in train while making sure that the workers had a big share in the ownership. We created a workers share ownership and also made sure that the regulation of the industry was tightened up so that you would continue to have a five day week delivery. When it came to the sale, of course the mechanics of it were handled by advisors and officials but I am the Secretary of State. I had to take responsibility for it. What I did do after the sale had taken place was ask one of Gordon Brown's ministers, a man called Lord Myners, to go back over what we had done and ask, 'Did we get this wrong?' His conclusion was that we didn't. The price when it was sold seemed in retrospect to be relatively low but it was relatively low because at the time the unions were threatening a strike in the industry. That was one of the things they were doing to try to discourage what was happening. And there were other risks involved. I think that the correct judgement was made. Subsequently, although the price shot up, it then went straight back down again. It is trading now above the original sale price, but not massively so, and what I think happened in the wake of the sale was a kind of speculative bubble. The bubble subsequently burst and you have now got a more realistic price.

BIGSBY There is one thing you say which rather surprises me in your book. You say you can foresee the time when we would join the Eurozone. Surely there are so many structural problems with the Eurozone that it is hard to think of the circumstances in which we would, isn't it?

CABLE I am not promoting the idea but I think it is always very dangerous in politics to use the word 'never'. It is certainly clear at the moment that the Eurozone is not functioning properly and there are various reasons for that. It worked pretty well initially because the Eurozone countries were able to take advantage of cheap credit to finance imports from Germany and southern Europe. It worked admirably for a while but when the system came under stress, which it did during the financial crisis, it was clear that they didn't have a satisfactory mechanism for dealing with imbalances within the Union and in order to have mechanisms for sorting out imbalances you need to have a much closer political union than actually happened. The Germans would have had to agree, for example, to have a much larger transfer of money to areas in deficit. That's how the United States works. There is a system of transfers between States of the US federation and there would have to be an accepted discipline by countries that have deficits that they will meet their obligations, but these disciplines were simply too weak. The Germans were not willing to make adequate transfers or agree to debt relief and so you had this horrible mess that we have had in the last two years. But I think it is quite possible that the Eurozone will be made to work. I think it is quite possible and I think we might find, in a decade or two decades' time, that not being part of it is a problem. So I am holding out for what is probably quite a distant possibility, but the one thing I am trying to avoid doing is using the word 'never'. It is a very dangerous word.

AMIT CHAUDHURI

Amit Chaudhuri, novelist, critic, musician, was born in Calcutta in 1962 and grew up in Bombay. He was educated at University College, London, and at Oxford University. His novels include *A Strange and Sublime Address*, *Afternoon Raag*, *Freedom Song*, *A New World* and *The Immortals*. He is also the author of poetry and short stories. His awards include the Betty Trask Award, the Commonwealth Writers' Prize, the Encore Award, the Los Angeles Times Book Prize and the Infosys Prize. He is Professor of Contemporary Writing at UEA.

This interview was recorded on November 11, 2015.

BIGSBY You were born in Calcutta and grew up in Bombay, though these are not the names now preferred. I seem to remember you saying that you regard the new names as in bad taste. Why?

CHAUDHURI Yes. Calcutta is a word that Indians have used when speaking in English about the city which has other versions of that name in other languages. In colloquial Bengali it is Kolkata and I have always called it Kolkata when speaking to somebody in Bengali. In Hindi people used to call it Calcutta. So it has several names and those names have histories. At some point, maybe in the 1990s, a group of people decided to go to the government and ask them to change the name in English from Calcutta to Kolkata. My problem with that word, in English, is that it has no history. It is a dead word. It hasn't accumulated any resonance. The word Calcutta in English has a conflicted history. It has a very interesting political and cultural history. Kolkata is dropped from above and is a dead word, a word without a history. It is a political gesture and also a literary gesture. It is a utopian word, like Xanadu.

BIGSBY Is it a different city in each language?

CHAUDHURI It might be. It is certainly a different city when Calcutta, in the English language, becomes Kolkata or Bombay becomes Mumbai. Mumbai is a post-globalisation ambivalent city in comparison to the Bombay of clearer demarcations. With Mumbai the demarcations are no longer clear. Who are the people who are making money? Who are the criminals? Who are the politicians? When I grew up in Bombay, in the 1960s and 1970s, people who acted in Hindi cinema weren't actually allowed in some places. There was no written law against them inhabiting certain parts of the city but they wouldn't be sold property there. They were discouraged in a tacit way from moving there and so they had their own neighbourhoods, but that changed. What we are looking at in the case of Mumbai is a different city where the earlier kind of divisions are much more blurred.

BIGSBY You have said that you were unhappy growing up in Bombay. Why?

CHAUDHURI I was unhappy because I was growing up in father's Bombay, which was a corporate world.

BIGSBY He worked in biscuits.
CHAUDHURI Yes, a biscuit company called Britannia Biscuits, which was at that time a subsidiary of a British company which had its own smaller companies here like Jacobs and Peek Freans.

BIGSBY But with free access to biscuits why were you unhappy?
CHAUDHURI That is a good question, because I did have free access to biscuits. I suppose I was unhappy because I grew up in these neighbourhoods which were really wonderful and extremely privileged in a city which by then had become the financial centre of India. I grew up in multi-storey buildings and we soon moved from a third floor apartment to the twelfth storey. It was a figurative and also literal rise in terms of my father's company career. When he was promoted from Finance Director he moved to the twenty-fifth storey apartment.

BIGSBY Did you get unhappier as you went up?
CHAUDHURI I did. Then my father retired and moved to a third storey apartment in the suburbs of the city. It is a Christian area and you could look out onto the street and actually see people, spend a lot of time on the balcony.

BIGSBY Your father suffered under Partition. Did that have an impact on him because he went on to be successful? Was that all forgotten?
CHAUDHURI My father moved to Calcutta as a student of English Literature in the forties and then, soon after Partition, moved to England in 1949. By then he had moved towards commerce, so he came here to take professional exams in taxation and accountancy. The sense of loss was there. There was a great resentment about Partition, about losing the homeland, which came out more in the women's talk to do with the role of the Muslims, but it was interesting to me, and instructive on some level, that when they spoke

about Sylhet, which is where they came from and which went to Bangladesh, this kind of talk to do with loss, or even blaming somebody, wasn't constant. There was no consciousness of being on the periphery, growing up in a small town, in comparison to Calcutta. It was as if they were right there in the centre of history and being in the centre of history meant not only the centre of politics, the freedom movement, but also literature. I never grew up encountering anybody who seemed to have a sense of being on the periphery. They seemed to have a sense of being idiosyncratic, provincial, and yet being in the centre all at the same time.

BIGSBY You grew up at first not hearing the English language. Your parents used Bengali although they were fluent in English.

CHAUDHURI Yes, when I was very small my parents only spoke to me in Bengali.

BIGSBY Why?

CHAUDHURI Because of Bengali pride in the language. When you look at the Bengali you are not looking, as you might with other kinds of Indians from other parts of India, at those who are part of an ancient tradition, but at somebody who came into being in the late eighteenth, early nineteenth century. The Bengali was a kind of arriviste social climber who came into his own in the nineteenth century as a modern. This meant a great investment in aspects of modernity including language and literature, so they wouldn't dream of speaking to me in English when I was small.

BIGSBY Don't you do the same thing with your own child?

CHAUDHURI Yes, I have done the same thing with my daughter. I didn't do it programmatically but I just couldn't bring myself to speak to her in English. Aspirational classes in India who aren't Bengali quite often take the decision these days, or have in the last fifteen years or so, the time of globalisation when English worldwide has become the language of globalisation, to learn English. The Chinese, the French, the Germans, everybody has some English now, so the aspirational classes in India speak to their children in English quite early on. I, however, without doing it programmatically found I was repeating what my parents had done to me, speaking to her in Bengali and she picked up English from her friends in the building.

BIGSBY By your mid-teens you were speaking in English and began writing.
CHAUDHURI Finally, yes.

BIGSBY Writing stories in English and also poetry, because you wanted to be a poet.
CHAUDHURI I began writing stories when I was about five or six years old, not as a great genius.

BIGSBY So you were writing in English.
CHAUDHURI I had to because I was in the foremost English language school in Bombay. I was admitted to school when I was five years old without any English and that was a problem because it was an English language school. The headmistress said to my mother, 'He will pick it up. Just give him Ladybird books and comic books to read.' So, at the age of five, I began to read about Peter and Jane going to the beach and comic books at the same time. I picked up English maybe in about two weeks.

BIGSBY In two weeks?
CHAUDHURI I must have. I was a child and there wasn't a huge lag between this piece of advice, me reading Ladybird books, and then beginning to write what was my first story, a story about a dog. I only know this because my mother has told me several times about how much she liked that story. So I wrote this story about a dog and I think I became interested in writing mainly because of discovering a language and then showing off that I had discovered it. So I became interested in writing very early on and, yes, I did become more interested in verse and in poetry than I was in prose.

BIGSBY You were eventually going to go to England, to University College, in London. Was England what you had expected or had your model of it been formed partly by literature, by what you had read? Was it a shock or did you immediately accommodate to it?

CHAUDHURI I had been to England as a child in 1973. I was eleven years old. So I had been to England and the reason I had been to England was that, as I said, my father worked for a company which was a subsidiary. That justified his trip to Britain but he also brought me along partly because I had a heart murmur and he wanted that investigated, so the trip to London also involved a journey to Harley Street to see a doctor. What was my sense of England in 1973? I could sense this world of insipient and conflicted multi-culturalism, encountering Indian immigrants, curry smells, black immigrants, hostility towards them, nice English people, leafy suburbs or areas at Belsize Park where my uncle still lived, English food. The only exotic things were Hungarian goulash or beef stroganoff. That was my first encounter with England. Also the cold toilet seats, even in the summer. All of that.

BIGSBY You said that you went to England to be a great poet, not a poet but a great poet?
CHAUDHURI A world famous poet.

BIGSBY A world famous poet. So that is why you went to University College.
CHAUDHURI It was a legitimate plan, wasn't it?

BIGSBY But you also said that while you were there you cultivated loneliness.
CHAUDHURI Yes.

BIGSBY It is one thing to be lonely but surely another to cultivate loneliness.
CHAUDHURI Let me connect what I am about to say to what you have just said about my wanting to be a world famous poet. Then I will come to the loneliness but I also want to address further the question of culture shock which you brought up, to compare what I felt in 1973 with actually moving to England as a student ten years later in 1983 and beginning to live there in Thatcher's

Britain and her ideas of the new Britain, her suspicion of immigrants but also her encouragement of business and trade, all those paradoxes. So I would say that the culture shock for me involved silence, encountering silence. It also involved the weather which was such that you closed the windows. You were much more with yourself, in a room, than in India. I became far more aware that in India you are basically always distracted or decentred.

BIGSBY I was struck by the fact that you have described your sense that in England we not only close doors but we lack balconies. You aren't hit with the noise of the neighbourhood, its vitality and energy. We tend to draw the curtains and stay within. That became a real contrast between the two cultures to you.

CHAUDHURI Yes.

BIGSBY You went to Oxford, ostensibly to do a PhD but not really because you seem simply to have wanted to extend your visa in order to write a novel which you started before you went to Oxford. Why did you have to be in England to be a writer? Why couldn't you go back to India and be the writer?

CHAUDHURI I just thought that if I were to get published in England, and get some acclaim over here, it would be an easier passport to fame and glory.

BIGSBY You were a cold-hearted, ambitious individual.

CHAUDHURI The reason I was waiting for fame and glory was that I began my apprentice period quite early, jubilantly writing that story about the dog soon after I had picked up the language. That apprentice period basically meant infatuation with literature, infatuation with poetry and then infatuation with voices, the voices of writers, and taking on those voices and those styles.

BIGSBY Your PhD was on D H Lawrence's poetry but meanwhile you were writing novels.

CHAUDHURI The whole apprentice period had me experimenting with other people's voices and styles which I think are fantastic. Then, when I was thirteen or fourteen, I would pick up these idioms and styles and reproduce them and think, 'Fantastic. I am just as good as Walt Whitman, because I have written something which sounds exactly like him, so acclaim can't be far away.' So this is the reason I was expecting acclaim at any moment because I found it so easy to reproduce these voices. I thought if they are famous then this fame has to come to me quite soon. This was the whole apprentice period and then came adolescent unhappiness, which also fed into my writing and my love of literature until I began to realise that at a certain point my material was joy and not unhappiness and that material had to do with the quotidian, the ordinary, rather than the important things.

BIGSBY That is really quite crucial and is evidenced right from your first novel, *A Strange and Sublime Address*. Salman Rushdie's *Midnight's Children* is a monumental attempt to capture India whole. You are at the other extreme of this. You are interested in the moment, the facticity of things. Objects almost become animate. You slow action down so that you can look around a room. You mention the quotidian and effectively that is what it is about, what makes your work distinct, I think, from any other writer that I know of and in writing it you had a draft which you then cut down and down until it was actually very short.

CHAUDHURI The first novel, yes.

BIGSBY Shorter than it finally turned out to be.
CHAUDHURI Yes.

BIGSBY Was that the moment you discovered what your style would be, no longer modelling yourself on other writers as you had when you were younger? Suddenly, you knew what you were doing.

CHAUDHURI I would say the first moment was reading *Sons and Lovers* by D. H. Lawrence which was recommended to me by my tutor at UCL, Dan Jacobson. He said, 'You know you haven't read enough prose. You have read a lot of poetry but you haven't read enough prose. You should start reading it a little bit more.' One of the novels he recommended was *Sons and Lovers* and what struck me was that it was a story in some ways to do with the provincial and the quotidian, the commonplace, opening out to me a world which was not the English drawing room of the nineteenth century novel. It was possible to write about a man like Walter Morel and his wife, who are really provincial people but who had their counterparts all over the world in modernity. So one of the things I began to see in them was their counterparts in Bengal, a man soldering things, working in the mines, coming back whistling, happiest when he is working at home. I recognised him. The thing that struck me about that book was that there was no meaning coming from elsewhere, which is what I identified modernism with, mainly because, as a young man, I was taking it in through people like T. S. Eliot. I was reading Eliot in a particular way and seeing the whole modernist project as being about the collapse of western civilisation, of organic European values which had been lost. With Lawrence there seemed to be no harking back to anything. He seemed to be saying, 'This is where it is. You know this is important.' Towards the end of his life he would say, in that rather weird book called *Apocalypse*, which is his gloss on Revelations, that 'whatever the dead or the unborn might know they cannot know the marvel of being alive in the flesh' and that belief is contained in *Sons and Lovers* which is a jettisoning of nostalgia for some meaning from elsewhere. He is saying embrace life. This is what you have. That spoke to me. I realised that this was me rather than the pose I was assuming of being eternally despondent about something.

BIGSBY We tend to think of profundity as to do with depth but there is a profundity in surface as well, and you are interested in surface, the moment by moment surface?

CHAUDHURI Yes, I am interested in surface. I would throw out depth in the sense that Lawrence threw out the idea of legitimacy having to come from somewhere else. I am interested in all kinds of re-orderings, the reordering of the idea of what is important and what is not. If you are saying that the commonplace is important, a kind of reordering is taking place which one hopes is not becoming a kind of fetishisation of the holiness of the ordinary.

BIGSBY There is no hierarchy?

CHAUDHURI No hierarchy. Maybe the protagonist is the progeny of the Renaissance project of the person being portrayed being at the centre of the universe and the universe being like a photographer's studio arranged around him, this man being the subject of the photograph or the painting. I was not interested in that protagonist being at the centre but the relation between that protagonist and his surroundings which immediately brings the object, the quotidian, what is pejoratively called the setting, into the foreground. There could be reasons to do with temperament that dictate that compulsion to do away with the centrality of the protagonist. Susan Sontag talks about Walter Benjamin being drawn to objects. The melancholic is drawn to objects more than to people so, who knows, there could be psychological reasons.

BIGSBY Another aspect of that first novel becomes something of a template for your later work in that it features a character who moves from one city to another, from Bombay to Calcutta. You are drawn to moving your characters around.

CHAUDHURI Yes, well spotted. I finally realised that maybe I am not so concerned about plot, although my books do have some kind of a plot, some sort of a story, and lots of things happen in them I must assure you, but most of them do involve a change of location. It could be a holiday, a break. He lives in one place and goes somewhere else. He goes to another city, or a different part of the city. All the books seem to have that so you are looking at a limited span of time in which things are exactly as they are but changed because there is a change of scene and to me that is a definition of the poetic text in contrast to narrative. This is how I think of it. The narrative is about the accommodation of detail, information in the best sense, so that by the time you have finished the narrative you do feel that you know more about that world and those people in it than you did when you began the narrative. With the poetic text, or the poem, when you end you are not sure what you have learned that you didn't know earlier. In fact it is possible partly because of the length of the poem but partly because of the nature of this experience. It is possible to finish reading a poem and re-read it immediately. One can read the same poem several times. Narrative, however interesting it is on a literary level, will satiate one particular desire in you which then will not need to be addressed and so you won't need to read it again. Very rarely would you want to start re-reading a narrative text immediately upon finishing it. The desire to know more about the life than you did when you began has been satiated by the time you finish a narrative. With the poem something else has happened. A change has taken place but it is not that kind of change. You have not learnt anything more than you did when you began the poem.

BIGSBY In your second novel you have a character who is Indian living in England and is trying to decide about his identity, the extent to which he remains Indian, the extent to which in some ways he is becoming English, which is of course the dilemma of immigrants. There is a strong autobiographical element in your work. Indeed in one novel you actually name some people who are relatives of yours. Was that dilemma about identity one that you felt or was that just a construction?

CHAUDHURI Whatever the book is, and whatever it seems to be to readers, I never thought of it as an exploration of identity. I saw it as a further exploration of narrative in terms of what I could do, given the fact that I had begun to write novels. But I didn't seem to be a novelist in any kind of conventional, recognisable, sense. In fact I felt I was getting further and further into a hole. I got into the hole with *A Strange and Sublime Address* and then further into the hole with *Afternoon Raag*, so the intention was to keep getting further and deeper into the hole of being in the wrong place.

BIGSBY But you have always felt as though you were in the wrong place, haven't you?

CHAUDHURI Yes, I have. But that first novel was an exploration of narrative, to do something with the novel which shouldn't be done maybe.

BIGSBY It begins with a poem.
CHAUDHURI Yes.

BIGSBY The reason for that being?
CHAUDHURI I felt I shouldn't waste that poem. I had written it, so I should put it somewhere. But the poem is about the music teacher's death and the music teacher and his death figure in the book which is why the poem forms an epitaph.

BIGSBY There is another side to your career. Music. When you were growing up you played guitar but then you set it aside. You had listened to western music, but put that on one side and turned to classical Indian music. Your mother was a singer, though not quite in the tradition that you were going for. Western music, then, remained remote from you for a decade and a half.
CHAUDHURI Yes, sixteen years.

BIGSBY Then it suddenly comes back and you see connections.
CHAUDHURI Yes, I see connections. I had an ideological moment when I was sixteen or so when I suddenly became aware that at that time, living in Bombay in the 1970s, where a lot of great performers and singers were performing at their peak, it was a very good time for Indian classical music, so it was impossible to completely shut it out, however much you might want to. And there was no kind of barrier in any way between those of us who were interested in western rock and pop music, though we wouldn't have thought of it as western necessarily, and Indian music, partly because of bands like The Beatles and the Rolling Stones doing what they did in the late 1960s, flirting with Indian classical music. So you had to flirt with it as well. Once you began to flirt with it, you suddenly realised what amazing stuff was going on. Then what happened to me is I got more and more drawn to it and for many reasons just gave up

western music because I had this ideological moment like a religious conversion. To me, it was not authentic, though what we are calling western music is completely authentic to Bombay because it is very much a part of Bombay history. It just seemed inauthentic because Indian music is deeply imbricated, for want of a better word, in the weather and the light and times of day. Raags are time specific. You sing them at a particular time of day or even at particular seasons. There are certain raags you can only sing during the rains, for instance, which means that they are interwoven culturally, as a language might be. Just as we use the word 'evening' to mean evening, the raag is similarly referential. It is not mimetic, so you might have a morning raag and an evening raag which has exactly the same notes. In western music on some level it seems mimetic because you think to yourself minor means sad, major means happy, dissonant means terror. You don't have that humanistic mimetic dimensionality in Indian music. It is deeply, almost linguistically, interwoven into that world, into that universe which is India. So I had that conversion. But when I came here I heard the great Canadian singer-songwriters like Neil Young and Joni Mitchell who I think is the greatest singer-songwriter of the twentieth century. If somebody had said you are going to be listening to Indian music again in 1999 I would have said, 'no, that is impossible' but when I came here what was happening was Culture Club, Frankie Goes to Hollywood, Relax and Duran Duran. At that time I was thinking I have to shut it out and that facilitated my total immersion in Indian music for sixteen years.

BIGSBY Your new novel is set in 1985. Why then?
CHAUDHURI It is based on my uncle. He was a bachelor. He never married. He came to England in 1961 becoming a manager in a shipping company. He always lived in the bedsit that he had occupied as a student in Belsize Park. He never left that bedsit. He was my sole contact in London when I was a student here, in terms of family and in terms of general human contact because I wasn't very much in contact with human beings at that time except my uncle and a very few other people. This

uncle was a strange man, an unforgettable character, and I finally convinced him to return to India. He said he never wanted to return because he had nothing but contempt for the Bengali middle class and for his family to whom he used to send money. So I said, 'You have to come back, I am getting married.' This was in 1991, and I persuaded him to come back for my wedding. Once he went back to India he didn't want to go back to England. He completely reneged on everything he had said earlier and it was typical of him.

He just began to spend more and more time in Calcutta but because he was not a property owner he used to stay in relatives' houses. About ten years after he had returned to India I bought a charcoal sketch by an Indian painter, F.N. Souza, who I greatly admired, and I put this charcoal sketch up in the drawing room in the flat in Calcutta. I bought it because it was affordable. His prices have now gone through the roof since he died but at that time I bought it for £700 which for me, for a picture I admired and by India's greatest modern painter, was amazing. He thought that a huge amount, so he came to me and said, 'I hear you have bought a painting for 55,000 rupees and where is it?' So I showed him the picture by Souza and he said, 'you might as well have paid me 55,000 rupees for farting' because his speech was littered with references to Tagore and poetry and scatological stuff in both countries so I said, 'But this is a great painter. What a wonderful sketch this is. How can you say that?' And he said, 'Yes, I grant you that what an idiot produces and what a genius produces often look exactly the same.' Having said that he went off. I did say to him 'notice that the sketch looks a lot like you' because Souza had done a self-portrait which looked a bit like my uncle and they both loved life. The difference was that my uncle loved Tagore, while Souza hated him. So he went off and I was thinking that the person in the sketch looked a lot like my uncle and then I recalled that Souza had named the sketch 'Ulysses' so I thought, yes, my uncle is actually a bit like Odysseus, in that he can't travel sometimes as he would want to. Then there was his life in shipping, so I began to think of taking this really reckless plunge into writing a book where I would cast my uncle as Odysseus. I was thinking of taking the cue from *Ulysses* in the novel by Joyce partly because I was thinking of my journeys from Warren Street to the bedsit in Belsize Park, ending up in the kitchenette pouring water for myself as the journey that Telemachus had made. So I had that vision. This is Telemachus's journey.

TRACY CHEVALIER   GLENN PATTERSON

Tracy Chevalier was born in Washington D.C. in 1962. She graduated from Oberlin College in 1984 and in 1993 gained a Master's degree in Creative Writing at the University of East Anglia, studying under Malcolm Bradbury and Rose Tremain. She subsequently settled in England. Her first novel, *The Virgin Blue*, was published in 1997. She followed this with *Girl in a Pearl Earring, Falling Angels, The Lady and the Unicorn, Burning Bright, Remarkable Creatures, The Last Runaway* and *At the Edge of the Orchard*. Her awards include the Barnes & Noble Discover Award and the Ohioana Book Award.

Glenn Patterson was born in Belfast in 1962. He obtained his BA from the University of East Anglia (UEA) before completing his MA in Creative Writing at the same university, studying with Malcom Bradbury and Angela Carter. His first novel, *Burning Your Own*, appeared in 1988. Subsequent books are *Fat Lad, Black Night at Big Thunder Mountain, The International, Number 5, That Which Was, The Third Party* and *The Mill for Grinding Old People Young*. He is a winner of the Rooney Prize for Irish Literature and the Betty Trask Award.

This interview was recorded on November 6, 2013.

BIGSBY Tracy, you were born in Washington D.C. but your father's parents came from Switzerland?
CHEVALIER Yes.

BIGSBY And your father was a photographer for the *Washington Post*. I wonder if you have inherited anything of his concern with the visual. You have said that you yourself are a rotten photographer but surely the visual plays a major part in your work?
CHEVALIER Yes, it does, though I am not the person who naturally reaches for a camera when we are in some interesting place. I don't paint and I don't draw, but I spend a lot of my time when writing imagining the scene in my head. I then write down what I see. It is almost like making a film and I think that it might be something to do with our generation growing up watching so much television and films. I think we were incredibly affected. I was certainly affected by the visual even if I didn't express myself in that way. It is still how I write.

BIGSBY When you were young you were interested in writing but I get the impression that what really interested you was books and that you could easily have become something else connected to books.
CHEVALIER I used to say I was going to be either a writer or a librarian because that was where I got my books from. I used to go to the library every week and the children's library knew me really well. They would set aside a book for me. It was where I thought books came from. I don't think we ever went to book stores. I don't know why but the library was everything to me and then, later in my teens, I discovered there is this thing called 'publishing' and I guess I lost a little confidence in the idea of writing, as you often do as a teenager. So I thought, well, maybe I will go into the book-making side of it. I will be an editor and that is what I did for a while.

BIGSBY You went to university in Oberlin, Ohio, which seems to have been a special place for a number of reasons.
CHEVALIER Yes. Oberlin is a small liberal arts college

founded in 1834 by radical religious visionaries. It has always been seen as a very progressive place. In the 1830s, 1840s, 1850s it was a hot bed of abolitionism, and it is still like that. I think that is why I went there because I knew it was going to be very progressive, left-wing.

BIGSBY Perhaps we will come back to that later because it has a special significance in relation to one of your books, in fact your most recent book, but as part of your course you spent a semester abroad in England. What was the significance of that?

CHEVALIER In my junior year I went on what they called the Oberlin London Semester for English Majors. There were eighteen of us who went over with a professor and lived in London and went to the theatre twice a week. We would read a play, discuss it in the morning and then go and see the production that night before discussing it the next morning, which is the most amazing way to learn about theatre. It was fantastic, and we read twentieth century British novelists as well, reading Virginia Woolf's *Mrs Dalloway* and then following around where she went in London. It makes all the difference.

BIGSBY And when you graduated you came back to England.

CHEVALIER I fell in love with London when I was a student and when I graduated I didn't know what to do. I didn't want to go into publishing in New York. It was too scary. So I came to London for six months and then I met a guy.

BIGSBY From?

CHEVALIER From Northern Ireland, which is where Glenn is from, so that accent always makes me sit up. It ended badly but I stayed and worked in publishing. I was an editorial assistant on Macmillan's *Dictionary of Art*. I spent a year typing letters and chasing up people who were writing articles for it. Vermeer had not come into my head by that point though years later I thought, 'who wrote the Vermeer article?' It was somebody I had not heard of but I was not focussing on the art part of the job. I was just glad to get a foothold in publishing.

BIGSBY And you were writing stories on the side?
CHEVALIER Yes, I started writing short stories at night. I just felt this itch. People ask me why I write and I don't really know. I just feel I have something to communicate and I keep coming up with stories or characters or strange situations and I just want to make them into something. I think because my childhood was spent so much in the worlds that I was reading about, I got used to moving away from reality. It may also be partly because my mother was ill when I was a kid. She got sick when I was three. She had an enlarged heart and died when I was eight, so I had a lot of time where I had to be quiet, or I had to be on my own. I think the books were a comfort, both when she was ill and then after she had died. My aunt used to quote me as saying, 'I never felt lonely if I had a book.' So those other worlds became incredibly important to me, and they are to this day. That is what I do every day. I sit down and I get back inside a world, but the difference is that this is one I am creating.

BIGSBY And then you chucked up that job and came to UEA?
CHEVALIER I did. One day I was riding a bus into work and read an article by Louise Doughty who had gone to UEA and done the MA in Creative Writing a couple of years earlier. I had vaguely heard of it but then I read the article and when I got into the office and my boss came up to me and said, 'Tracy why haven't you done blah blah blah blah blah and why are you being blah blah blah?' I remember standing there looking at her and thinking, 'I have got to get the hell out of here. I am going to apply for that creative writing course.' It was weird because even as I had read the article I didn't think that it was for me but suddenly, an hour later, I thought, 'Ah, I get it. I get it.' So I came here.

BIGSBY Let me pause you there for a moment while I turn to Glenn. As I gather, you might very well have been born in Canada.

PATTERSON My grandparents went to Canada in early 1953. My parents had met the New Year's Eve before and they met because of Babycham, which is a shameful thing to admit. They were in separate dance halls in Belfast. In dance halls in those days you couldn't get a drink inside. You had to get a chit to go out to get a drink and then come back in again. My dad and his friend left this dance hall and there was only one bar in Belfast in those days that was serving Babycham. It had just come in, so they went to get this sophisticated Babycham drink and on their way back they passed another dance hall and went in and he met my mum. Shortly after that my grandparents emigrated and my mum was seventeen and was staying behind. Then her brother fell ill, so my mum followed her parents and my dad, having got a taste for my mum, as well as Babycham, went out after her and they married there. All my brothers were born in Canada so, having had three Canadian boys, they decided to come back to Ireland and have an Irish girl to complete the family. God knows I tried. I did all in my power.

BIGSBY Yours is a Protestant family and you have talked about going on Orange Lodge marches when you were young. At that age nothing seems strange. How old were you when you began to feel that was a little odd?

PATTERSON There were two great opportunities for licence in my teenage years, one was New Year, when you just went and asked girls for New Year's kisses, and the other was the July 11, before the big Orange parade. There would be bonfires and you would get Eleventh Night kisses, so that was it. You got drunk and you got kissed, which seemed to me like quite a good thing for people to do. I didn't question the politics behind it for quite a long time. I grew up, in the 1970s, on very ordinary housing estates and those post-war housing estates became very polarised, entirely Catholic, entirely Protestant. I was going to school in the city centre and mixing with people, middle class people, and then going back home to my housing estate which was dominated by sectarian politics and paramilitary organisations. It was a very odd teenage period.

Then I went to Canada in 1978. I was sixteen at this stage. Earlier, one of my brothers, having come back to Belfast at the end of the 1950s, in his early twenties, had been chased out of Belfast by a loyalist paramilitary organisation. I didn't know this. Having been chased out he then went to Toronto and promptly joined an Orange Order Flute Band, which is bonkers. So I went to visit him in 1978 and I was standing on Young Street, the longest street in the world, to see my brother's band march, because they have a Twelfth demonstration in Toronto, and I looked up the street and all I could see was Young Street going forever in either direction and in the middle of it was this small huddle of Orangemen playing their flutes. There is a particular thing about Orange marchers which is that you are not supposed to cross the road in the middle of the march. It breaks the magic spell, and so there are these men with little staffs under their arms watching vigilantly in case any Toronto pedestrians should try and cross the road and I think at that moment I just thought, 'This is fucking nuts.'

BIGSBY As we walked across you were invoking Seamus Heaney and you are actually based at the Seamus Heaney Centre, but why is that in Belfast?

PATTERSON Seamus Heaney was born in Bellaghy in County Derry and he came to Belfast as an undergraduate and studied at Queens University, Belfast. You see, I have been primed. You have to rehearse this before you leave Belfast. He studied at Queens and lectured at Queens University. So about ten years ago they set up the Seamus Heaney Centre for Poetry. There was a time when I thought all of Northern Ireland would end up named after Seamus Heaney.

BIGSBY It is just that he made a political decision to move south.

PATTERSON He moved south, in about 1972, which wasn't a bad time to move south it has to be said. If you had to leave Belfast at any stage, 1972 would have been the year to go.

BIGSBY You didn't go to Queens but came across to

UEA as an undergraduate. Was that a move away from something as much as a way towards something?

PATTERSON It was. It was a little bit as Tracy described it except that in my case I didn't read an account. I was given an account by a friend who told me this garbled story about a student who had gone to this university in East Anglia where he hadn't done any work for three years and at the end of three years was called in and asked what he had been up to and presented this portfolio of short stories at which they pronounced him a genius. They were published and that was Ian McEwan. I thought, 'I could probably do that.' I could certainly do nothing for three years, though whether I would be pronounced a genius at the end I didn't know – but I was willing to give it a try.

BIGSBY Of course that wasn't quite Ian McEwan because he didn't do a BA at UEA. He did the MA. So, you weren't tempted to stay on in Belfast?

PATTERSON Well, yes. My girlfriend was still at school and she had told me if I left Belfast that was it. We were finished. So I stayed on for a while. I worked in a book shop so, a bit like Tracy with the library. Being in Belfast, it was very hard to get hold of books but the boast of the shop that I worked in was that we could get books faster than anybody else. That was because of me. People would come in and ask for a book and, if we didn't have it, I would be sent to run to the warehouse and get the book and then run back with it. I loved working in the book shop. If you have worked in a book shop, if you have been a publisher, that love of books is really important.

CHEVALIER People are always asking me what should I do if I want to get published. I say you have to read a lot, and they say should I go do an MA in creative writing or a night class and I say, that is fine but the most important thing is to read.

BIGSBY Tracy, is it here, at UEA, that you began working on your first novel?

CHEVALIER Yes, I started in my second term. I had never had an idea big enough to fill a novel. I had always had ideas that were short story size but I had turned thirty or thirty-one and was getting more interested in my family history so I wondered about my father's family, the Chevaliers, from this little town in Switzerland. My grandparents had emigrated to the States with my dad when he was five but my ancestors had lived in this little town in Switzerland for centuries since, apparently, 1572. They were Huguenots in southern France who after the massacre of St Bartholomew in 1572 fled and eventually ended up in this town. I didn't know any of that but I found out about it and I started thinking. One day I was sitting in the library pondering it in my mind and I had just heard that my sister was moving to southern France and I thought, 'oh, she is moving back' and it was like a circle getting closed. So I started thinking about the cycles of immigration and whether problems and characteristics in families can continue throughout the centuries. If a family is prone to internal strife does that happen centuries later? And so that was what gave me the spark for *The Virgin Blue* and I started writing that when I was here.

BIGSBY What was that course like for you? Was it just a case of buying a year of time or were there other things – the teaching, the other students?

CHEVALIER It was a combination of all of those things, though I think that probably for me the most important was the time bought. I had always worked full-time and crunched my writing into odd periods of time so that meant sometimes it took a year to write a short story. I just wanted a year off. I wanted to step outside of the stream of my life and have a year where all I did was write, so that was what it was most useful for. It was of course useful to have other people who were doing the same thing. We would critique each other's work and it was helpful having that audience, the deadlines, all of those practical things. A couple of my friends said, 'Why don't you just take the tuition money, live off of that, and write at home instead of coming to UEA?' And I said, 'I need the discipline. I need the little piece of paper at the end that tells me I have done it.' Maybe a lot of people don't need that but I felt that was what I wanted to help to get me launched.

BIGSBY Glenn, diid you start *Burning Your Own* here?
PATTERSON I did, and I started out of sheer terror. Malcolm Bradbury taught the first term while the second term it was Angela Carter and the way the cycle fell I was the first person to present work to Angela Carter, the week after Christmas, and I was absolutely terrified. We were all terrified of Angela and so I thought I had better have something because I had been writing some short stories. So over Christmas I wrote the first chapter of my first novel, just to have something more than a short story. I wasn't very good at writing short stories so I thought I had better have something for her. She was brilliant, absolutely fantastic. I was trying to describe Angela Carter's technique to somebody, her way of talking, which was that she would speak and then she would look away in the middle of a sentence and everybody in the room would follow her eyes to see where this sentence was going and then her hand would start to do this as she circled. It was a bit like a lasso. We would all follow and then she would get the word, and it would always be the right word. It was just brilliant, the way she did it, and I remember her going with the lasso as she talked about what I had given her. My first novel has a character who appears to live on a rubbish dump in the first couple of pages and somebody in the group said, 'It appears he lives on a rubbish dump. Is that possible?' and she lassoed the sentence and said, 'When readers open the book they enter into a contract with the writer. Anything can happen and the writer's only job is to stick to the rules they have created and if you deviate from them it has to be for a reason.' That was it. Brilliant.

BIGSBY That was a novel set just before the Troubles in Ireland.
PATTERSON Yes, 1969.

BIGSBY After finishing your degree you didn't go back to Northern Ireland. You moved to Manchester at one stage.

PATTERSON I did, yes.

BIGSBY Did writing the second book, *Fat Lad,* lead you back to Northern Ireland again?

PATTERSON I had these grand ambitions for the first novel and it was meant to be narrated from the present day looking back to 1969 and to the childhood of the narrator. I just found I couldn't do it. It was hard enough to write one part of the story, so the second novel, which I started to write in the late 1980s, took up the story I suppose I had been trying to write in the first novel. I was, as you say, living in Manchester – which is so close to Belfast that when you fly they used to send you your sandwich the day before so you could eat it because they didn't have time to serve it on board. That is how close it was and I just found I was going backwards and forwards to Belfast and so much had changed, everything was changing. It was changing quite quickly and I became very interested, and I still am, in the city and how all cities rewrite themselves on the landscape. Belfast, in particular, is interesting because it's all built on. The city centre is on reclaimed land so it is the most unpromising place to build a city. They started it four hundred years ago. So I began writing the novel about change and cities. It just happens that when I write about cities Belfast is the one I know best so I tend to go there.

BIGSBY While you were at UEA a student said, 'You are lucky because you have got Belfast.' I got the impression that at that stage you rather resented that remark – but it is what you have got, isn't it?

PATTERSON What she said was, 'You are lucky you have got something to write about. You have got the Troubles', which is a very different thing, but that is just something that happened in the history of the place. I wrote a novel called *Number Five*. I knew somebody who used to refer to his novels by number – 'When I was writing number one, when I was writing number two...' – so I thought, right, I am going to call one *Number Five*. I had just finished the fourth one but it's about a house in Belfast over a period of forty-five years and I just wanted the bit that is called 'The Troubles' to be part of what that house and the occupants of that house go through. Actually the story is about the city and the story of the people who live in it.

BIGSBY Tracy, you moved on from *Virgin Blue*, which is set in two time scales?

CHEVALIER When Glenn was talking about having these grand ideas for his first book, I was exactly the same. At one point it was going to be set in four different countries and four different time periods. Everything was huge but in the end, once you start writing, the moment you set a sentence on a page, you can just hear doors slamming, all the possibilities of where you could go. Writing is a constant choice between shall we go this way or that way? Oh, we are going this way, OK, that way is shut. It gets more and more focused and so it ended up as two different time periods and two different countries, France and Switzerland. It was much more pared down. Funnily enough, I still go through this. I am going through that now with a book I am working on. I keep thinking it's going to be these different things and actually in the end it becomes smaller, but the next book, *Girl with a Pearl Earring*, was much more focused from the start because the day I started researching it I found out I was pregnant and I knew I wanted to finish the book, or at least a draft of the book, before the baby came because I wasn't really sure what my brain would be like after that. As it happens someone had complained they can't focus at all and get anything done when they are pregnant. For me it was just the opposite so my publisher is always saying, 'Could you have more kids please?' I knew this was going to be a linear book. Structurally it is not experimental at all. It is from one point of view. It originates from the painting and one, two, three, go. I just went.

BIGSBY This is what a nine-month book looks like?
CHEVALIER It's never been that easy again, sadly.

BIGSBY But you had that picture, Girl with a Pearl Earring, on your wall when you were a teenager.

CHEVALIER From the age of nineteen, yes, but I was thirty-four or thirty-five when I had the idea.

BIGSBY So what triggered it?

CHEVALIER I don't know. I was lying in bed one day. I had been looking at it for years and I had gone through various stages of why I loved the painting so much. When you first see that painting the first thing you think is that the colours are so beautiful, the blue and the yellow, the shadow on her face, the way he has rendered her face. It is just so realistic and yet it is not realistic. There is something so 'other' about her. Eventually I reached the point where I just thought there are so many contradictions in this seemingly simple painting. I can't tell if she is happy or sad, if she is rich or poor because from her clothes it is hard to tell. Is she saying I love you or I hate you? Is she thirteen or thirty? The whole painting is unresolved and that is why it is a masterpiece. You never really know what she is thinking. You can write or read a whole novel about her and still not know what that look on her face means. So I was lying in bed one morning and just idly looking up at it and I thought I wonder what Vermeer said to her, or did to her, to make her look like that. That was the first time that I thought the look on her face, and all that ambiguity, might have to do with him rather than just her thinking about herself being a model. Suddenly the painting became a portrait of a relationship rather than a portrait of a girl and I thought I wonder what the relationship was? I looked it up and nobody knows who she is so I thought, well, that is me sorted, the whole field is open and they don't know much about Vermeer either so I could make up a lot. It just came to me really quickly, the whole story.

BIGSBY So what followed were four million copies, a film, a play. Presumably this must have taken your breath away a little?

CHEVALIER Yes. It doesn't happen immediately so my breath got taken away in very slow motion, but, yes, I was pretty astonished because I was expecting it to sell to family and friends and if I was lucky sell 500 copies.

Then it would remainder and that would be the end of it because it doesn't sound sexy, but a lot of people love this painting and I think that there is a desire to know what is going on in her. I think a lot of people who know the painting think that maybe this is going to tell them, so they read it to see if they can find out. Of course, by the end it is still open, which is a good thing, I think. Always leave some openness.

PATTERSON Can I just say four million. God help us, that's amazing.

BIGSBY And translated into thirty-six languages.
CHEVALIER Yes. It is kind of crazy.
PATTERSON I was going to say one thing about book selling that I had forgotten. You were talking about books getting remaindered. I remember being sent into the stock room and ripping the jackets off paperbacks because that is the only bit that the publishers want. It was like the pelt of an animal. They used to throw out the actual text at the back of our book shop. I would be in there ripping the back off books. This was just before my first novel came out so it was like an education. When I was in Toronto last month doing a reading as Writer in Residence at a university I went down Young Street again. There was a second-hand book stall and the first thing I saw was one of my own books, presumably the only book of mine I think you can get in Canada. At the reading somebody asked if my books were available in Canada and I said, 'if you are really fast you can get round onto Young Street,' and I was thinking I could have bought it for a dollar and sold it for twelve. My little hungry children. They left the books outside the shop at night and there was one I wanted to buy, not my own, and I didn't know what to do, whether to try and post the money through the door or to leave a little note saying I have taken this book. Then I thought, if I touch it cameras will catch me. So I just left it but they left them outside all night, a dollar each I suppose.

BIGSBY Turning to one of your novels, *The International* is set in a bar.
PATTERSON Yes, that's true.

BIGSBY There is a certain thread that runs through your work.

PATTERSON I used to be a member of the Real Ale Society here at the UEA because the girl who was signing people up was so beautiful that I signed up for the Real Ale Society. We used to go around places in a van and try real ale and I remember going into a house in Burnham Thorpe, where Nelson was born.

CHEVALIER Did you have Nelson's blood? That is clove cordial and rum mixed together in that pub.

PATTERSON It may have been the fourth one we went to that night so I have no idea. They got us a drink from the back. I honestly do think that 'public house' are two of the most beautiful words together in the English language, but in Belfast, in the 1970s and 1980s, if you wanted to kill people, generally the easiest place to find them was in a bar. So, they were bombed, there were people shot in them. We lost a lot of the city centre night life and I think that cities lose something vital if they lose public houses. Also I like drinking, so I have indeed occasionally written about bars.

BIGSBY This is a novel set in the past.

PATTERSON Yes, January 1967. Tracy, I was listening to you talking about *Girl with a Pearl Earring* and I think it is extraordinary that sometimes the books you write you have been looking at for years. I knew about the International Hotel because it is right behind the City Hall in Belfast and my dad used to go there for works parties. He worked in the shipyard and then the aircraft factory, so I had always known about it, but one day the name came into my head, *The International*, what a great name. I just thought, that's a great title for a book. Suddenly, when you find yourself thinking about wanting to do something, it is as though everything just comes towards it at speed and within a matter of hours this particular novel started to come together.

I had a friend and I went to ask him about the International Hotel to see if he could help me do some research and he pointed across to a man at the Belfast Public Records Office and said, 'See that guy over there? He used to work in the International Hotel.' So I went to talk to this man and he had been the junior Under Manager on this particular day that I was interested in, which was January 30, 1967, when the Northern Ireland Civil Rights Association had its first meeting in the hotel. In retrospect it was a very important day. At the time it was barely recorded and I asked him what he remembered about the meeting and he said, 'Well, it was a political meeting, so we knew we would need extra bar men.' So I just thought, that's it, that's exactly what I wanted to write about. I wanted to write about what it was like then, not how it looked looking back at it. I suppose you are always looking, aren't you, for some new way of coming at the world.

CHEVALIER And the best ideas come together fast I think, definitely.

BIGSBY We were talking about the success of *Girl with a Pearl Earring* but that set the bar rather high for you and you had a little bit of trouble with your next book.

CHEVALIER I had a kid by then, so my time was taken up by being a mother and I had to learn to deal with that. But also there was suddenly an expectation on me from publishers and readers. I had so many people say, 'Write about another painting. Are you going to write about the Mona Lisa?' and I thought, yes, they want me to write 'Woman with a Pearl Necklace', the sequel to *Girl with a Pearl Earring*, and I just didn't want to do that. So I wrote something as different as I could which was *Falling Angels*, a book set in Highgate Cemetery. It is about two families during the Edwardian period who have graves side by side. I wrote the whole first draft in the third person and I hated it. I cried when I re-read it and I ended up chopping it all up and rewriting the whole thing in the first person from twelve different points of view. Then it worked, but it was a real panic.

I don't know if you have ever had this, Glenn. You read what you have written and just think, 'This isn't working at all.' Then you just despair and think I have just wasted a year, a year-and-a-half, two years, however long, and it's like lead. It is terrible. Then you think, I will just try this and suddenly it works and it lightens up the whole thing. It is wonderfully magical, that feeling, but it is pretty terrifying until you get to that point where you figure out what to do. That is where an editor can come in, but at this point it was so awful that I didn't want to show it to anybody, so I figured it out myself, though I have certainly had editors help me a lot over the years and I am grateful for it. I think because I was an editor myself I value the outside look in.

BIGSBY Your first book was in two time periods but thereafter you moved back into the past and there is one thread that connects every writer in this festival. They have all set books in the past. Why do you in particular turn to the past?

CHEVALIER I think I do it to escape myself because I don't want to write about myself. I can't imagine anybody would find my life interesting. I realise of course that I don't have to write autobiographically but when I write about the present, which I do in short stories sometimes, I find I can't get away from me so I like to escape the present day. I get so much of the present day in television news and newspapers; apart from living it, why would I want to write about it, too? So I like getting outside my comfort zone. You try to find something different. Some people go to different countries and some people write genre novels, turning to the future, but I go to the past. Also, I think that over the years, as I have gotten older, I have understood the value of trying to figure out where I am, not just by looking at myself all the time in the present and what I am going to do in the future but by adding a third dimension by looking backwards and seeing, and understanding, just how insignificant I am.

BIGSBY You most recent book, Glenn, *Mill for Grinding Old People Young* – which, incidentally, is the name of a bar – shifts back in time to look at an earlier Belfast.

PATTERSON *Mill for Grinding Old People Young* was the name of an inn in Belfast in the 1830s and I just read it one day. The only other reference to it is in *A Tale of Two Cities*. The bar sign was some elderly people walking towards a mill hopper and then coming out the other side all sprightly. I was just so fascinated by this. My younger daughter had just been born and she woke during the night. I was trying to get her back to sleep and was just rocking her and saying the mill for grinding old people young, the mill for grinding old people young, the mill for grinding old people young. Do you ever get that thing where you almost see a novel like a balloon and you just see it's wonderful and are so dazzled by it. Then all the air goes out of the balloon when you wake up and you realise that the only way to inflate this balloon is one word at a time so I just decided I wanted to write something called *The Mill for Grinding Old People Young*.

It was time specific. It only existed in the 1830s. It actually has very little to do with the Inn. What I discovered was that there were all kinds of interesting things happening then. Belfast was a sizeable merchant town in the early 1830s and within about twenty years it turned into a major industrial city. One of the reasons it did was because of something very mundane. Belfast's river used to come up towards the High Street. It was very serpentine and the merchants of the time wanted something straight to get to Belfast Lock so that the big ships could get up faster to make more money. When they did this cut they dumped all the silt on the east bank of the River Lagan and that turned into the shipyards of Harland and Wolff, birth place of the Titanic. That was what made Belfast the major city and they did that with the silt that they were digging up. So I was interested in the fact that we don't always know what we are doing. I suppose if there is one thing that the novel is about, it is how history will look at us, how it will judge us on what we think we are doing, what history will tell us we were doing.

CHEVALIER I thought you were going to say the reason Belfast got big so fast was because there is this mill where people go in and they come out young and the population just expanded like crazy.

PATTERSON Yes, that was the science fiction one that I didn't get round to writing. Incidentally, did you know that *Game of Thrones* is filmed in Belfast? It is filmed in the paint hall which is where the ships used to go to get painted and stripped down. It is now a major film studio and they film all those studio-based shots of *Game of Thrones* in there, including a lot of sexual practices that were still technically illegal about three years ago in Northern Ireland. No wonder people are queuing up to be extras for that.

BIGSBY Tracy, when you were writing *Girl with a Pearl Earring* is it true that you were trying your hand at painting?

CHEVALIER Yes, because I was going to be writing about a painter I took a painting class in order to get a feel for the paint. I was absolutely terrible at it but I just wanted to have some hands-on experience of it.

BIGSBY And then in *Remarkable Creatures*, which involves fossil hunting, you went fossil hunting.

CHEVALIER It is kind of on-the-job training. I just felt I couldn't write about a fossil hunter without doing it myself. In my most recent book, *The Last Runaway*, the main character is a quilter, and I also felt that I couldn't possibly write about it without doing it myself, so I did and now I still do.

BIGSBY It is a novel in which someone goes from this country to America, to Oberlin, the opposite of what you did.

CHEVALIER I am not sure I ever would have been a writer if I hadn't moved to England because it is being an outsider that sets me slightly apart from what I am writing about. That is really crucial. This is my seventh novel but it's the first time I have felt far enough away from the States – twenty nine years of being away – to be able to write about it. So there is a lot of me in it, even though it's going in the opposite direction to my own journey. It's that feeling of displacement that is important.

BERNARD CORNWELL

Bernard Cornwell was born in London in 1944. He was adopted and raised in Essex by two members of the Peculiar People, a strict religious sect. He worked as a teacher before joining the BBC and then Thames Television. He moved to the United States in order to marry his second wife, at the time an American travel agent. His first novels, *Sharpe's Eagle* and *Sharpe's Gold*, appeared in 1981 and marked the beginning of an immensely successful career which involved several series of books including further novels featuring Richard Sharpe, a trilogy set in Arthurian Britain, *Grail Quest* novels and a series focusing on the Anglo-Saxon kingdom of Wessex. He has also written thrillers and four novels set during the American Civil War.

This interview was recorded on October 27, 2014.

BIGSBY You were born as a result of a fairly brief affair between a Canadian Airman and a WAAF which, for people below a certain age, was the Women's Auxiliary Air Force.

CORNWELL It was a disastrous love affair. My mother was a working class girl from East London. Her name was Cornwell. My father was an upper-middle-class Canadian officer in the Royal Canadian Air Force. When I met him first I was fifty-eight and I remember saying, 'Tell me about my mother because I have never met her and I probably never will. You are the only person who can tell me anything about her.' He said, 'I don't know anything about her. It was a one-night stand.' I said, 'Was she pretty?' 'Of course she was pretty,' he said, 'you wouldn't be here if she wasn't.' That was that. A year later I met her and asked her and she said, 'The bastard. It was seven months.'

BIGSBY There was one stage when you said that you weren't going to look for them, but then you did.

CORNWELL I had known their names since I was about ten years old. What happened was that I was in Vancouver being interviewed by a reporter from the *Vancouver Sun*, and he was obviously bored to death. He was just asking the standard questions and I thought, OK, I will wake you up. He asked, 'Is there anything you want to do while you are in Vancouver?' I said, 'Yes. I want to find my real father.' It was really as stupid as that. I gave him his surname, which was Uhtred, and within two days somebody got in touch with me and said your father is William Uhtred and this is his address and phone number.

BIGSBY And that name was going to become quite important to you.

CORNWELL Yes. Maybe this is the moment to explain what a historical novel is. Historical novels have a big story and a little story. The big story is, can the South win the Civil War? The little story is can Scarlett save Tara? What you do is you flip them. You put the big story in the background and the little story in the foreground. I always wanted to tell the story of how England came into being. That is a big story, a very big story, but I didn't have a little story but then, when I met William for the first time, he said to me, 'You know we have a family tree and it goes all the way back to the sixth century.' It turned out to be quite genuine. Their name had been Uhtred and they had owned Bamburgh Castle, so that gave me my little story. The little story was how the hell does this family hang on to Bamburgh Castle, or Bebbanburg, as it was then called, even though the rest of northern England had been taken over by the Danes?

BIGSBY Let me take you back to your early years. You ended up in an orphanage and then were adopted by the Peculiar People, and I am using that word in several senses. Can you explain what was peculiar about them?

CORNWELL The Peculiar People was a sect in south east Essex. They were fundamentalists, evangelical Christians. My mother, Dorothy Cornwell, had me for two weeks. She said she was lying in bed one day and this couple came in, stood at the foot of the bed and looked at us. She said to me, 'I could tell they weren't cuddly,' and, oh God, she got that right. The Peculiars were not cuddly. I hated them. When I was seven years old my new mother said, 'I wish we hadn't adopted you.'

BIGSBY And your father would beat you?

CORNWELL Yes. I think he was rather a good man but he was completely obsessed with this religion. I guess the distinguishing feature of the Peculiars is that they wanted to keep me separate from the world. The name came from the Bible: 'I shall make thee unto me a peculiar people says the Lord thy God.' I think that is Deuteronomy. They had this enormous list of things that were sinful – blondes, cosmetics, alcohol, tobacco, cinema, television, so this became my wish list. I was beaten for reading *Treasure Island* because this was not considered suitable reading. I once counted that there were seventy-six Bibles in the house. The Peculiar People have virtually disappeared. They changed their name in the sixties to the Fellowship of Independent Evangelical Churches, which was really chickening out.

BIGSBY   And they are still there, in Essex.

CORNWELL   I gather there is one church, a chapel in Tillingham.

BIGSBY   There are a few in East London but they are mostly in Essex. Anyhow there you were, beaten if you read anything other than the Bible, or anything that was not approved. You were rescued, though, because you were sent to a boarding school.

CORNWELL   Yes. He reckoned the local schools were simply not religious enough and so he found a low church boarding school which was actually terribly civilised. So, yes, I was rescued.

BIGSBY   And there you could read?

CORNWELL   Yes, you could read whatever you liked, and I did.

BIGSBY   You were only a teenager but was it then that the idea of writing occurred to you?

CORNWELL   I think so. I think even when I was fourteen, fifteen, I had the idea that writing was better than working, and so it has proved.

BIGSBY   You went on to university, which presumably was antithetical to the values of your parents.

CORNWELL   They didn't like it because they were very suspicious of education. What made the Peculiars peculiar, what was special about them, was that originally they rejected all medical attention, a bit like Christian Scientists. I think it was in 1911 that there was a big diphtheria outbreak in Britain and the Grim Reaper went through The Peculiars with great enthusiasm. Some of them were prosecuted for not giving medical attention to their children. So then the sect split into two and there were the Old Peculiars, who went on rejecting medical attention and going to prison, and the New Peculiars who didn't. They got back together again in the 1930s but I remember even when I was ill, as a child, the elders of the church were brought in to lay their hands on me. I remember five ancient men standing round the bed pressing their hands on my head and saying, 'God come and cure this child,' which he didn't. Dr. Acres was called in and he had to do the job instead.

BIGSBY I love the irony that the Old Peculiars were against alcohol and Old Peculier is the name of a beer.
CORNWELL Yes, I drink it. Thank God it is exported to the States.

BIGSBY So you went to university to study theology. Was that a case of know thy enemy?
CORNWELL It was, and I came out the other end feeling as if I was now totally equipped to fight an enemy that no longer existed, so it was a complete waste of time.

BIGSBY The Peculiars were also pacifists. So inevitably you tried to join the army.
CORNWELL Yes, that was part of the wish list. They totally disapproved of military service, which in some ways was quite brave of them. In the First World War a lot of Peculiars went to prison rather than serve. In the Second World War the government was far more sensible and said that if they served in the ambulance service or the auxiliary fire service then that would be fine, but their hatred of military service certainly interested me, just as they hated high heels, cosmetics, blondes and alcohol, and all those things that have illuminated my life.

BIGSBY There was something else they were against, television. So you joined the BBC and ended up in a fairly elevated position in Northern Ireland at the time of The Troubles.
CORNWELL I loved it. The BBC love acronyms and I was H to the CAGTVNI. I would get memos saying Dear H, CAGTVNI. It stood for the Head of Current Affairs Group Television Northern Ireland. When I was in Belfast they appointed an Assistant Regional Sound Engineer and they put his acronym on the door. I was walking past and there was a guy painting it. I said, 'Are you sure you are meant to be doing that?'

BIGSBY So there you were, launched on a career you were enjoying, and then you gave it all up.

CORNWELL Yes. This is thirty-six years ago. Jeremy Paxman and I were supposed to be doing a programme on a government green paper on the future of industry in Northern Ireland. They then delayed the issue of the green paper by two weeks so we were suddenly without a programme and I looked at the diary and noticed that the Northern Irish Tourist Board were bringing travel agents from America to persuade them to see Ulster as a tourist destination. This was crazy. It was the second worst year of The Troubles and they were bringing these innocent American travel agents to Belfast and Derry so I thought, OK, I am going to film this. I remember talking to a guy at the Northern Irish Tourist Board and he saw trouble coming. He was not an idiot. He said, 'Bernard, you are going to be disappointed. The American travel agents can't put two words together. They are hopeless. You are not going to get an interview out of them. They are as dumb as stumps.' He was very, very convincing. So Gavin Esler and I flew to Edinburgh where these travel agents were to see if any of them could actually stitch two words together, and he was pretty well right. They were as dumb as stumps. Then the lift doors opened and a blonde walked out and I said to Gavin, 'I am going to marry that one.'

BIGSBY And that is what stopped your BBC career?

CORNWELL It stopped everything. I am still married to her.

BIGSBY So you followed her to America. Did you expect to be able to move into the media when you first got there?

CORNWELL I had a job with WNET in New York and they said to me, 'You have to get a Green Card.' I went along to the American Embassy and said, 'I want a Green Card,' and they laughed . 'Join the line.' So I said to Judy, 'I am coming anyway,' and she said, 'what are you going to do?' and I said 'I have always wanted to write a book.' It was insane, really insane.

BIGSBY So in order to survive, to have some income, you wrote a book but I seem to remember you analysed other books before setting out on it?

CORNWELL Yes, I did. I took three books, one was a Hornblower, maybe two were Hornblowers, and I broke them down. If you are going to build a better mousetrap, what do you do? The first thing you do is you go and buy every mousetrap on the market and see how they work, and you throw out what you think is a bad idea and you keep what you think are good ideas. So you do that with books. I analysed them. I made these huge charts: what happens in each chapter, how much is flashback, how much is action, how much is dialogue. I sadly lost the charts long ago.

BIGSBY So you began to develop a formula?

CORNWELL Yes, sure, absolutely. Look, I am not in this to win the Booker Prize. I am in this to make money, so you look at books that have made money and you think, well what is he doing and how has he done it? I remember when I first started to write one of the most difficult things was to move characters from one room to another, so you go and look at the people who have done it before and say, 'Oh, that's how you do it.'

BIGSBY And this was going to be the first Sharpe novel. Why that location for that book?

CORNWELL Because when I was a kid I discovered Hornblower. I loved Hornblower. I didn't realise until much later that C.S. Forester didn't like writing Hornblower. He was published by Little, Brown. Forester lived in California and Little, Brown were in Boston in those days and whenever Little, Brown's profits began to look a bit low, a guy called Angus Cameron would be given a suitcase full of whisky bottles and told to fly to California and persuade Forester to write another Hornblower. You asked why that setting? I can remember when I was sixteen or seventeen there were no more Hornblowers to read and what is the next best thing. In the real histories of the period, I discovered stories about Wellington and the army and I used to think wouldn't it be wonderful if there was a Hornblower on dry land?

I used to go to W H Smith looking for this series that didn't exist and, at some point in my twenties, probably when I had just joined the BBC, a dim light went on in my head saying, 'Why don't you write it?' But I never did because I was too busy, so that when the time came to be with Judy I thought, OK, that is what I have always wanted to do, write Hornblower on dry land. So that is where it comes from.

BIGSBY Did you have difficulty placing that first book?

CORNWELL Actually, no. I had a flat in London and sold it to a literary agent and I thought, OK, this is great because I now have a contact in the business and I sent the manuscript to him. It came back with the speed of light, saying nobody wants to read about the British Army. So that was bad but having worked in television I had a connection with another publisher, so I sent it to him. I didn't know him that well, and I knew it had to be published in London not New York. I actually got an offer and I didn't know what to do because the offer simply wasn't sufficient for me to live on and write the next book. So I didn't accept it and about a week later we had been invited to a Thanksgiving day party in New York and I was standing on a balcony looking at McDonalds' All America High School Band that was high-stepping past us on, whatever it was, Central Park West, and a voice behind me said, 'They do this sort of thing frightfully well, don't they?' So, being a brilliant conversationalist I said, 'Oh, you are English.' 'Yes,' he said. I said, 'What do you do?' He said, 'I am a literary agent.' I said, 'Oh good, because I have just written a novel,' and he said, 'fuck' and walked away. So I followed him into the party and said, 'I have had an offer on my novel.' Now he is a literary agent so his eyes are really doing the whole fruit machine thing, and he said, 'what's the offer?' I said, '£3,000 world rights.' He said, 'It must be a fucking awful book.' He turned round and walked away again. So I got him a third time and said, 'Please read my novel,' and he said, 'Oh God, dear boy, if you must. I will meet you in the Oyster Bar, Grand Central Station, tomorrow, midday.' So the next day I went into the Oyster Bar at Grand Central Station and I gave him the manuscript and we had a very awkward lunch. He phoned me that night at seven o'clock and said, 'How much money do you want?' and within two weeks I had a three-book contract, and within a month that was a seven book contract. So, no, it wasn't difficult at all.

BIGSBY But how much of a slow burn was it to establish yourself with those books?

CORNWELL My then, and present, publisher said it is going to take five books to make you a best seller. I don't know whether a publisher today would say, 'OK, we will lose money over the next five years on the grounds that we believe that after five years it will be all right.'

BIGSBY At a certain stage would come the television version of the Sharpe novels. Was Sean Bean the original choice for that?

CORNWELL No, Sean got the part because he looks like me though the other guy would have been very good, that was Paul McGann. They started filming in the Ukraine and after two weeks or three weeks of filming they were playing soccer on the beach. They had lots of Ukrainian extras from the Ukrainian army, so it was the crew of actors and technicians against the Ukrainian army and poor Paul fell over and did something to his knee, something dreadful. He couldn't walk for six months and what resulted was the biggest insurance claim in British television history. They had ten days to turn the thing round and they hadn't even given Sean an audition, but he was the only actor who was available to come and do it, so they had no choice. Sean was terrific. My idea of Sharpe was quite different but Sean was perfect, and he just took over.

BIGSBY Did it change your approach in subsequent to the book?

CORNWELL Yes, everything. Sean is wonderful. He is grumpy, just like Sharpe, and I think Pete Postlethwaite, playing Hakeswill, was much better than my Hakeswill, much better, so Sean took it over and I thought he was great.

BIGSBY Roughly half of your books have been written about Sharpe. But you have written various other series, many set in medieval Britain. And you have written a book about Agincourt. What does surprise me is something you have said about the speed with which archers can release arrows, which I found astonishing.

CORNWELL A modern Olympic bow has a draw weight of about forty pounds. That is the same as lifting forty pounds. The archers at Agincourt had a draw weight of over a hundred and twenty pounds, some of them up to probably a hundred and fifty. We know that because we have got some of the bows. This is phenomenal, and we have found archers' graves and their bones have grown bigger because of that, to serve as anchors for the muscles. I found a guy who spends most of his life at Warwick Castle entertaining the tourists and he can draw a one hundred and twenty pound bow. We set up a Frenchman-sized target at one hundred and fifty yards and then timed. He sent, I think I am right, sixteen arrows in one minute at one hundred and fifty yards, and of the sixteen arrows twelve hit, and the other four would have hit the guy next to him. The greatest expert on a long bow is the actor Robert Hardy and I talked to him and he said, 'yes, sixteen, seventeen, easy, no problem.'

BIGSBY So at any one time there would be thousands of arrows in the air.

CORNWELL Oh, thousands. I think there were probably 5,000 archers at Agincourt and the first line of Frenchmen at Arms consisted of 8,000. So these 8,000 guys have got to cover about 250 yards through incredibly thick mud up to their knees. It probably took them ten minutes, each of them wearing seventy pounds of armour. They were unbelievably brave, and they are being shot at by these 5,000 guys. 5,000 times ten is 50,000 now multiply 50,000 by 15 and that's how many arrows probably hit those 8,000 guys. It is incredible that they reached the English line but by that time they were exhausted and had to advance with their visors down. It must have been awful. Even if you are hit by what they call 'a blunt', which is an arrow without a head, it will knock you back two paces. The force behind those arrows was extraordinary and so these poor Frenchmen, brave guys, struggling through the mud, were being hit by these arrows and even if the arrow didn't pierce the armour it would knock them back. It was like walking into steel hail.

BIGSBY A common element in your work is war, and you have said that that is a gift to a writer. In what sense?

CORNWELL I always think of the Sharpe books as basically adventure stories. I am not writing literature, I am writing adventure stories and war is this incredibly rich background. It is a kind of instinct as to how you shape a novel. All I know is that you are telling a story and you have to satisfy the reader. Every new novel I start I think I can't do it, this is not going to be good enough. I go down to three or four hours sleep a night which lasts until the novel is finished.

BIGSBY I said you have written various series and one is the Arthurian one, which in the past you have said is your favourite. Why is that?

CORNWELL What drew me to it is that these stories are at the tap root of British history and I really wanted to do something different. I wanted to put Arthur into a believable sixth century environment and try and de-mystify. I am fascinated by the relationship of myth and reality and I really did do an enormous amount of research. I was reading everything there was on Arthur and was getting bored to death by it. I had allowed myself six months of really intense reading then I got bored and one day I thought, let's just try a chapter. I didn't know whether to write in the first person or third person so I thought today I will just write a chapter in the first person to see if I can make it work. I had never written in the first person. It was, say, September 7. By December 19, the book was finished. I just went 'vroom!' It was great, just wonderful, and the second and the third were the same.

BIGSBY To what extent are you looking for the gaps in history that you can occupy?

CORNWELL One of my favourite books is *Sharpe's Tiger*. It is about the Siege of Seringapatam, and in the siege the enemy is the Tipu Sultan, who in many ways was rather an admirable man. He died in what is called The Watergate, a tunnel under the very thick walls of Seringapatam, and when he died he was festooned with jewels, rubies, pearls and diamonds. He was plainly killed by a British soldier but no British soldier ever came forward and said, 'I killed the Tipu,' obviously because he had stolen the damn lot and didn't want any officer asking 'Where are the jewels?' So some guy, probably from a Kentish regiment, got away with it but we don't know who. Well, boom, enter Sharpe.

BIGSBY When you write, as you do, about Stonehenge, you have to invent a great deal of that world. Do you like it when there is less historical material to deal with, or do you need an historical framework?

CORNWELL I don't care which way. I found *Stonehenge* incredibly frustrating simply because I think I failed to make up an adequate theology, to be honest. It is not one of my favourite books. But you do other stories, like *The Fort*, where you have an immense amount of material. I think I had fifteen diaries and ships' logs to work from. I really don't care which way it is. I like making up dark ages stuff, but I also like working from this very informative framework too.

BIGSBY You have now turned to Waterloo, but not, as with Sharpe, in fictional terms. So why Waterloo and why non-fiction?

CORNWELL This is one of the greatest stories of history. It is an extraordinary story. For a start, everything that matters takes place in four days, so it is very, very, tight. The second thing is the extraordinary fact that the two greatest soldiers of the age, who had never met on a battlefield, were about to do so. It has this immense drama. It has a unity of time. It is a very small battlefield. So it is this extraordinary story of a rivalry between two great men in what is obviously a very important battle. So why this book? One reason is that it is such a good story. I am a story teller, so I wanted to tell the story again and it is quite a long time since a story teller has told it. There have been a lot of books on Waterloo which are technically incredibly interesting, but not necessarily told by a story teller. I always say to people that if you want to know about the Peninsular War go and get Charles Esdaile's wonderful book, *The Peninsular War: A New History*, and it is a great book, but it won't keep you up at night. You can put the book down and go to sleep. I have failed if you are not still reading at half past eleven.

BIGSBY You quote Wellington as talking about the impossibility of describing a battle, especially if you are in it. And that presumably is the challenge for you because it wasn't just one battle. It was effectively three battles.

CORNWELL Yes, Wellington said that to write of battles is as impossible as writing the story of a ball, a dance. You can't tell what happened in that swirl of ball gowns, scent, champagne and flirting. Who can say what happened and when? So you just have to try and sort it out. In the book I say that many of those who survived that field left their memoirs. People made huge efforts to contact survivors and say what happened, but there are still things we don't know.

BIGSBY How far did the French lose that battle rather than the English win it?

CORNWELL Oh, they lost it. Right from the start Wellington is praying for time. He knows that his position is incredibly fragile, that the French, if they are given enough time, are probably going to break his line. He only makes a stand on that ridge because he knows that Blücher and the Prussians are coming to his aid. As it turns out, the Prussians are held up and are late, though it's not their fault. Napoleon delays the battle by two hours on a day that Wellington is praying for time. Napoleon gives him time. That was a huge mistake. Then Napoleon detaches Grouchy, with 33,000 men and ninety-six guns, and they are wandering off like Alice in Wonderland not doing a damn thing. If they had been on the battlefield Wellington would have lost. Napoleon was not on his best form, we can say that.

BIGSBY And it was an incredibly brutal battle.
CORNWELL Oh awful. It was dreadful, horrible.

BIGSBY There were 20,000 amputations without anaesthetic in that battle and you talk about what came to be called 'Waterloo Teeth'.
CORNWELL After the battle people went round the battlefield with pliers and pulled out the teeth from the dead, and maybe from the wounded too, and sold them to dentists. For years afterwards if you got false teeth they were called 'Waterloo Teeth'.

BIGSBY You are a prolific writer of novels but you also have an interest in theatre where you live in America. Do you play English parts or American?
CORNWELL I play American roles.

BIGSBY How is your American accent?
CORNWELL Not good. I don't like it. I started playing mostly Shakespeare, but it has expanded.

BIGSBY Is the acting completely separate from the writing?
CORNWELL Totally separate. Writing is a solitary vice and I like being alone. You listen to characters in your head. If I am writing a book I hear conversations between the characters who are nothing to do with the book. It is one way you get to know the characters, listening to them talk to each other. I know it sounds crazy but then suddenly, in the summer, for three months, I work with this Rep Company of drama students who are usually very bright and very talented, irreverent and fun. I spend three months with thirty-, forty-, twenty-something-year-olds and it is great. Then I go back to writing again.

RICHARD DAWKINS

Richard Dawkins was born in Nairobi, Kenya, in 1941 and is an evolutionary biologist. He was educated at Oxford University. His first book, *The Selfish Gene*, appeared in 1976. Other books include *The Blind Watchmaker*, *Unweaving the Rainbow*, *The God Delusion*, *The Greatest Show on Earth* and two volumes of memoirs, *An Appetite for Wonder: The Making of a Scientist* and *Brief Candle in the Dark: My Life in Science*. He is a Fellow of the Royal Society and the Royal Society of Literature.

This interview was recorded on October 21, 2015.

BIGSBY Richard, you grew up in a colonial world, presumably with all the trappings of that.

DAWKINS Very much so. We had servants. We had tea in the garden with beautiful silver teapots and cloths over them. It was a very gracious kind of living but on the other hand we had an earth closet not a water closet. So it was a mixture.

BIGSBY The family moved within Africa to what is now Malawi, where you grew up, before leaving at the age of eight or nine. Have memories of Africa stayed with you?

DAWKINS They have been obliterated by more recent memories. Memory is a funny thing anyway. I think that all our memories are to some extent obliterated by later things, hence false memory syndrome. I think we don't really remember what happened as though it was a cine film. We remember our memories of memories of memories and they get distorted as time goes by. They get overlain.

BIGSBY You left Africa and came to a boarding school in this country. What was your experience of that?

DAWKINS Going to boarding school at the age of seven is no fun and I do remember that I used to have fantasies that the matron would turn into my mother. She had dark hair like my mother and so it wouldn't have required a very great miracle to achieve the transformation. So I suppose that I was one of many who were taken away from home too early. I wasn't bullied myself, thank goodness, nor did I bully, but I witnessed bullying and now in adulthood I can't understand why I didn't intervene. I can't understand the cruelty of children who do the bullying or those who don't bully but are indifferent to the suffering, which is very considerable, of those who are bullied.

BIGSBY I am surprised you weren't bullied because at that stage you had a stammer.

DAWKINS I did have a stammer, yes, but I don't remember that as being a cause for bullying. It wasn't a very bad stammer, I suppose, though I had trouble saying my own surname, Dawkins, because it begins with a D which is a difficult letter to say. At my later school we had an Army Cadet Corps and I was tormented by the ordeal of having to march out in front of a General who had come to inspect. We all had to march out, salute, and say, 'Cadet Dawkins, Sir.' I rehearsed this and finally managed 'Cadet Dawkins, Sir' and got over it but it was a difficult moment and when, in class, we had to mark our own tests, if I got ten out of ten I would actually sing out nine because I could say nine and I couldn't say ten.

BIGSBY From there you went to Oxford where you read zoology. Your father had been a botanist, but when you were young you were more inclined to read.

DAWKINS Yes, I was. My father wanted me to be out in the great outdoors with the wind in my face looking for flowers and birds and things and I would creep rather shamefacedly upstairs to my room and read. Nothing very edifying, I hasten to say. It would be Biggles or Bulldog Drummond or something like that. I once visited the Monastery in Brno, in what is now the Czech Republic, home of Gregor Mendel, the founder of genetics, and I was shown the library in this Austrian-Czech monastery. It was filled with English schoolboy books, Biggles, Arthur Ransome, Percy F. Westerman. What they were doing in that library I don't know but they were there, along with Mendel's own copy of *The Origin of the Species* in German, with underlinings to show that Mendel had actually read it.

BIGSBY When you were at school you went through a fairly intense religious phase, did you not?
DAWKINS Yes, though I wouldn't say it was that fanatical.

BIGSBY But you have described being tempted to go down to the chapel at night.
DAWKINS I did, that's true.

BIGSBY That's intense.
DAWKINS What can I say? When I was a child I spake as a child, I thought as a child, I understood as a child,

but when I became a man I put away childish things.

BIGSBY And was it *The Origin of the Species* which converted you, or perhaps unconverted you?

DAWKINS I think it was my father who first explained Darwinian evolution to me. I didn't quite get it at that point but I got it a bit later at school.

BIGSBY You went on to do a PhD in animal behaviour, in particular to do with the self-grooming of flies and pecking instincts.

DAWKINS It was a kind of Popperian analysis of what goes on inside an animal's head worked out purely from the behaviour that emerges from the animal. So you don't cut the skull open but think up possible hypothetical models of what might be going on inside. You use algebra to deduce predictions from the model and then test the predictions on the behaviour that emerges from the animal. In this case the predictions came out remarkably successfully, which is in some sense weak evidence that the model is correct.

BIGSBY I once made a programme for the BBC about Darwin. We went to his house and later did an experiment on ants to see if they can hear. We found an ant colony and played them Mozart and punk rock. Rather more significantly, ants posed a problem for Darwin, did they not?

DAWKINS Yes. I think that Darwin actually got one of his sons to play the bassoon, but that is an aside. The problem that ants posed was that worker ants are sterile. There are several different kinds of workers in any one ant colony: minor workers, major workers, soldiers with great big muscular jaws. They are all clearly adapted to particular functions in the nest but because they are sterile they obviously can't pass on their characteristics by any form of heredity because they don't have offspring. Darwin worked out that what they were doing was working for the reproductive success of their mother, who does of course pass genes on. In modern genetic terms we would say that copies of the mother's genes are in the soldiers and the workers and, although the workers are sterile, the genes make them do things which contribute to the reproduction of those very same genes in the mother. Darwin used the analogy of agriculture where a farmer wishes to have good quality meat from his cattle. The ox itself, which produces the meat, has been slaughtered. It doesn't reproduce, but Darwin said we go with confidence to the stock and that is the analogy with going to the queen who passes on the genes.

BIGSBY I read another explanation of how that works which is that there was an earlier form of ant colonies in which they were sexualised but that that led to competition, which in turn led to the breakdown of colonies. Is that at all plausible?

DAWKINS Not as you have described it, no. I don't think that is plausible. I don't think it is necessary because the Hamilton theory, which I have just outlined, is utterly convincing and sufficient.

BIGSBY You spent some time in America, at the University of California, Berkeley, as an assistant professor. This was at the time of the Vietnam war.

DAWKINS A very young assistant professor. And I marched with the best of them, or the worst of them, against the war and was tear-gassed. I was only there for two years but they are pretty firmly imprinted on my memory. It was a wonderful time with the revolution in the air. Bliss was it in that dawn.

BIGSBY You came to the idea of *The Selfish Gene* really quite early. You referred to it in a lecture and then you began a book, but you put the book to one side.

DAWKINS Yes. The idea really wasn't mine. I was simply putting it into different words. It really dates from the 1930s but it had never been put into quite these words. I put it into words in lectures in 1966, 1967, 1968 and then, in 1974, started writing it as a book. It was the year of the three-day week in Britain, which meant there was no electricity and I couldn't do my experiments, so decided to write a book instead. But unfortunately – or fortunately, as the case may be – the three-day week came to an end, so I shelved the book for another three years and then went back to it when I had a sabbatical.

BIGSBY And the essence of that idea is that it is the gene that is the significant element not the individual, not the group?

DAWKINS The gene is the only permanent entity. The individual dies having reproduced its genes, and so it is genes that go through generation after generation after generation in the form of copies of themselves, the good ones, where good simply means that they do go through many generations. The good ones are good because they are good at building bodies, good at contributing in co-operation with other genes, to do whatever the species does, fly or swim or dig or swing through the trees, and do it well. Another way to look at it is to look at it backwards, to say that every creature that is alive is descended from an unbroken line of successful ancestors. That is obvious but it is important because it means that every creature alive has inherited the genes that made its ancestors successful at becoming ancestors. Every single one of your ancestors lived at least long enough to achieve at least one heterosexual copulation. Lots of their rivals didn't succeed in doing so. They died, or failed to attract a mate. We are all descended from a progenitorial elite of animals that were good at surviving and we have inherited the genes that make us good at surviving in whatever particular way our species does it.

BIGSBY And the individual is the vehicle.

DAWKINS The vehicle, or the temporary survival machine that works to survive, pass on its genes, and then die.

BIGSBY Were you surprised by the success of that book; after all, it sold a million?

DAWKINS I jokingly referred to it while I was writing it as 'my bestseller' but I didn't really think it would be, so yes, I was surprised.

BIGSBY In Darwin's time there was a collision between science and religion and that is no less true now.

One of your most successful books is *The God Delusion* which has sold three million copies and been translated into thirty-five languages. Was that a battle that it was inevitable you would fight?

DAWKINS   I suppose all my books have been written on the assumption of a lack of religion but this was the first one where I came out and wrote a whole book about it. I originally suggested it to my literary agent John Brockman in New York in about 1998, I think, and he vetoed it at the time because he said you couldn't sell a book like that in America. Then about six years of George W. Bush changed his mind and he told me 'now is the time to write *The God Delusion*'.

BIGSBY   And here we are sitting in Norwich, which, according to the last census, is the most irreligious city in the United Kingdom.

DAWKINS   Oh, bravo.

BIGSBY   But who were you writing it for? Presumably not for the convinced religious person because the whole point of religion is that it turns on faith and no amount of evidence that you present will alter that. It will simply be regarded as a test of faith. So if you are not writing for them, who are you writing for?

DAWKINS   I think I was probably writing for those who vaguely think of themselves as religious but haven't really thought very hard about it and are therefore sitting on the fence. They are very numerous and I found this out with an opinion poll that my foundation, The Richard Dawkins Foundation for Reason and Science, commissioned in the week after the 2011 census. The 2011 census, you will remember, contained religious questions. You had to tick which religion you belonged to, or not, and we, in my Foundation, suspected that the people who tick the Christian box were probably in many cases only doing it for form's sake. So we commissioned a polling organisation to give supplementary questions to a sample of those who ticked the Christian box and with interesting results.

The number who ticked the Christian box had dropped from 74%, I think it was, in the 2001 census to 54% in the 2011 census. We then took a sample of the 54% and asked them supplementary questions such as, 'Do you regard Jesus as your Lord and Saviour?' 'Do you believe in the virgin birth?' 'Do you believe in the resurrection?' 'Can you pick the first book of the New Testament from the following list of four: Matthew, Genesis, Acts and Psalms?' I think it was 39% of those who called themselves Christians who were able to pick Matthew out of that list. We asked them, 'Why did you tick the Christian box?' giving them various alternatives, and the most popular answer was, 'Because I like to think of myself as a good person.' So I think that really answers your question. There are people who call themselves Christian because they like to think of themselves as a good people. We asked them, 'When you are faced with a moral dilemma, do you turn to your religion to solve it, or do you turn to this, that and the other?' and only 10% said they turn to their religion when faced with a moral dilemma. So, I think the number of people who officially call themselves religious, but actually are not, or are sitting on the fence, are ripe for a book like *The God Delusion*.

BIGSBY Surely one of the surprises is that we entered the twenty first century, an age of science and technology, but also, it has turned out, an age of fundamentalist religion.

DAWKINS It's true. Fundamentalist Christianity is pretty strong in America. It isn't in this country, though fundamentalist Islam is becoming stronger here and in the world. But even in America the number of people who profess no religion at all has now grown to 20%. It is not as high as in this country, or in Scandinavian countries, but it is growing higher, so I see the broad sweep of history as moving in the right direction with occasional blips going in the wrong direction.

BIGSBY You took part in a series of television programmes on atheism with Jonathan Miller and something he put to you had to do with the sense of wonder, something we tend to associate with literature, the romantic poets for example. You have argued for the wonder implicit in science but said that when scientists invoke wonder there is a minister in the bushes who the moment he hears the word 'wonder' leaps out and claims you for religion.

DAWKINS I have written a whole book about this, *Unweaving the Rainbow,* which is about the poetry of science and I follow Carl Sagan, among others, who saw the whole universe as a kind of poem. When you look down a microscope you see the extraordinary complexity of life which may exist only on this planet. We have no evidence that it is anywhere else, though I suspect it probably is for statistical reasons, but when you think that atoms bumping into each other, following the laws of chemistry, following the laws of physics, have, through this remarkable process that Darwin discovered, evolution by natural selection, unfolded into prodigies of complexity and apparent elegance of design, trees and birds and dolphins and kangaroos, bacteria and humans with brains that have evolved to become so big that they have actually managed to work out where we all come from, I think that is an astounding, wonderful fact and worthy of great literature. I don't really know why the Nobel Prize for Literature has never been awarded to a scientist.

BIGSBY You invoke writers but as a scientist you yourself turn to metaphor, to analogy.

DAWKINS Very much so, and I like to think that I have a sense for cadence, for the rhythm of language, as well as for imagery, and it is the facts of life, the facts of the universe, which move me in that direction.

BIGSBY How does the gene impact on consciousness?

DAWKINS Via the brain in a very indirect way. The gene is naturally selected through generations to specify a recurrent embryonic process starting with a fertilised egg in every generation and this embryonic process gives rise to nervous systems, and nervous systems in advanced mammals become very big. Brains become very big in humans. We are put into the world to survive and reproduce. In the course of that we evolved brains so big that we can now do mathematics and philosophy and poetry and music and this is way, way removed from the original quote 'purpose' for which we were put into the world.

BIGSBY   I can see that the brain evolved. Isn't consciousness something else? A sense of self-awareness?

DAWKINS   Well it is something very mysterious. I don't think it would be right to say that it is something other than a manifestation of brain activity but it is a very peculiar manifestation of brain activity, one that baffles philosophers. We each of us know internally that we have consciousness. We have no absolute way of being sure that anybody else does and that shows itself in our uncertainty about whether non-human animals have it. We really argue by analogy. I believe everybody in this room has consciousness because I have and I know that everybody in this room came into the world in the same kind of way as I did and there is no reason to think that I am peculiar, no reason to be a solipsist in other words, to believe that I am the only one who has consciousness. There is a lovely story about Bertrand Russell. He had a letter from a lady which said, 'Dear Lord Russell, I am so pleased to hear that you are a solipsist. There are so few of us around these days.'

BIGSBY   I gather that you have won a minor battle. Anyone who has stayed in an American hotel knows that they will find a Gideon Bible in the drawer, but you are fighting back?

DAWKINS   I had a letter a couple of weeks ago from the landlady of a small hotel in the Lake District, The Mortal Man, which said that they have decided to replace the Gideon Bible with *The God Delusion*. So this is a hotel everybody should visit.

BIGSBY   You are a scientist but you have also become a major figure in the promotion of the understanding of science. Indeed that was the title of a professorship that you held and, as you said earlier, you have established a foundation. What is its purpose?

DAWKINS   It is a foundation for reason and science

and that pretty much says it really. It is actually two foundations, one in Britain – that was the one that did the poll I referred to – and one in America with the same name which is rather more active and has an actual office and salaried staff. It raises money to pay those salaries. The American foundation has a number of projects going. One is called Openly Secular, which is an attempt to persuade Americans that it is not true that everybody in America is religious. American politicians believe that to be true, which is why so many of them lie about their religious beliefs. All 535 members of the US Congress claim to have religious belief and that is statistically an obvious nonsense. It can't be true because it means that all 535 members of the US Congress are either religious or liars. You can't blame them for being liars because they think they have got to lie in order to get elected. The Openly Secular campaign is an attempt to disabuse them by getting people to stand up and say, 'I am not religious.' We are doing it using YouTube films, getting celebrities to come out. It is a bit like the gay campaign which has been so successful in the last few decades in which people have transformed being gay from being something you kept quiet about to being something you take pride in. So we have taken a leaf out of their book and are trying to emulate them. I suppose that is the main thing we are doing in America, though there are other things as well.

Next year is the ninetieth anniversary of the famous Scopes monkey trial in Tennessee so we are sponsoring ninety productions of the play *Inherit the Wind*, which is a fictionalised version of it, in schools all around America. We are also setting up a programme to train middle school teachers to teach evolution. A lot of middle school teachers of science in America don't have a science degree and they don't feel confident enough to teach evolution because they don't feel confident at coping with the push back, the sheer aggression they get. We are trying to stiffen their spines by teaching them how to teach evolution.

BIGSBY You were a very early adopter of the computer and I don't mean by that using the computer. You have programmed computers and developed a programme which was almost a demonstration of evolution.

DAWKINS In those early days you couldn't use a computer unless you programmed it and so I did in lots of different languages. I even built my own word processor with which I wrote *The Blind Watchmaker* but I did write the programme you referred to and which is a representation of evolution by artificial selection. From patterns on the screen you can choose from among randomly mutated forms which ones are going to breed. You can breed whatever you like. I have managed, starting from trees, to breed insects and weird castles and I think, on one occasion, a passable caricature of the Wykeham Professor of Logic.

BIGSBY You insist that evolution is not about progress, in the sense that it is not about moving from simple organisms to mankind, but there can be other kinds of progress.

DAWKINS Yes. Certainly you should never think of evolution as being drawn to a particular end point like mankind. I think it is not unreasonable to see trends towards greater complexity, not in all cases but in cases like the evolution of the eye, the evolution of complex organs. They have to start in a primitive state, hardly functioning at all, and then eventually reach a state like the modern eye where it really is a very, very efficient camera focusing very precise colour images, capable of extremely fine discrimination. That has got to come about by gradual steps, gradual degrees, and that implies progress. There has to be progress from an ancestral state, where the ancestral eye could hardly see anything at all, maybe just the difference between light and dark, moving steadily upwards towards a beautifully functioning eye such as we have today. So there is progress in that sense, but it is not progress towards a particular species like humanity.

BIGSBY There is something else that you say that interests me. You say, strip God away, strip faith away, and it can seem a bleak, cold universe dictated purely by chance. You are born at a particular moment, in a particular place and as a result have a particular religion, maybe a particular ideology. You go into one room rather than another and you marry someone as a consequence of that. It can seem as though we are indeed the tennis balls Shakespeare talks about and yet you are saying that that raises the stakes so that creating meaning becomes that much more significant?

DAWKINS Yes. I think we are extremely lucky to be here, if only because a particular sperm had to meet a particular egg I mean, and that wasn't a sufficient reason for us to be here. There is a poem by Aldous Huxley which expresses this very well, it goes, 'A million million spermatozoa, all of them alive; out of their cataclysm but one poor Noah dare hope to survive. And among that billion minus one might have chanced to be Shakespeare, another Newton, a new Donne – but the one was me. Shame to have ousted your betters thus, taking ark while the others remained outside! Better for all of us, forward Homunculus, if you'd quietly died.' So we are incredibly lucky to be here and I think that should make us feel grateful, not grateful to any particular individual, but just grateful to the happenstance of being here and determined to make the most of our time while we have got it. We haven't got it forever, so let's make the most of it. Let's work to have a good life and let's work to understand the process that brought us here in the first place.

MARGARET DRABBLE   EIMEAR MCBRIDE

Margaret Drabble, DBE, FRSL, was born
in Sheffield in 1939. She is a graduate of
Newnham College, Cambridge, and joined the
Royal Shakespeare Company in 1960 before
turning to the novel. She has published eighteen
novels, beginning with *A Summer Bird Cage* in
1963. She has been awarded the Golden PEN
Award by English PEN for her distinguished
service to literature. Among her books are *The
Realms of Gold*, *The Middle Way*, *The Radiant
Way*, *The Witch of Exmore*, *The Peppered
Moth* and *The Pure Gold Baby*. She is also the
author of biographies of Arnold Bennett and
Angus Wilson, and is the editor of the *Oxford
Companion to English Literature*. Her book
*The Pattern in the Carpet: A Personal History
of Jigsaws* appeared in 2009.

Eimear McBride was born in 1976. Raised
in Ireland, she moved to London at the age of
seventeen, intending to be an actress. She then
wrote a novel, *A Girl is a Half-Formed Thing*.
After many rejections it was finally published
nine years later, in 2013, by Galley Beggar,
a newly-established Norwich publisher (she
was by then living in Norwich). It became a
publishing sensation, winning the Goldsmiths
Prize, the Geoffrey Faber Memorial Prize, the
Baileys Women's Prize for Fiction, the Kerry
Group Irish Fiction Award and the Desmond
Elliott Prize.

This interview was recorded on
November 12, 2014.

BIGSBY Margaret, since you were last here, eight years ago, you have published a novel, a book of short stories, and what, on the face of it, was a strange book, a book about jigsaws, though it turned out to be about something else as well.

DRABBLE I wanted it to be about jigsaws but my publisher wasn't enthusiastic. He kept telling me what you really want to write is a memoir. I didn't want to write one but it turned out to be half and half. I didn't want to write about me but realised I could write about my aunt who taught me how to do jigsaws. So in a way it is a tribute to her, but also I learnt a lot about jigsaws and completely enjoyed the research. So it was a bit of everything.

BIGSBY Writing about a member of your family could be dangerous territory. It has been for you in the past. I take it that you had found a member of your family who was not going to be a source of problems for you?

DRABBLE Well, she was dead. I saw a lot of her and she saw a lot of me, and no guilt attached to my relationship with her at all. We were very fond of one another and writing about her was a pleasure. It was a tribute to her because she was a remarkable woman though in some senses she was a very ordinary woman. She was just a primary school teacher who had no children but loved her nieces and nephews.

BIGSBY The book is a little like a jigsaw. You go off in various directions, have various pieces which slowly fit together to form something. I presume that when you started you didn't know that.

DRABBLE No, I really wanted to write a little book about jigsaws that would be sold in museum shops with a jigsaw in the back flap. I thought this would be a really big seller but oddly enough the publishers didn't go for it at all.

BIGSBY One thing that you contemplate is the contrast or comparison between jigsaws and writing except that with a jigsaw the complete picture is known before you start, and you start with the corners, and the edges.

DRABBLE Yes, corners, but when I start writing a novel I have no sense of a frame or of the corners or edges. I just begin at the beginning and hope for the best. I don't really have a plan until I am halfway through. As to jigsaws, I find them very soothing. I do them listening to the radio. You need to have something to do. I don't knit, so I do jigsaws. I find them really quite calming.

BIGSBY They do seem to major in nostalgia. They feature thatched cottages or bucolic scenes.

DRABBLE I did do a huge battle scene once. There was a ruined windmill. It was the battle of Valmy and was bought for me by my grandson. He said, 'I thought this looked just great for you,' and I said 'What, all these dead horses?' He said, 'Yes, they are great, aren't they?' And it was wonderful to do but not peaceful – no, not peaceful.

BIGSBY You also say that they can be therapeutic. You mention the fact that you turned to jigsaws when your husband, Michael Holroyd, was extremely ill.

DRABBLE When I say it was calming that was because at the end of an hour you had done a piece or two and you had got somewhere. It took your mind off things. Also when Michael was very ill I found I couldn't read. I couldn't find the right book to read. My mind was turbulent and I couldn't settle to reading very seriously. I certainly couldn't write, so the jigsaw got me through that five o'clock, six o'clock time in the evening before we could start watching a DVD. It was just a great comfort to me. It took me out of my brain. It was good.

BIGSBY For all that, you say something very surprising in the book and that is that you keep the telephone number of the Samaritans to hand and that more than once they have stepped in. That really surprised me but it is true, isn't it, that your parents suffered from depression too?

DRABBLE They were both quite depressive. My mother was very depressive and I am afraid to say she was on medication most of her adult life. They never revised it, never tried to find out what was the matter with her. They just gave her pills. My father just took it on the chin and went on being depressed. He was more stoic than she was. I have very, very low patches and there have been one or two moments in my life when there has been absolutely nowhere to turn without causing great upset. That's what the Samaritans are for. I greatly admire them. I know people who have been Samaritans as well as people who have turned to them. Just to have an anonymous person on the end of the line can be a great help.

BIGSBY When you are in that condition can you write?
DRABBLE Sort of, yes.

BIGSBY And does writing play a part in reaching out beyond the world you have suddenly been trapped in?
DRABBLE Yes, though I don't want to overplay myself as a depressive because I don't stay down for very long. I don't stay seriously down. In fact I have been OK for quite a little while now so let's hope this isn't bad luck talking about it. I come up quite quickly. I am very volatile of temperament and I think as I get older there is no point in getting really depressed. It doesn't get you anywhere, though ten years ago I did feel that it got you somewhere.

BIGSBY How?
DRABBLE You were confronting something terrible and you had to know it, but now I think there is no point. I have grown through it. I get very depressed but I now say to myself, exactly what my father used to say to me, 'Just keep going, keep doing things and it will go away. Go for a walk, do a bit of vacuum cleaning,' and I do find the vacuum cleaner very comforting. My father used to be the same. He used to find things to do, and it does get you through.

BIGSBY A novel does end up with a completed world. Is there something inevitably reassuring about that. Whatever the tone of the novel there is a beginning, a middle and an end. There is a structure, an arc to characters' lives. There is something essentially reassuring about form in any kind of art, a frame, or a containing field.

DRABBLE I think I agree with you. There is something very satisfying about getting to the end and deciding that it has completed itself, but I have to point out that all my novels, apart from one, have an open ending, so it is as though the characters can continue. I am very un-keen on killing people.

BIGSBY Iris Murdoch talked about her novel as 'a house for free characters.' Is that how you think of it?

DRABBLE That is very nice, yes. Jane Austen talked of a group of families, which is a similar idea, a group of interactive people. The novel is the house, the house is the novel, the village is the house while a lot of people interact who don't really exist. There is something rather wonderful about that. They don't actually exist except within this space that you have invented for them which to me becomes totally real. Even if the book is not very good, it is real to me.

BIGSBY Eimear, you were born in Liverpool but at the age of three you and your parents went back to Ireland, which is where they came from, though not to Northern Ireland, where they had lived, presumably because of what was happening there.

MCBRIDE That's right. Because of The Troubles.

BIGSBY How Catholic was your upbringing?

MCBRIDE Very Catholic, like everyone growing up in rural Ireland in the 1970s, 1980s and early 1990s. It was mass on Sundays and, in times of stress, mass every day. There was confession twice monthly from the time I was seven until I was about sixteen.

BIGSBY At the age of seven you had to come up with sins?

MCBRIDE I did confess a lot of sins, I have to say. I also experienced a lot of the charismatic movement that was such a big part of Irish life at that time and that I later included in my book because it was so odd. It took me a number of years of living in the UK to realise that it was odd to see people speaking in tongues and communing with the Holy Spirit in the back kitchen on a Tuesday evening.

BIGSBY How does that go together with Catholicism?
MCBRIDE I think it was part of a movement, a social movement, where people were trying to take control back from the church and bring the idea of spirituality into the home, make it more part of their lives and less about being preached at. But as with those movements generally it ended up building its own power structures and becoming destructive in fairly similar ways.

BIGSBY The first place you lived was very small with, I imagine, not a lot to do, but you then moved. Did you have access to books? Were you writing as a teenager?
MCBRIDE Yes, I was, since I was a small child. I was always keen to write. I grew up in Tubbercurry, County Sligo, which is kind of half-horse town. In terms of books you could only get Mills and Boon in the local library. That was it. But my parents were very keen for us to read and no matter how straitened our circumstances were would always show up with armfuls of books at every birthday and Christmas. Then, when I moved to Castlebar, which was a horse-and-a-half, it had a great library and if it didn't have anything in it would order it for you. That made a huge difference.

BIGSBY You were eight when your father died.
MCBRIDE That's right.

BIGSBY Did you feel a trauma then or was it displaced until later?
MCBRIDE No, I was very close to him and he died very quickly. He died from cancer. It was just eleven weeks from diagnosis to him dying and it was very traumatic for me, my brothers and my mother. It was something I have carried along all my life but in some way I felt as though maybe I was safe because that was the bad thing that would happen in my life and after that there would be no more bad things, that would be it, but I was wrong.

BIGSBY Yes, you were. At the age of seventeen you went to London. Were you going towards or were you escaping from?

MCBRIDE A bit of both. I was dying for the city. I wanted to get there, I wanted to be in a place where no one knew me and start again, so I went to drama school.

BIGSBY Why do you say that you wanted to go somewhere where no one knew you to start again?

MCBRIDE When you grow up in a very small town and everyone knows you it becomes quite constricting after a while. So to go somewhere where no one knows you is a relief. You begin to be the person you imagined you were going to be in your teens. At seventeen you will come to London and everything you were before will be gone and you will become the confident, exciting, talented, interesting human being you always knew you were inside.

BIGSBY And you had wanted to be an actress when you were younger.

MCBRIDE After my father died my mother sent me to drama classes to bring me out of myself a bit and I really loved it. So I decided that I wanted to act. I always thought I would keep writing along with it but I thought acting would be first. So I went to the Drama Centre, which was a very odd school. It had a very odd reputation at that time. It was a 'method' school.

BIGSBY Known as the trauma centre.
MCBRIDE Yes, that's right.

BIGSBY The trauma centre because of Stanislavski.
MCBRIDE Yes, because of Stanislavski. They enjoyed breaking you down and making you rebuild yourself which, at seventeen, is probably less complicated than it would have been now. It was very exciting, very intense, but where a lot of drama schools will use Arthur Miller, Eugene O'Neill, Tennessee Williams and then contemporary writers like Caryl Churchill, they were very obsessed with the Histories. We had to start back at the Greeks and read everything all the way up. But not

the contemporaries. So it was a strangely literary training for an actor but a useful one for a writer.

BIGSBY Has any of that stayed with you? Stanislavski, after all, is concerned with affective memory, reaching back into the past and you certainly had incidents in your past to go back to.
MCBRIDE Absolutely. Character is what I am interested in and my whole approach comes from that background. Most of *The Girl is a Half-Formed Thing* is about trying to make language represent the experience of an actor recreating a character. It's about trying to make that character, make language do it instead of the body.

BIGSBY It was about this time I think that the bad thing happened?
MCBRIDE Yes.

BIGSBY That is to say your brother had a brain tumour. At first you simply visited but then you went back and were with him while he was dying. That really seems to have sent you to pieces a bit.
MCBRIDE As I said, I think I had in some way made my pact with life. Losing my father was on the understanding that that was it. After that there wouldn't be anything else, so losing my brother destroyed my whole sense of security in the world, my whole sense of safety in life. Now I understood that anything can happen, at any time, to anyone. There is nothing between you and the edge. That was a big realisation for me. It was not only dealing with the grief of losing my brother, who was twenty-eight and didn't want to die – and it was hard to watch him die – but there was also the fact that my whole understanding of life was broken apart. It was at that point that I realised I didn't want to act and that in some way I had been using that to hide from life, or control life maybe.

BIGSBY Was it then you went off to Russia?
MCBRIDE About a year after that I went to Russia for four months.

BIGSBY And was that giving you a chance, in a different place, to reconstruct yourself?

MCBRIDE Yes, absolutely. I knew I needed to be away from everything that I knew, and from everything that I had expected myself to be, and start again. I had always wanted to go to Russia so I went there and I did some English teaching. I wandered around and went to the theatre a lot. I went to concerts and I did the ballet and immersed myself in culture, which really helped. It was at that point that I realised it was time to start taking writing seriously. So when I came back that is when I began working on it.

BIGSBY But you had another little minor bad thing happen, that is to say your notes for the novel were stolen?

MCBRIDE Yes. When I came back from Russia I had to do a lot of temping work to pay the bills. I would get up at five in the morning and write. Almost all of it was rubbish but I was teaching myself how to write and how to be disciplined, just to understand how to do it. Then, about two years later, I knew I was going to have six months when I wasn't going to temp and I would be able to write. If I was ever going to write the novel, that was going to be the time, but about two months before that someone broke into my house and stole my handbag in which were all my hand-written notes, because I didn't have a computer.

BIGSBY That should be a disaster.

MCBRIDE It should, and I spent a lot of time running round rooting through bins in Tottenham, shaking my fist at the sky. But in reality it was a good thing. Someone did me a good turn by accident.

BIGSBY Because when you started again it was different.

MCBRIDE It was different, and also I wrote with a huge sense of panic because I knew I only had a short time. I had to get the novel out but I wasn't looking back at things and thinking 'oh, that is great. I must try and get that in there somewhere' and then just forcing things in that didn't belong. It was really good to just start from the beginning and go all the way through to the end.

BIGSBY Margaret, you, too, began as an actress.
DRABBLE I did indeed.

BIGSBY Why did you pack it in?
DRABBLE Well, I wished I hadn't. But it just didn't work out that way because I kept having children and it was a very inconvenient career. Anyway, I was very restricted in my range. I could only do tragedy. I was a tragedy queen and I couldn't sing and I couldn't dance and I couldn't do comedy, so it was a rather small range of parts. It was perfect at university, where you can do all the classic tragic heroines, but not good for a career.

BIGSBY In your jigsaw book you talk about writing as an illness. What did you mean by that?
DRABBLE It has become a kind of illness. When I started off it was something I did instead of being an actress, and instead of looking after my children all the time, then it became a terrible habit and then an illness because I have tried to stop and I can't because it is what I do. Eimear is too young to know about this, but it is a really lonely career. You just spend a lot of time sitting by yourself and you don't really belong anywhere except in the weirdness of having readers who write to you and who enjoy what you are doing. Meanwhile, though, you are just sitting there being nobody and that's not good. So it is a kind of illness you try to escape but there is no escape once you are in the habit of being a writer.

BIGSBY When you were here eight years ago you said that the novel you had just published then was probably going to be the last one. One thing you talked about was the fact that you had had trouble with family, because you had written about family, but also trouble with lawyers. I said to you, 'Why don't you write a book to be published posthumously?' And you said that you had had the same thought and had written the first paragraph but didn't feel able to continue. The book you mentioned then had the same title as the book you have now published. What changed, and why at that time did you then feel inhibited about going on with the book?

DRABBLE I was inhibited because of the subject matter and because I knew I was going to have to get consent from one individual in particular. I do remember exactly saying that here and I went off and didn't really want to write it but, as I say, writing is an illness so I kept on having to go back to it. I didn't show it to anybody, or tell anybody about it, or do anything for about four years, which is so unlike my normal pattern. I was perfectly happy to leave this book unpublished forever if the person whose consent I had to get said no, so it was as though I was writing just to write the book and not for publication.

BIGSBY Could you explain why you had to get permission?

DRABBLE The subject of the book, *The Pure Gold Baby*, is a child who has learning difficulties. The child is based very closely on a person I have known of from before birth and who is celebrating a fiftieth birthday in January. So for fifty years I have known this young person who is not so young now though of course the mother is the person I really know. The mother is not at all like the mother in the novel – well, a bit like the mother in the novel – but the child is very like the child in the novel and the child will never know I have written this book because the child can't read, but the mother, of course would recognise everything I was putting in there and so I just didn't know how to tell her.

BIGSBY So you might have had to throw it away if she had said no?

DRABBLE Yes, and I was really lying awake night after night feeling really quite ill. I had reached a stage in the book where I knew it was OK and that if she liked it she liked it, and if she didn't like it there was nothing more I could do with it, but she did like it.

BIGSBY Towards the end of the novel the narrator says that she doesn't know whether she had the right to write the book. Is that you?

DRABBLE Totally me, totally me. I had no idea whether I had the right to write it, but when my friend said OK and seemed actually positively pleased about it, and it had certain consequences that were good in every practical sense from the point of view of the subject matter of the book, I knew I had done the right thing, maybe not artistically but in human terms I had done the right thing.

BIGSBY You quote a number of writers who had children with learning difficulties; some distant, like Pearl Buck, but also Arthur Miller and Doris Lessing. Miller is dead but was Lessing still alive when you wrote it?

DRABBLE Doris was still alive but she wouldn't have known by that stage what I was writing about.

BIGSBY That was because she was suffering from Alzheimer's, but you can see the ethical problem. We have ethics committees here at the university. If you are engaged in certain kinds of research you have to go before them and explain what the ethical implications of that are. There is, surely, a minefield here because Doris Lessing's son was still alive, as was Arthur Miller's.

DRABBLE It is a huge problem. In fact I didn't really worry about Doris. There is only one sentence about Doris in the entire book and I have known her for forty-to-fifty years, so I felt, OK, I can write one sentence about her which isn't even critical.

BIGSBY The book is partly written in the third person, partly in the first and partly in the first person plural.

DRABBLE I started writing this book in the third person, from the point of view of the mother, and then realised I simply couldn't be that intrusive. I couldn't do that. So I got a device whereby the narrator is telling the story of her best friend, who she knows very well but not totally right through because you never know anyone totally right through. The first person plural, the kind of 'we' voice, I wanted to give the sense of this neighbourhood of people back in the 1960s bringing up their babies and all the things they did, we did.

I just enjoyed looking back to that community of young mothers which I no longer belong to.

BIGSBY Towards the end of the novel the narrator says, 'I didn't observe all of this.' It is as though you are trying to account for the fact that there is this shift in the narrative voice.
DRABBLE Yes.

BIGSBY I am interested in a word that you use. It is there on the first page, but it recurs. The word is proleptic.
DRABBLE Whenever I look at the word proleptic I get really worried by it because it is a slightly worrying word. It means foreshadowing. I think creative writing classes actually teach foreshadowing, which certainly wasn't a word I ever knew. I did know the word proleptic because we did it as a figure of speech at school. I think it means seeing the future. It's like *déjà vu* a bit, but not quite, knowing you have seen it. In Jess's case the whole story unrolls from the fact that she has this child with difficulties but she has a foreshadowing of it before she has the baby. It is like re-reading your life. As I get older I find I do this more and more. What triggered that? Why has this happened? It is as though you may have known but you weren't sure that you had the proleptic knowledge. It is just a word I have always been interested in.

BIGSBY The title refers to the baby, who ages physically but not in other ways, but the book becomes less a story about the baby than about people who are getting older. You are watching an ageing process that is going on because you have a fixed point against which to judge it in some way.
DRABBLE Yes, she doesn't grow old. Pearl Buck, who had a brain damaged child, wrote a book called *The Child Who Never Grew,* and that is true of Anna. She never grows. She remains unknowing. I think the book is about her but it is also about how her life of not knowing is contrasted with the ageing and responsibility of those who have to take responsibility for her, not knowing where they are going to be in ten years' time themselves.

BIGSBY So doesn't that mean that it is also partly about change?

DRABBLE It is about change and ageing, yes. It is certainly about ageing but it is about changelessness.

BIGSBY Eimear, you were explaining that you had to go back to the beginning again with your novel but this time there was a particular influence at work, that of James Joyce.

MCBRIDE Yes. While I was doing my terrible temping jobs I decided that I would read *Ulysses* because I hadn't. I was starting this one particularly awful job in a records department of a bank in the city and so I stuck *Ulysses* in my bag and got on the train at Bruce Grove. I opened it and started to read and when I got off the train at Liverpool Street I just knew everything I had done before was going to have to go in the bin. That was day zero for me. From that point on it changed everything for me, in bad ways and good ways.

BIGSBY Then you finished the book, sent it off to agents and publishers and nine years later it was published and then almost by chance.

MCBRIDE That is right. I had sent it out for quite a few years and received glowing rejection letters which said, 'This is a great book. We love it. It is so well written but we don't know how to sell it,' and that was it. Or they said, 'Our marketing department doesn't think it fits into any niche so go away.' So after about five years I put it in the drawer and a few years after that my husband and I moved here to Norwich. One day he was in the Book Hive, a local book store, and was having a chat with Henry Layte behind the counter. Henry asked him what his wife did and my husband told him the story and Henry said, 'Some friends and I are thinking of setting up a little press. Do you think she would let us read it?' and I said, 'Fine.' I was seasoned in rejection at this point so thought, 'I have heard it all before. I will never hear from them again,' but they came back and they liked it. They said, 'We don't have any money and are just about to publish our first book but can we come back to you when we are a bit more ready?' I said, 'Fine.' A year later they came back and said, 'OK, we still don't have any money but we know a bit more about what we are doing so can we publish it?' And I said, 'Yes' and it came out in June, 2013.

BIGSBY   And you were offered a six hundred pound advance?

MCBRIDE   Six hundred pounds. They beat me down from a thousand.

BIGSBY   And by my calculation the awards you have received add up to something like £60,000. There is a rhythm to this book, and it takes you a page or two to get into it, but what alarmed publishers was that you invent words, you run words together, you will have ten words, each one with a full stop after it, so that the punctuation, the syntax, is radically changed, hence the letter saying this is wonderful and impressive but how can we sell it? What led you to that particular approach to language? It is called *A Girl is a Half-Formed Thing* and in the sense she is never formed because she is fractured by various things that happen and I suppose the language is equally fractured, reflecting something that is going on inside her. Is that how you thought of it?

MCBRIDE   It is, but also because of my theatre background I was very interested in trying to provide the reader with a different kind of reading experience. So rather than writing the book for myself I felt as though I wanted to see if it was possible to do something else for the reader as well. Again I stole wholeheartedly from Joyce and his conviction that there is part of life that is not adequately described by straightforward language and that sometimes if you want to talk about those aspects of life, about the life that happens in the corner of your eye or in the depths of your soul, sometimes straightforward language won't do. It won't convey the depths of it. In order to do that you have to try and make language work a bit harder, work in a slightly different way, so I thought, 'well, I will have a go.' I didn't know that it would work. Some people would despise it and some people love it but I thought it was worth trying.

BIGSBY You must have hesitated a bit because beneath this language there is arguably a familiar Irish novel, with its invoking of Catholicism and sexual molestation, with echoes of Edna O'Brien and Anne Enright.
MCBRIDE I hear that a lot and I understand what you mean, but at the same time when an English writer writes about the war no one goes 'oh, it's another English novel' though English writers write about that a lot because it is an important experience in the country. In the same way, Irish writers are drawn to those things because those stories are still unfinished for us.

BIGSBY I mentioned Edna O'Brien and Anne Enright who among other things deliberately set out to introduce a female perspective on sexuality, because there were plenty of male accounts.
MCBRIDE Yes. I really wanted to try and write about female sexuality in a different way. What was important to me was to write about the girl's sexual experience and her sexual exploration and to write about it in a non-judgemental way, to try and keep morality of all kinds out of it and just allow the reader to look at her and see what she does to herself because of how she has been reared to think about herself. But I didn't want to be standing there saying you must feel this now, you must think this now, you must feel critical or you must feel disgusted or you must feel whatever. Female sexuality is something that is so criticised from every angle, at all times, by everyone. I wanted to try and break out of that a little bit, just for a short time.

BIGSBY I have mentioned the traumas you have experienced and there are two major traumatic episodes in your novel. One is the molestation by her uncle when she is growing up. This happens first when she is very young, though it gets very complicated later on. The other source of trauma is the fact that her brother has a brain tumour. I am interested in your tactics and strategies for handling that. This is a book which is dedicated to your brother, who, as we said, had a brain tumour. I have read interviews by you in which you wanted to distance yourself from that connection and others in which you say it is part of your attempt to come to terms with that fact.

MCBRIDE I knew when I wrote it that people would assume it was very close to me and it is important for me to say that the boy in the book is not my brother. It is not based on my brother. He had a completely different life and an independent life, but I am interested in how such things are dealt with within the family and outside the family, how other family members feel about them, how well they can be spoken about or not. At the beginning of Margaret's novel we see the dawning realisation by the mother. She knows, already, what no one else does, that something is not quite as it should be and that interests me a lot.

BIGSBY Your novel is surely about love and about loss in many ways. The love is for the brother but the loss is quite fundamental to her. She begins almost to destroy herself, dismantle herself. What is the force of the ending to you?

MCBRIDE It's a sad ending. The whole point is that she spends her life trying to become, to overcome and to become, to be free to make decisions, even tragic decisions, even terrible decisions, but to be able to make them, to own the decisions she makes in her own life for herself. At the end of the novel she does do that and I wanted to write about that in a way that was uplifting. I get very annoyed when people say, 'oh why can't it end on a note of hope?' I just think hope is not a destination. Hope is the journey. She makes her own way and that is what she wanted to do.

BIGSBY The book has been dramatized.
MCBRIDE Yes, it has. They asked me if I would adapt it and I didn't have time but the director had done literary adaptations in the past and so I gave her the right to cut the novel. She wanted to present it as a one woman piece so I said she could cut it. She wasn't allowed to add to it. She wasn't allowed to use anything out of context, but she could cut it down to a performable length. I recorded the audio book in the summer and it is seven-and-a-half hours end to end and the play is an hour and twenty

minutes so that tells you how much cutting she had to do. She would send me drafts and occasionally we would disagree over something that she had cut. She was very patient with that process and then I went into rehearsal. I was nervous about meeting the actress because when I had heard other people read it they had sounded as though they didn't understand it, but as soon as she read it I knew that she understood. Though she read it quite differently to how I read it, she had made it her own and so I was very pleased with it. I was nervous to see it, the final product, but they did a really good job so I am very, very happy and I am hoping it will tour.

BIGSBY When you thought the book would never be published and you put it away you started on a second novel.–
MCBRIDE I did.

BIGSBY Where is the second novel?
MCBRIDE Sitting on the desk.

BIGSBY How much of it is there?
MCBRIDE Oh, loads. It should have been finished this year but suddenly this got published and so I went round doing other things. It will be finished next year instead.

BIGSBY In the same mode, with the same attitude to language, or is it different?
MCBRIDE I made this language to tell this story. That is what it was there for, so it can't be the same but I am interested in language. It is a different story, about different people, so it has to work in a different way again.

BIGSBY Margaret. Does the fact that you originally said you weren't going to write another novel but have now done so, mean there is going to be another novel?
DRABBLE If I ever finish it there will be, yes.

BIGSBY How far are you along with that?
DRABBLE I call it the point of no return because I have invested so much time in it that I think I will finish it.

I thought the last one was un-publishable. I think this is un-publishably depressing.

BIGSBY Eimear, you said something interesting about realism. You said that you felt that it had in some way exhausted its possibilities.

MCBRIDE When people talk about the death of the novel, I get so irritated but I do think that there is something to be said for saying that the novel has to learn to work in different ways. I don't mean all novels, but people who are interested in trying to do something else to make it work in a different way. I do think that there is not much point in all the realism and literalism in the same way that it was for the Victorians. You don't have to describe different landscapes and clothes or what the dinner looked like because if someone wants to know what it looked like they can look it up on the internet. The novel can look inside the person in a way that nothing else can do. Words can do that. They can uncover more, can make meaning deeper and richer than anything else because you have your frame and anything can happen inside it. It is up to you to plumb it.

STEPHEN FRY

Stephen Fry was born in London in 1957. He grew up in Norfolk and was educated at Cambridge University. He is a comedian, writer, actor, director, presenter, whose voice is familiar from audio books (J.K. Rowling's Harry Potter series, Douglas Adams's *The Hitchhiker's Guide to the Galaxy* among many others), video games and advertising. His many television appearances include *A Bit of Fry and Laurie*, *Jeeves and Wooster* and *Blackadder* as well as the long-running *QI*. In film he has appeared in *Oscar Wilde*, *Stormbreaker*, *The Hobbit: The Desolation of Smaug* and *The Hobbit: The Battle of the Five Armies*. He is the author of novels and three volumes of autobiography, the most recent of which being *More Fool Me* (2015).

This interview was conducted on October 8, 2015.

BIGSBY You made a programme for television called *Who Do You Think You Are?* in which you traced your heritage. On the one side, the Fry side, that led back to the workhouse and prison. On the other side it went to middle Europe and Auschwitz, because you are Jewish by virtue of your mother. I got the impression that the Jewish part didn't really mean anything much until you made that programme.

FRY That is more or less true. To me it reinforced the horrific, arbitrary, nature of the racism that underpinned the Holocaust. Having a Jewish mother would certainly have meant that I would have been disposed of and, as E.M. Forster wrote in the 1930s, around the time of the rise of Oswald Mosley and the Blackshirts, 'I think it very probable that even the Prince of Wales could not mention by name his eight great-grandparents, and he comes from the most famous family in the world. Yet each one of those great-grandparents is as responsible for his existence as the other, not just the one called Windsor.' We all have two parents, four grandparents, eight great-grandparents, sixteen great-greats etc. Very quickly it encompasses the whole of mankind and yet there is a huge determination on the part of people to determine themselves by their identities. On the one hand we all want to be global brothers and sisters, we all want to be connected, we all want to say we are one, we are one world, one people, but on the other hand we want to say, 'I am Welsh. That is who I am, not just what I am. I am Scottish and you are British and I don't want to be a Brit.' It is a very curious paradox that underpins so much, particularly over the last two hundred years of human history, and continues to do so.

Being Jewish is not a religious thing to be. Sigmund Freud, who was an atheist, would have been put in the gas chambers if he hadn't escaped to Britain, as would Einstein, as were many Jews who were, you might almost say, the fathers of modern atheism, the grandmothers of modern atheism, given people like Hannah Arendt. So, yes, it was actually the word that did it. I remember I couldn't help swearing, and I was crying. It was a ridiculous thing. There is an archive in which we got as far as my grandfather's family. Then there was a document which said, 'died Auschwitz Camp.' It was that word, Auschwitz, the darkest word in human history. I have never particularly wanted to be Jewish, with all those rules about eating shellfish or genital mutilation, or any particular decision by any given Israeli government. It has nothing to do with me. I will not take blame for it, will not respect it just because of my genes. On the other hand, if someone says, 'You are a Jew, aren't you?' I will say 'Yes.' I am not going to deny it but if that means I have to get put against a wall and shot, that is a peculiar thing. We define ourselves by our enemies rather than our friends. But while on the subject, there is no more extraordinary subject than the Holocaust.

I did a documentary on Wagner, a composer and dramatist, artist, about whom I have extraordinarily ambivalent feelings. Some people have extremely clear feelings of morbid dread and hatred. Others offer insane worship. I am somewhere in-between but I spoke to this remarkable woman called Anita Lasker-Wallfisch, who at the age of fifteen was taken to Auschwitz and survived only because she was a magnificent cellist. You can't quite believe you are talking to a chain-smoking survivor of Auschwitz, with a clear memory, about this extraordinary experience for a teenage girl to go through, and she told me a story. She said, 'I was on my bunk with a friend and was picking the nits from her scalp while she was doing the same for me, a daily ritual, when the camp doctor came in. I am sure you know his name. It was Josef Mengele,' the man who cut open identical twins, cut open pregnant women, put dyes into people's eyes without anaesthetic and did the most unspeakable and barbaric things you can imagine. He pointed to Anita and she said, 'My bowels turned to water. I thought, oh my God, he wants to see what's inside a musician's brain. Maybe he thinks we have a different brain shape from other people and he is going to cut me open while I am alive. Then he pointed to my instrument and I thought, oh, he just wants me to play. So I took my cello, followed him into his office and played.' I said to her, 'Do you remember what you played?' and she said, 'Of course. I played two cello suites by Bach and I played Traumerei by Schumann which is one of the most transcendentally beautiful pieces of music ever written.'

So here was this fifteen-year-old girl with a shaven head and a hideous uniform in the corner of the office of one of the most wicked people that ever drew breath, playing this music which was floating up. It is such an extraordinary idea. Then I said, 'What happened then?' She said, 'He clicked his fingers and waved me away.' I then said possibly one of the stupidest things anyone has ever said, and yet a very understandable thing, 'Did he thank you?' She said, 'Oh poor darling, you still don't understand. Do you thank your telephone when you finish a conversation? Do you thank your dishwasher when you take out the last plate? We were not human beings. We were untermenschen, subhuman. That is why they could do what they did.' I thought of course, it is so obvious, and yet it isn't obvious because to none of us does it seem even remotely possible that we could regard any type of fellow human as subhuman, who could do the kinds of things that were done. Yet in our own lifetimes these things have been done, and continue to be done. As we speak someone is being tortured.

When I said she was a brilliant cellist I really meant it. She survived the death marches, as the Germans emptied the camps for fear of the Russians approach and marched west, marches on which nearly all the prisoners died, of oedema, starvation or being shot and left to die, but she survived and fell into the hands of the British, came to Britain and was the co-founder of the English Chamber Orchestra, with which she remained for decades. So she is not just an amateur. She is a very serious musician. I then asked a really important question, artistically, 'So is there an aversion effect now? Are Bach's first two cello suites, and Traumerei, poison for you?' She said, 'No, no, they can cut off your ears, they can kill your mother in front of your eyes, they can pull the genitals from someone and stuff them in their mouth – I have seen things no one should ever see – but what they can never do, no one can do, is make something that is beautiful not beautiful.' The triumph of the music was an extraordinary idea. It was one of the most powerful moments of my life, talking to that woman.

BIGSBY Several times in your books you say that you wanted to belong. Does that mean you felt excluded?

FRY Utterly inexplicable. It is an imp that has lived inside me for as long as I can remember. I probably over-do the luxurious bliss of my childhood. I lived in a largish country house. There was a cook and there were gardeners and a tennis court, and even a badminton lawn. It was a gorgeous place and if I had been a normal child I would have relished and loved it, though my parents were not particularly interested in television. My father was an extraordinarily hard worker and a magnificent pianist though he would never play if he knew I was listening, or anyone was listening, so you had to creep around the house and just catch a bit of Beethoven or Brahms or something, but otherwise it was remote. The great Sydney Smith said in a letter, 'You ask me where I am, how it is like in this new parsonage, this new living that I have. I think I can best answer by saying that I am simply miles from the nearest lemon,' and believe me we were miles from the nearest lemon so I did feel short-changed to some extent.

BIGSBY So it was as though life was going on somewhere else?

FRY Life was going on somewhere else. It sounds such a stupid thing but I envied people who had wall to wall carpeting. I thought that was the most luxurious thing.

BIGSBY Central heating?

FRY Central heating and mains water. We had a pump system and had to pump the water from an underground aquifer and from rain water, and the fuses were always going, those great Victorian ceramic ones.

BIGSBY So is this why you now belong to so many clubs?

FRY Probably. I don't think it was a sense of being Jewish particularly. Sexuality of course had something to do with it, growing up in the 1960s and 1970s, knowing that inwardly one was somehow different. I remember having seen a production of *The Importance of Being Earnest*, Anthony Asquith's film version on television,

and being utterly captivated by the language of it –
'I hope, Cecily, I shall not offend you if I state quite
frankly and openly that you seem to me to be in every
way the visible personification of absolute perfection.'
I just hugged myself at the idea that language could
be used to such extraordinary effect. I came across a
book called *The Trials of Oscar Wilde* and realised, with
a growing sense of dread as I read this book, that this
man's disastrous ending, his imprisonment, two years of
hard labour, his exile, his miserable alcoholic absinthe-
dependent-utterly-impoverished-sham-filled ending,
seemed to be the natural ending for anybody cursed with
this sexuality, this nature. I would go to the library where
almost all the books I read, and there weren't many,
seemed to suggest the same. There is a marvellous book
called *Escape from the Shadows* by Robin Maugham, and
I read about the number of his friends who committed
suicide, the number of his friends who were arrested,
and I thought, 'God, I am going to end up in police courts
or in some sort of seedy world of shadows and denial, or
something ghastly. Then I saw the film *Victim*, with Dirk
Bogarde, when I was about fifteen.

BIGSBY So there was this sense of being an outsider.
FRY Doom, utter doom! There were no role models.

BIGSBY In reading what are now three volumes of
autobiography, I get the feeling that one of your motives
in writing them was that you wanted to close the gap
between your own sense of yourself and other people's
perceptions of you, indeed to understand yourself.
FRY I think that is very perceptive. I think that is right
and I sometimes accuse myself of a sort of literary self-
harm because I almost deliberately set out to expose
some part of myself and then drip lemon on it to make
it sting. It is almost as if, every ten years or so, I have to
force the world to think, 'Oh God, Stephen. I thought
I liked that chap but he turns out to be a complete tosser.
Why go on about being gay, being bipolar? Why go on
about having taken drugs? Well, I am afraid the only
thing you do when you write is go on about things.

BIGSBY You were sent off to boarding school at the age of seven. Your schooling was not an ultimate triumph because you got thrown out, having taken to stealing from your school mates, though you were clever enough not to steal a large amount. You took a small amount from each of them, which is how banking fraud operates, as it happens.
FRY Christ, I never thought of that.

BIGSBY And you were living dangerously, literally dangerously, because at one stage you would walk on the parapets?
FRY Yes, I was rather obsessed with walking on the roof of the school and chapel, looking down on people.

BIGSBY You then stole a credit card and what you did with it was rather strange. You went through various counties spending to sustain this artificial character that you created for yourself.
FRY Yes.

BIGSBY But that is odd.
FRY Pathetic is one word for it. I never presume to psychoanalyse myself. I just lay bare the facts as honestly as I can, as honestly as memory allows, though memory is a very unreliable narrator. The great Vladimir Nabokov wrote a book called *Speak, Memory*.

BIGSBY The interesting thing is that he remembered different things in different languages.
FRY Yes. It is astonishing and very interesting. Steven Pinker cited him as an example of how different parts of the brain store different information in different ways. Lies are a very good example. If a lie is told early enough, and repeated enough, it becomes a truth, that is to say you won't fail the lie detector. But a recent lie is hopeless because it doesn't reside in the experiential part of your brain. Generally speaking, I try and be as absolutely candid as possible, except where other people are concerned. This is not because I am a saint but I really do not think it is my business to write about the secrets of other people.

BIGSBY But that trail of things – walking on the parapet, having the credit card – reads like someone who wants to be caught because you could certainly never get away with the credit card.

FRY Yes, completely. My parents said that at the time. They said it is so obvious you wanted to get caught. At school they sent me to a psychiatrist, who was the classic Harley Street sort of psychiatrist with a huge Montblanc pen and a big sheet of paper. He would write down things. When I made a film about being bipolar, called *Manic Depression and Me*, we visited my school and my housemaster had kept what in those days would probably be called a mimeograph that my father had made of the psychiatrist's analysis of my mind. He had put the word 'bipolar,' question mark, and the word bipolar was not used at all. We are going back to 1972, 1973 something like that. I would have been identified as ADHD, Attention Deficit Hyperactivity Disorder, today. I qualified pretty much on all of those things. You have only got to skim through the reports to see he was writing out all the symptoms for ADHD. 'He seeks attention at all times but cannot focus, cannot possibly for a single moment settle down. He is a disruptive influence on everyone else, is always buzzing around, won't shut up.' It is just plain ADHD, which is very often what leads into bipolar disorder, or a strange satellite of it.

BIGSBY So you followed the family tradition and went to prison?

FRY Yes, it turns out that on my father's side there are many fine and noble civil servants and war heroes, who were skipped over by the squalid sensation-seeking BBC, but, yes, as it happens, on the distaff side of my father's family we go proudly back just a few generations to less reputable people. I don't think anyone ever said it better than John Lennon, 'In the end we are all fucking peasants as far as I can see.' That is one of the profoundest statements anyone ever made. It is true of grand cuisine and it is true of grand people. We were all peasants once and sometimes you go a few steps further back and there is a story of a workhouse. At school I was occasionally called 'unco' which was a school term for uncoordinated.

BIGSBY You don't throw very well.
FRY I don't throw well. How did you know that?

BIGSBY Because I saw you on QI trying to throw something.
FRY You're right. I don't throw well.

BIGSBY And you can't dance or sing.
FRY There are people who say everyone can sing. Not true. I actually have it on the highest authority in the land. I did a film once with John Schlesinger and when I was kindly invited by the Schlesinger family to the funeral I found myself standing and sitting next to Paul McCartney and I did what I always do at church services, or synagogue services, when the hymn comes or people are singing round the piano, I mimed, breathily so it sounds as though I am singing but no notes come out because I don't want to distress people. About two thirds of the way through the second song or hymn, Paul McCartney said, 'You are not singing. You should be singing.' I said, 'I can't sing,' and he said, 'Of course you can sing, everyone can sing.' So when the third song came up I thought, fair enough, so I sang and he just nudged me and said, 'You are right. You can't sing. Shut up.' So I have it from the horse's mouth.

BIGSBY But you did once sing on television.
FRY Yes, but I had to go and see a hypnotist in order to do it. It was a most extraordinary experience. The hypnotist, rather pleasingly, was Hungarian. I don't know why but the accent made it more enjoyable. He said, 'What is exactly the problem?' and I explained that I needed to sing live on television because there was a programme called *Saturday Live* and Hugh and I had written a sketch which involved me singing. I realised by Thursday that we had painted ourselves into a corner. I said to Hugh, 'I have got to sing,' and he said, 'Yes, but it's not really a song. You know you can do it.' I said, 'It is not just that I don't hit the notes, I can't even come in on time. I lose the ability to count. Everything goes in a blur.

It would be like someone who has stage fright having to stand up on a stage in front of 8,000 people. I wouldn't find that a problem at all but if I had to sing even one line I would have very, very, projectile diarrhoea.' I don't know why I needed to say that, but I went to see this chap and he said, 'I am going to ask you to put your hand on your thigh. You may do this if you wish. It may help. Feel your hand sink into the flesh of your thigh. Now I am lowering you down a well, right down where it is very, very, dark but the rope that is keeping you from falling is my voice. My voice is keeping you from falling down into the dark. You may close your eyes. You feel very relaxed now. Everything is very calm. Now I will invite you to suggest to me reasons why you can't sing, because you have a good ear and you can hear tunes and recognise them. Why can't you sing?'

I am no great one for hypnotherapy necessarily but what it did was it uncovered a memory in me of being a seven-year-old at that prep school where we had to sing a hymn that the music master thought the school didn't know. He would play it on the piano and teach it to the school and this hymn was quite unusual in its harmonies. I did my best at it and a prefect, whose name I remembered instantly while I was down the well, Graham Kirk, pointed at me and said, 'Listen everybody. Fry is singing flat,' and the master said, 'All right, everybody except Fry shut up.' He played it and I sung it on my own. I was trembling like an aspen and the whole school burst out laughing. I had completely forgotten this incident but he reminded me of it, so he said, 'What is the cue that your partner is saying?' Unfortunately, the answer was, 'Hit it, bitch.' Then I was supposed to sing. So, 'Say this again, please?' he said. 'Hit it, bitch.' And he said, 'So when you are hearing the words, "Hit it, bitch," then you are released from the power that Graham Kirk had on you and you can sing. Now I will pull up the rope, and I count down.' So the following Saturday, and you can see it on YouTube somewhere, I do sing and I seem to get away with it, but unfortunately I had to ring up Hugh Laurie and say, 'Could you in twenty minutes time call my mobile and say, "Hit it, bitch," so that I can sing?'

BIGSBY Let me take you back. You are one of the only people to emerge from prison and have an epiphany. You turned yourself around and went to Cambridge where you met Hugh Laurie, which was probably the most important thing that happened to you at Cambridge.

FRY Obviously the praise for that must go to my parents. I was constantly causing crises, constantly causing family conferences and anger and the slamming of doors, all the miseries of adolescence I went through. Somehow they believed in me. My mum had never doubted for a second that I would go to Cambridge, and not only that but that I would get a scholarship to Cambridge, not even when I was lying on the prison floor with the shadows of the bars of the prison on me. She still somehow knew, although to be fair to myself they had rightly given up on financially supporting me. So when I came back from prison on probation I said, I will go to Norwich City College. It was their second day of registration for a one year course in A levels and I was the last in the queue. I said, 'I want to do A levels in History of Art, French and English.' The man who was interviewing me said, 'English has gone. English went yesterday.' And I said, 'No, no. I really have to do English because I am going to go to Cambridge and I have to get a scholarship. I will work and I will pay for it myself and I will pay the invigilator for me to do the exam.' He looked at me and after what seemed an hour while he just looked at me he went, 'I don't know why but, yes, all right.' He ticked my name off so I went to City College, to whom I shall forever be grateful. I owe them everything. So I did the A levels and I got the scholarship to Cambridge and then I thought, was it Winston Churchill who said, 'Young men sow wild oats and old men grow sage' and, well, it is time for me to grow tweed, if not sage, and I will stay here in these safe ivy-clustered walls and won't dare venture outside again and tempt this weird mind of mine.

BIGSBY And you did very well, academically. In the first part of your degree you got a First, the best First in the university.

FRY In English Literature, yes.

BIGSBY But you threw yourself into other things. You seem to have signed up for everything in terms of drama. You had played the witch back at school in *Macbeth* but now you met Hugh Laurie, which was going to be a pathway into the Footlights. In the end you didn't get the First Class degree but you were in Footlights and a whole new realm had opened up to you. You had been intending perhaps to become an academic, maybe do a PhD, but in fact you were in a production that went to the Edinburgh Fringe, not only with Hugh Laurie but with others whose names would become familiar.

FRY Emma Thompson and Tony Slattery. Yes, it was extraordinary. There is one photograph I have from a late night revue we did in the second term of our last year at Cambridge. It was a sketch that Hugh and I had written about an American courtroom and it featured Hugh, Emma and Tilda Swinton. We counted five Golden Globes and three Oscars, plus God knows how many BAFTAs in that picture. At the time of course you felt like a timid mouse who is never going to make it because in the Footlights club room there are photographs of Peter Cook, John Cleese, Graeme Garden, Clive James, Douglas Adams and Griff Rhys Jones who were already famous and are all staring down at you, and you just thought the door has closed, especially as in our last year we saw Alexei Sayle on television and it was as though he was the equivalent of the Sex Pistols and you were Cliff Richard and Hank Marvin.

BIGSBY But the Edinburgh show then went to London, and Australia, and television got interested in you. Then you were asked to write the book for *Me and My Girl*, which was hugely successful here and in New York, and you were doing commercials and voiceovers for outrageous sums of money. Suddenly money came tumbling down on you.

FRY Absolutely, yes.

BIGSBY And you weren't hesitant in spending it.

FRY No, I wasn't. In my second book, *The Fry Chronicles*, everything begins with a C because it outlines my addictions and ends with the final one, candy sugar.

I lived for it. I stole money for it. I would go and raid the tuck shop, raid the kitchen, in order to steal the huge lumps of caterer's jelly. It was almost as if it was a sexual act, having sugar, and then cigarettes is another C, and of course credit cards. And the first thing I did when I got money was get credit cards of every conceivable kind.

BIGSBY Suddenly you were belonging.
FRY Because it is a way of belonging, and clubs was another C. I joined every club imaginable.

BIGSBY And cars and computers?
FRY And cars and computers, classic cars, computers, and a country house. So it was a very peculiar time for someone who always thought he was an outsider. It is a strange thing to say because so many people think of me as a quintessentially English person, whatever that means. Of course the two most quintessentially English people, Winston Churchill and Agatha Christie, another two Cs, were both half-American, so perhaps that is what makes someone quintessentially English – someone who isn't actually English, so they try that little bit harder to be English.

Then there is the whole sexuality thing which makes one feel alienated. A part of me yearned to be a part of the tribe and another yearned to be apart from it. One desperately wants to be like Ibsen's *Master Builder*, he who stands strongest is he who stands most alone, to be apart from everyone else, to be an utter individual who is not part of the tribe. Yet whilst standing alone on the touchline looking at the grubby rugby scrums, the flannelled fools at the wicket and the muddied oafs at the goals, as Kipling put it, feeling superior because you have got a copy of Mallarmé's poems in your pocket, another part of you wishes you could be with them and join in their songs. Actually, I thought I felt spring and nature and love in a way that nobody else had, except artists like John Keats. I thought of all those people who were at school with me. Have they noticed a dewdrop falling from a lime tree in spring? Have they seen a back-lit thrush as it is hopping from twig to twig not wanting to burst into tears? Am I the only one who is like that? No,

I am not. I can read Wordsworth and does that make me soppy and if so is that soppiness something to do with my sexuality because I couldn't really get into the idea of playing rugby.

BIGSBY The thing that seems to connect your acting, writing, conversation, presenting is a revelling in language, but I wonder if you don't also use language to deflect, to hide behind, to misdirect.

FRY Yes, yes. One of my early literary encounters was Anthony Burgess, who always sent one scurrying to a dictionary. I enjoyed that experience and I do like sharing words, but I know sometimes it can look like showing off. It is a fault I share with Will Self, who also likes the ten dollar cigar word as opposed to the two nickel cigar word, as the Americans put it. Sometimes I use a word and explain what it means and they go, 'Well, why couldn't you have said that?' I say, 'I am sorry. I just have this appalling habit of using one word where twenty would do.'

BIGSBY You spoke earlier of your addiction to things beginning with the letter C. One such has been cocaine, which you started taking in 1986 and continued taking for fifteen years. In your new book you include diary entries, one for 1993.

FRY It starts when I am off it because I am writing a book and that is very important to me.

BIGSBY But in that 1993 diary entry you explain that you went to the Groucho club, had a vodka, took a line or two of coke, played poker till four in the morning, got up at ten, Hugh came over, wrote some scripts, did a voiceover and so on. When I read that entry it seemed to me that the behaviour you describe could be a function of your bipolar condition, staying up endless hours, engaging in frenetic or dangerous activity as you had at school when you were walking the edge at the top of the school.

FRY It is very extraordinary you say that. I was talking to my psychiatrist a couple of weeks ago. He is a wonderful, steady, very firm Irish fellow who is very concerned that I don't drink too much and that I don't take on too much, that I don't burn out, that I continue to live a happy successful prosperous and fulfilled life for as long as possible without burning candles at both ends, without alcohol, certainly without drugs but also without taking on too much work, just enjoying life. And he said, 'I am afraid it has been apparent to me now for a year, though I haven't really said it to you because I wanted to find the right time when I felt you were stable enough, but your diagnosis has always been Cyclothymia, which is what they call in America, 'bipolar light'. But, he said, I am afraid that is not the correct diagnosis. You are bipolar one. He said don't be upset by it, and above all please don't just go home and check the difference in Wikipedia or anything stupid like that. I can tell you the difference. There is no real difference. You are still the same person. It is a bit like a climatologist saying we are living in a time of climate change and the climate is going to get a bit worse, so you have to be more alert. You have to have a bigger store of umbrellas and you have to make sure that the roof tiles are more firmly hammered in, you have to up the insurance. Just be aware. It is a chronic condition. That doesn't, of course, mean severe. It means you have it all the time. It is a thing you manage, cope with, but never stop having. Bipolar one is a chronic condition and you just have to learn how to cope with it.

I don't say this in the book, because I think it would have been cheating since it wasn't what I thought at the time, but looking back I think, of course, I was going through very strange mood swings. I had every reason to be absurdly happy because I was making a lot of money, I had a country house, I could do whatever I liked. I could never dream of turning right when I got into an aeroplane. The beautiful things of the world were opening up in front of me like blossoms, and yet I was utterly empty inside, utterly unfilled. Part of it was love, but part of it was that my moods would change. And if you don't know that what you have got is actually a recognisable disorder, you reach out for the first and most obvious things that can change your mood. If you can afford it those things will be alcohol, which is most affordable, which will numb you if everything is just getting on top of you, or cocaine, which will just bring you up and make you party and make you go to bed at four in the morning. I have the constitution of an ox. I would not recommend it. I should probably be dead. I don't say in the book, 'this was the reason I took the drugs' because I didn't know then and I think it would look rather paltry, as if I was trying to excuse myself. I have been a bit upset by some of the responses. Some people have said, 'Oh, another showbiz blah. I took drugs. Poor me.' I deliberately tried not to say 'poor me'. On the other hand, nor did I want the other posture, which is just as revolting, braggadocio: 'I was so cool. I just took drugs everywhere.'

BIGSBY Though the everywhere, which you do list, included Buckingham Palace, which is why you are not getting a knighthood?

FRY Exactly, which is why I won't be getting a knighthood. The reason for that list of places was just to show that it was impossible for me to go out, even to somewhere like Buckingham Palace, without my little friends in my wallet. It absolutely looks weird to me now, and I don't know how much my close friends noticed it. The occasional intervention was attempted but I was far too skilful at deflecting it and saying it wasn't a problem.

BIGSBY You mentioned that you made a film about bipolar disorder, in fact two films, in which you interviewed not just actors and people in the arts but those in other areas of life. You asked all of them whether, if there had been a button they could press that would free them of that disorder, they would press it. As I recall, only one person said they would do so.

FRY You are absolutely right.

BIGSBY And you wouldn't have pressed the button. Why not? Is it because that is who you are? It is what gives you the energy and imagination and drive that you have?

FRY It comes from the classic professor of philosophy who when opening his lecture on ethics will usually say, 'I have a button here. Believe me, it works. If you press this button, and any of you can come forward and press it, there will be no starvation, there will be no child abuse, no child malnutrition, no disease from cancer, there will be no murder, there will be no war, there will be no crime, absolutely none of that will happen. There will be peace and there will be no transgression and there will be no cruelty and there will be no pain. But, there will be no Mozart, there will be no art, there will be no love, there will be no humour, there will be no friendship, there will be no painting, there will be no literature. Who wants to press the button?' Nobody. We live in a bipolar world in that sense. We take it somehow as a bargain with this bizarre cosmos into which we have contingently been flung.

BIGSBY But there is a high risk because we used to call it manic depression and the other side of it is depression. You may be subject to it but you can't prepare for it.
FRY You cannot.

BIGSBY And when you are in there and the door closes behind you, there doesn't seem to be a door to open.
FRY No. There is no future. There is nothing. It is a nothingness. It is quite extraordinary in every degree. When you are hypomanic you are filled with grandiosity, with optimism. The future is a palpable real thing that you can help create, make, shape, and that you can do things in. You can make art in it, you can change the world through charitable enterprise, through ideas, through setting up companies or setting up foundations. You know you can help people, help yourself. You say yes to so many projects, to so many ideas, to life. Everything is bright and for some people it becomes very extreme. It leads to the extremes of exhibitionism, to over-shopping. You just buy stuff, and everything is just great. It is fantastic. When you are depressed it is literally the opposite. There is no future. The future is just a black wall that almost touches you. The last words of Kenneth Williams' diary are, 'Oh, what's the point?' That is exactly what anyone who has ever suffered depression will know. There is no point to anything, which, of

course, we know to be true as far as we can tell, unless you have the consolation of a particular faith. There is no point, but there being no point doesn't usually worry us. Most sane, stable, people are not worried by the fact that there is no point to our existence. Great artists like Samuel Beckett say we live our lives being punished for having committed the crime of being born, which is how the Catholic Church would have it. Even without the Catholic Church, a lot of us feel that somehow we have done something wrong but at least we endure.

I used to be asked what I thought were the greatest qualities a person could have and I always used to say kindness, which I hold by. Cheerfulness is another, curiosity. Somebody once said to me that curiosity killed the cat and I said, yes, but it launched homo sapiens. We would not exist without curiosity. It may well have killed a few cats but it got us here, for good or ill. But as I have aged I have found something more extraordinary. Since I have had the good fortune to travel widely I have encountered people who are obscenely poor, and what I have witnessed is endurance. Why do women walk seven miles in the morning to the source of water with a pot on their head and then walk seven miles back, then pound maize into a porridge before feeding their children, digging in the garden while putting up with abuse from a drunken husband before doing the same the next day and the next day. They endure, and most human beings do endure. People in my position may be seen to be making a fuss about how life is terrible and unfair, and, of course, it is all of those things but we all try and help, where we can, in Syria or with the Ebola crisis, or wherever a handout is needed or a friend needs assistance, but we can be no help to anybody else unless we can endure.

BIGSBY But in your case depression led you to the edge, to the possibility of ending your life?

FRY Yes, two years ago it did. Two years ago was very, very, messy and unpleasant. It was in Uganda as it happens, a country I dearly love and which is in something of a terrible state thanks to the evangelical right of America. One night I was absolutely at my blackest. I had been filming during the day and I had to do what is known as a piece to camera after an interview with a really horrific man. I don't know whether that was the trigger for it, because you don't really have a logical trigger for depression. But for whatever reason I could feel that the crew could see the blood had gone out of my face when I was giving this piece to camera, that I had looked different. My eyes looked different, which is a big giveaway with me, as it is with a lot of bipolar people. I have noticed that the left and the right eye look remarkably different when one is going through a transitional phase, and the cameraman noticed it. He said, 'Are you all right?' I said 'Can we have a talk about this later? I will just do this piece to camera.' So, I did it and the director said, 'There is clearly something wrong with you.' They were worried about malaria, dengue fever, bilharzia, all the things you might have because you are in Africa. It never occurred to them that it was something inside. I said, 'I am just not really feeling with it. I won't join you guys for dinner.'

They went off to do some filming of the sunset and what are known as GVs, general views, and I went to my room . Then it slowly blackened, blackened, blackened and blackened, blackened, blackened, blackened. It just came down on me in a way it hadn't for many years and I absolutely could see no way out except to say goodbye. I lined up as many pills as I could grab, dozens of them, and a bottle of vodka. I downed it. I don't think I even left a note. This is awful for my family, and I am sorry they have to hear it, but it is better to talk about things than not to because, although I am past that age, suicide is the largest cause of death for men under forty-five in Britain, bigger than heart-attacks, bigger than road traffic accidents. It's a really important issue.

So I found myself just nowhere. I went straight into blackness and when I was discovered I was on the floor with broken ribs. I must have thrashed around in some bizarre state of horrific mental turbulence. I had three violently broken ribs virtually poking out of my skin and was alive, much to my distress. I was taken home and put into a hospital where I met this psychiatrist, who is now my psychiatrist, and for three days I was still absolutely enraged that I was still alive. I was just enraged that it could have gone wrong because it would have been so simple and so easy.

BIGSBY And yet you still wouldn't press the button, would you?

FRY Well, there is a good outcome to this. The reason we need to talk about Stephen is that he started me on a course of medication for the first time. You talked about language, and how I love it, and I have always essentially believed that the point of my being on this planet is my ability to put one word after another in the service of a sentence that may or may not amuse, tickle, delight, beguile, seduce, charm, persuade or do anything else. If I couldn't do that anymore because some pill has calmed me down but slightly zombified me, then it would be mortal agony to me. It would be taking away my personality. It would be essentially like the ending of *One Flew Over the Cuckoo's Nest*, a kind of lobotomy. I might be peaceful and at ease. I might be smiling, but I wouldn't be myself and I have never been able to bear the prospect of that. Eventually, when I finally realised that I was glad to be alive, I said this to the doctor and he said, 'Well, now we can try things out because I don't want you to be anything other than yourself, either.' So we tweaked this cocktail of medications which I have, which I am now on and have been on for two years. I have the odd manic episode but the depressive episodes have more or less gone away. So that is my mission. I am president of a charity called Mind. People may accuse me of going on and on about things because drugs are a very important part of mental health, street drugs. So many people with mood disorders turn first to speed, ecstasy, coke, drugs, alcohol, because it does something that nothing else can do. It takes them out of a bad place, or seems to. In fact, of course, it gets worse.

DAVID HARE

David Hare was born in St. Leonards-on-Sea in 1947 and was educated at Lancing College and Jesus College, Cambridge. He was a joint founder of the Portable Theatre Company, his first play, *Slag*, being produced in 1970. Among his many plays are *Plenty*, *The Secret Rapture*, *Racing Demon*, *Murmuring Judges*, *The Absence of War*, *Skylight*, *The Permanent Way*, *Stuff Happens*, *The Vertical Hour* and *South Downs*. He is also the author of numerous television and film scripts including *Licking Hitler*, *Wetherby*, *The Hours*, *The Reader*, *Page Eight*, *Turks and Caicos* and *Salting the Battlefield*. In 2015, he published *The Blue Touch Paper: A Memoir*. He was knighted for services to theatre in 1998.

This interview was recorded on
October 7, 2015.

BIGSBY You went to public school and have written about feeling out of place, not fitting. Is that because of your upbringing? You were encountering people who had completely different backgrounds?

HARE Yes. I wrote a play about my education at Lancing College which prompted a huge correspondence from people who had a common experience, who had the same background as mine, which was a lower middle class background. I was forced up through the system by being a scholarship boy. I only went to a private school because I won scholarships. I won scholarships wherever I went and that did give me a very acute sense of the class system. When I wrote this play about my education, *South Downs*, I tried to explain to the actors in it, teenage actors, what Britain was like in the 1950s and 1960s and when I explained it they just said, 'I don't believe it. This is impossible. How can that be?' It was as distant to them as Proust. It really was, and I realised that I thought I had lived through very uninteresting times, a feeling which my parents instilled in me by suggesting that I had had the misfortune to miss the main event which was the Second World War. I had been born after the Second World War and therefore I had missed the most significant and interesting years in Britain in the twentieth century. Now we were living in a period of calm and peace, so it did not occur to me, until I wrote that play, that the country had changed a great deal and that I had changed a great deal.

So I wanted to write a memoir which was about the theatre and the cinema that I first worked in, which was personal, about the effect of being a writer and how catastrophic it was really for my private life and, thirdly, that was also about the history of this particular time. When I tried to put those three strands together what I found oddest was that I had the field to myself. People born after the war are commonly thought to be narcissistic, self-obsessed and indulged, and yet if so why are there no literary memoirs of the period at all? Salman Rushdie has written a memoir but it was about being the victim of a fatwa, which I am hoping to avoid. The great literary memoirs of my time are by people older than me. Edna O'Brien's *Country Girl* is a very beautiful memoir as is Michael Frayn's book about his father, but they are probably both eighty now. It is very curious that the writing about the 1950s and 1960s is mostly by rock stars or sports stars. There is very little literary description about this extraordinary mid-century feeling in Britain and I wanted to get it all down in *The Blue Touch Paper*.

BIGSBY You mentioned *South Downs*. Why did it take so long to write that play?

HARE Because as a writer I have gone about everything arse over tip and I would recommend it to anyone who wants to be a writer. Most writers start by writing about their own experience. I started by writing about the Chinese revolution and the nationalisation of the railways, aid to the Third World, the financial crisis and the diplomatic process leading up to Iraq. I wrote about the world. I wasn't interested in writing about myself. I have only come to the notion of writing about myself in my sixties, and I have left it until then.

BIGSBY I wonder if the passage of time isn't what makes you able to write this as a comedy because it is extremely funny at times. If you had written it much earlier I wonder if you would have seen it in that way because there is some pain under the surface.

HARE Well it is what's called a bildungsroman, about how you become a writer or how you become an artist and so I can now see that there is a hilarious element to what I had to do in order to become a writer. You have to put your mind back to the 1970s, an incredibly contentious time. The folk memory of it is three day weeks, strikes, the lights going out, everybody arguing bitterly about everything. The dominant narrative that has been created is that Britain was in absolute chaos in the 1970s and that then Margaret Thatcher came along, organised everything, and everything has been fine since then. Well, as they say, history belongs to the victors because it is almost the exact opposite of my experience.

The 1970s were disputatious not just politically but culturally, so if you were identified with a particular theatre, or identified with a particular magazine or a particular newspaper, you were licenced to hate and you fought. As soon as my generation of playwrights appeared – Howard Brenton, Trevor Griffiths, Snoo Wilson, who came from the University of East Anglia – there was none of the ecumenical attitude there is now to new writing where they say, 'Let's encourage young writers.' The critics tried to kill us at birth, to throttle us at birth, because they so disagreed with what we wanted to do. Their opposition was principled. It was extremely painful to live through the 1970s because the internecine arguments were very, very bitter. On the other hand, to me that bitterness was a sign of vitality and although I got very hurt by it, and became a playwright at immense expense to my character as I feel, yes, it is comic now to look back at it. Nevertheless, I am essentially mounting a defence of the 1970s as a period in which we were all arguing about things which really do matter.

BIGSBY What was the price you paid to your character?

HARE I think playwrights by nature are uncomfortable people. As I became a playwright it became clear to me that an evening with John Osborne or Harold Pinter or Dennis Potter was not an entirely relaxed affair. These were all liable to explode at any point. So, if, like me, you had begun as a literary manager and your job was to meet playwrights, you did notice that they were incredibly touchy difficult people.

BIGSBY Especially Harold Pinter.

HARE Especially Harold, but your friend Arthur Miller could spread a little gloom around him at the dinner table, so it occurred to me that it was probably down to the nature of the activity, namely that it rips the skin off you. I keep people away from *The Great British Bake Off*. I get them into a room and then try to persuade them that their two-and-a-half hours, or two hours, is going to be well spent rather than being at home with the person they love and the television they want to see, something which requires less effort. Then I sit among them and I hear their reactions and a lot of those reactions are extremely hostile. That was especially true

in the 1970s. The reaction was very, very hostile. My
favourite reaction to a play of mine was when I heard
a couple leave the theatre and the woman put her arm
round the man and said, 'I am sorry darling. That was my
idea.' When you have heard those things so many times
they do have an impact on your soul. Unlike novelists,
we actually sit among the audience and we hear what
they think of us so we can't delude ourselves in the way in
which some novelists believe that everybody adores their
books because they don't actually sit while people read
their books, whereas I sit and hear what people actually
think. But I had always imagined that most playwrights
wrote out of anger. There is a wonderful line of Philip
Roth's. He says, 'A writer needs to be made angry in
order to see.' I think it is true to a degree but where I had
assumed anger was the only thing that motivated me,
actually the experience of writing the book has made me
realise that bewilderment is just as powerful as anger.
That is what I felt in Bexhill, where I was raised. I could
see it was a very repressed town in which the lid was
being kept on everybody, in which everybody had to
conform. I had a very powerful feeling that everybody
else understood the rules but I didn't. At Lancing, again,
I felt everybody understood the rules.

It is not that I am trying to break the rules, that
I am an anarchist, a rebel, it's that I simply don't
understand what the rules are and why the rules are
the way they are. So when I write a play I am often
proposing to the audience, 'Look, this is how I see the
world. Does anyone else recognise this?' And when
I write a successful play – *Skylight* is the obvious example
– a whole crowd of people rise and go, 'Fantastic, he
has said exactly what I have been feeling but nobody has
been saying it.' But when I write an unsuccessful play,
and it happened to me with a play called *My Zinc Bed*
where I thought I was writing about alcoholism and
about something which everybody could recognise,
I could just see this reaction in the audience as if to say
'I don't know that this seems very important to me.'
There was no hostility but there was this sense that
'he doesn't seem to be talking about anything that
interests me much'. So its that bewilderment which

causes me to ask, 'Does anyone here recognise what I am talking about?'

BIGSBY John Major once suggested that we should condemn a little more and understand a little less. It seems to me that you are the reverse of that, that the search for understanding is part of what lies behind your plays, plays about the different institutions in this country, plays about the Iraq war, privatisation, and so on. Understanding has primacy.

HARE Yes, though because I spend the whole day understanding I can be a son of a bitch in the evening and I think that is true of playwrights. They spend their whole day trying to see other people's point of view, what other people are going through. I am naturally very curious and I do very much enjoy the research projects I have been involved in where I go out and spend time, say, with the police or the clergy. I have a fantastic time when I am out there but it does mean that if you do that all day and try and look at the world from other people's perspectives, it can make you very, very selfish in your private life.

BIGSBY Let me take you back a bit. You went to Cambridge, largely because you wanted to study with Raymond Williams, who turned out to be another absent father because you hardly saw him at all. What did you go there to become? Did you have any notion of what was going to lie on the other side?

HARE I was being trained to be in the elite corps of literary critics. That is what reading English at Cambridge was about. You were being trained to find eloquent ways of expressing your disappointment with literature, and I trained with some of the most disappointed people in England. F.R. Leavis made a list. He was the God of the Cambridge faculty. He made a list of who was approved: Shakespeare, Milton, on and off, Donne, George Eliot, T. S. Eliot – end of list. Dickens was said by Leavis to lack the formal control of a great novelist and Thomas Hardy was just out to lunch. So now I just can't read criticism, this sense that literature hasn't done for you what you hoped it was going to do.

That is what I was trained to be, a critic, and that is why I revolted so against Cambridge.

BIGSBY But you were beginning to direct while you at Cambridge and continued when you left and formed Portable Theatre, which was, as its title suggests, portable, that is to say it moved around the country. It was a very in-your-face theatre, not particularly interested in aesthetics. Did you succeed in discovering the new audience you were looking for?

HARE We did to begin with, in the late 1960s. We were lucky enough to be one of the first groups to have this idea of taking theatre to prison camps, village halls, canteens, people's private homes, anywhere, and we bunged the play on to crash the problem of aesthetics. People do not go to *Hamlet* in order to decide whether to kill themselves or not. They go to compare Michael Sheen's Hamlet with Benedict Cumberbatch's Hamlet, with David Warner's Hamlet or Rory Kinnear's saying, 'Oh, I liked it better last week and he did that speech much better. The lighting was much better, the costume much better, I have never seen that play so well done. I have never seen that play so badly done.' We tried to crash that by just bunging plays on. We didn't even pretend they were well-lit or well-designed or anything like that. We were urgently trying to get the subject matter across. That was the aim of that kind of theatre and, yes, at first we did go to new venues but we noticed that one year we would go to a venue and suddenly the next year when we went they had built an Arts Centre and when they built an Arts Centre there would be people there saying, 'we think your costumes are better than last week's show but on the other hand your lighting isn't quite as good as the lighting we had last week' and you go, 'Oh my God, I have got to take aesthetics on. I can't pretend aesthetics doesn't exist,' whereas we did actually try to pretend that.

BIGSBY I once asked Arthur Miller why he wrote *The Crucible* so fast and he said, 'Because I wanted to get the news out.' You also wanted to get the news out.

HARE The charge against topical theatre is that it

dates. The charge is always, 'You are just a journalist running along behind the truck taking notes.' But if you write about something that has underneath it a classical conflict then writing that kind of theatre, which may be about something extremely contemporary, is curiously lasting. When people first saw the play I wrote about the diplomatic process leading up to the Iraq invasion, people saw it as journalism. But now when it is performed it is infinitely sadder because you can see the play as a classical tragedy. *The Absence of War*, which went touring earlier this year, was tied to Neil Kinnock and the failure of the Labour party, but twenty years on people can barely remember Kinnock and what happened to him, so now they see the play in the light of Jeremy Corbyn and what is going on now. It seems to shine completely differently. It is odd how topical plays, if they are underpinned with any real classical tension, will actually grow with time and not diminish.

People keep asking me if I am going to write about Jeremy Corbyn and I keep saying I have written about Jeremy Corbyn. It was called *The Absence of War* and I wrote it twenty years ago. As Leader of the Opposition Kinnock says, 'I would love to speak about nuclear weapons but I can't. Why? Because it is fifty thousand people's livelihoods. It's real lives, and I can't talk about it.' So everything that is happening now is all in the play.

BIGSBY You mentioned Snoo Wilson, who was a UEA student at one time. He played a role in you becoming a playwright rather than a director.

HARE Ted Hughes says, 'To emerge as a creative writer from Cambridge you have to avoid the gun towers and crawl out under the wire.' It never occurred to me to be creative because obviously I would have been shot down before I had tried to be creative with so many specially trained critics there, so it was only when Snoo failed to deliver a play that I had to write one. He failed to deliver it for the usual pathetic petty bourgeois reason that he had to do his finals. Some rebel.

BIGSBY One of the plays you wrote, called *Slag*, was an all-woman play and you write strong parts for women.

HARE I don't think I write strong parts for women – I just write parts for women.

BIGSBY But that is not necessarily so common. Why?
HARE It is partly that I was brought up among women. My father was completely absent and so women were the element in which I grew up. So when I started writing I started writing about women, because it was women I was interested in. I could see at some political level that it was completely ridiculous that the stage was not open to half the human race. They were not represented. It just seemed bonkers, but that isn't necessarily what a creative person responds to. You don't write to an agenda like that but, having said that, the leap of imagination that is needed to be something different from yourself is, to me, what inspires art. Writing about yourself, in spite of the fact that I have now resorted to it, has always seemed to me something I didn't want to do and what greater act of imagination could I perform than to imagine what it was to be a woman.

BIGSBY You worked for various theatres, subsequently, including the Royal Court, which comes across in your book as a centre of creativity but also as a nest of vipers.
HARE In those days people felt very strongly about the cultural organisation which represented their views, but their views were diametrically opposed to the views of others. I was the literary manager at the Royal Court. My job was to go round and see plays all over the place, new plays. I had to see them on behalf of the directors. When I went to see a play at the Royal Shakespeare Company I put in my usual chitty for three shillings and sixpence, which was the cost of the ticket and the supper that I was entitled to – one shilling for supper and two and sixpence for the ticket – and Bill Gaskill, the Director of the Royal Court, said to me, 'We are not going to pay you to go and see the work of that appalling company.' He said, 'If you want to go and see the Royal Shakespeare Company on your own time and your own money that is your business, but I am not going to subsidise you to go and see such terrible work.' That is what we felt.

We were at war and we stood for something which, crudely, was social realism, truthfulness, the portrayal of the working class, honest political work while they stood for fakery, conceptual productions, exaggerated acting, ridiculous speech. They were just wrong though that now has disappeared completely from cultural life. Joan Littlewood at Theatre Workshop in the East End attacked us all the time as middle class liberals. She called George Devine an anti-Semite on absolutely no evidence whatsoever. She said, 'I hate that anti-Semitic theatre.' That was the discourse of the day.

BIGSBY Your work came from the left but, by the mid-1970s, society was going the other way, and there was a brief hiatus in your career as the implication of that fact sunk in.

HARE Nobody saw Thatcher coming, did they? Of all the things that seemed likely in the 1970s the least likely was that there would be deregulation of markets, that workers' rights would be taken away and that capitalism would renew itself from within through these fiscal and political measures. I don't know of a single person who forecast that the developed world would lurch to the right and abandon the principles of the welfare state, so if you were on the left in the nineteen seventies you were caught out. I end my memoir deliberately in 1979 with my divorce, Thatcher's election and my finally writing a play that I am pleased with, which was *Plenty* in 1978. You had to think, well, hang on, I have been arguing for something which doesn't happen, so I have been rebuked by reality.

BIGSBY There is a line in your play *Gethsemane* which says that when you have a dark night of the soul you have to go on. Was there a sense then, as you reconstructed yourself, that you needed to go on in the face of the historical forces you describe?

HARE If you were a contemporary writer you were left looking very stupid, and that is what I felt. I felt that, having continually predicted that there would either be anarchy or some kind of apocalyptic breakdown in England in the 1970s, which is what everybody felt was coming, then you would be dishonest if you didn't face in yourself the fact that you have been wrong and so, yes, it did take me a few years to find a way of writing about Thatcher and I think you will find that it is significant that it took everybody a long time before the best work about Thatcherism began to appear, *My Beautiful Laundrette*, *Serious Money* or *Boys from the Blackstuff*.

BIGSBY I first tuned into your work with *Licking Hitler*, which was a film for television and is a reminder there was a time in the 1970s and into the 1980s when television was a place you wanted to be, a serious place. Large numbers of people watched and they were socially conscious plays. *Licking Hitler* was a film set during the Second World War about a black propaganda unit in which the classes come uneasily together. Their job is to tell lies in order to deceive Germans. They use radio broadcasts to spread defeatism. Then came *Plenty*, set after the war, at a time when lying has infiltrated society at large. There is a sense of betrayal of values which once seemed to bind people together, and I do feel that in your work there is a sense of loss, a loss of vision, of transcendence.

HARE I am constantly asked by producers to write plays about the National Health Service, to which I say, 'What am I meant to say about the National Health Service?' In 1945 it was wonderful, now it is not and there is a danger on the left of that being the only myth the left has. In 1945 everything was great and now everything is absolutely terrible, which plainly is not a way of engaging with the world as it is now, much as I may have lived through that story. But I do have the feeling that my life was literally cut in half at the age of thirty-two. We were heading in one direction, an assumption about the common good, an assumption about the welfare state, an assumption about the National Health Service, an assumption that the purpose of government is to intervene and help the weakest, then, for the last thirty or however many years, we have been heading in exactly the opposite direction and the division is so completely like a hairpin that it is impossible in writing a history like this not to remark on that change.

BIGSBY You have also written for film and as you know Jonathan Franzen was here recently, which must strike a rather sad note with you.

HARE Well, I spent three years writing the film of *The Corrections* and I wrote twenty-three drafts and in the end it was never made so it was heartbreaking, absolutely heartbreaking.

BIGSBY You began as a director, then you stopped but then took it up again both in the theatre and in cinema. What is the difference between directing in the cinema and directing on stage? Do you have more control in one than you have in the other?

HARE You are treated much better, yes. Everybody expects you to have the answers and so the great film directors that I have worked with are intensely collaborative and intensely open. The ones that you have to avoid like the plague are the lone genius figures who resent the idea that they don't create the whole movie. There are a lot of extremely intelligent people who argue that the auteur theory is what destroyed cinema. It was a completely ridiculous idea and indeed wasn't taken seriously by directors themselves and yet the director is plainly in charge on the set. But how much more power do they need? Do they also need to be told they are a great artist by everybody? And so all the intelligent directors who I work with are the ones who collaborate most, in other words who regard it as a team with the editor, the cameraman, the screenwriter, the designer as equal partners in the venture. The lone genius thing is just a madness.

BIGSBY And is that essentially the way you work when you are directing a play?

HARE Yes, the theatre is collaborative by definition. It is built into the theatre. The director will be absent when the play goes on. Then the director has no role whatsoever except to sit and fume and fumble in the distance. That is all you can do. I am working at the moment with a director and I can actually hear him at the back of the auditorium going, 'Oh no, no.' He is powerless because when the event takes place there is nothing he can do, whereas obviously in a film the director has power, meaning he or she creates it. When people ask me about the difference between writing for the cinema and writing for the theatre, the most significant difference is legal. Legally, in the theatre, I am contractually in charge. I am the playwright and if they do not do every word that I wrote I am entitled to take the production off. Indeed Harold Pinter did take off a Visconti production of *Old Times* on the grounds that they did not do the lines in the exact order that he had written them. Contractually, in the cinema, I am a hired hand, exactly the same as the assistant director, exactly the same as the script person. That is my status. I sell my labour, so when I sell my labour they are legally entitled to change my words. They own what I offer them. I give them words, they own them, and can do what they like with them. They don't have to appear on the screen. So obviously writers like going back to the theatre because legally they are in charge.

BIGSBY But there are directors who don't like the writer to be a presence in rehearsals because they are an alternative source of power?

HARE Those are people we call stupid directors, of whom there are always very many.

BIGSBY We talked at the beginning about the long period of time before you went back to write a play about your childhood. There is another example of such a gap. You went to Saigon but the film that came out of that appeared ten years later. Is that unusual or are there certain works of yours where it simply takes time for it to filter through in some way?

HARE I think that the twenty-first century has presented a great problem to writers. It is so eventful. Look at what happened in the first three years of this century. First there was an attack on mainland America and second the invasion of Iraq. I can tell whether you are left wing or right wing according to which of those two events is more significant. People on the right tend to say of 9/11 that, 'Everything has changed. The world will never be the same again.' After the invasion

of Iraq, people like me went, 'Politics will never be
the same again. This is such a radical event.' So there
has been a sense, particularly given my position as a
political playwright, of having to work fast to get down
the changes that are happening, and happening so
dramatically. Harold Wilson was much mocked in 1964
for saying that 'the white heat of technology is going to
transform people's lives' but he was only thirty years
out. He thought it was going to happen in the late 1960s,
early 1970s, but it started happening in the 1990s. He
was dead right about it. You can tell that in Jonathan
Franzen's new book he is trying to assimilate and deal
with what is happening at a time when it is happening
so fast it is almost impossible to keep hold of it.

BIGSBY I said earlier that in the 1970s and early
1980s television was a place people wanted to go, but
throughout the 1990s and the first part of this century
it seems to me that the BBC abnegated that role,
indeed British television as a whole, and lo and behold,
miraculously, American television suddenly started
producing first rate television drama. I wrote a book
about this but at the end of it I said, 'However, there are
the first signs that the British are coming back,' and the
work I quoted was your film for television, *Page Eight*,
which was to do with the relationship between MI5 and
politicians.
HARE I think it is true. I am still a Raymond Williams
fan and I find as the years go by that Raymond Williams'
thinking means more and more to me. What he said,
and this is why I wanted to study with him, was that
culture comes up from below. He said it is not the elite
talking to each other over teacups in an airless room, it
is the movement of ideas in society and that is expressed
through the people who call themselves painters and
novelists. He said that no sooner does somebody say
the novel is dead, than, suddenly, in Nigeria somebody
writes a great novel. It always pops up from somewhere
that is totally unexplained and so it is true, suddenly,
in American television there was a period of blinding
creativity, just as in Scandinavia. Who saw that coming?
I walked past a tattoo shop today and there was a queue

out into the street in Norwich and I thought that fifteen years ago they must surely have been thinking of shutting the tattoo shops, that the tattoo business was over. Now they can't believe their luck. Something is going on in society that makes people feel they want to be tattooed. I don't pretend to understand what it is since I don't carry any myself but plainly something is going on and it always comes from a direction where you are not looking. It is a democratic impulse and that, which Raymond taught me, has kept me going for fifty years.

BIGSBY In preparation for that particular television film you gave a lecture to MI5.

HARE Yes, I was asked by MI5 to go and give them a talk about the British theatre. I very much welcomed this opportunity. They were at a very low point in their fortunes because this was the end of the twentieth century and they were very upset that Ireland had been solved since so many of them were making a fat living out of Northern Ireland and they said, 'We do fear that we are in a business where there is not going to be anything to do any more.' They didn't quite see 9/11 round the corner and MI5 was caught with very few Arab speakers, and with almost no agents in place within the communities that they wanted to be in. They were really caught hopping but business is booming in MI5 now.

BIGSBY You once said you have tried to avoid genre but in *Page Eight* you have what is surely a spy thriller, a detective thriller. So you haven't actually kept clear of genre.

HARE Yes, to your credit you have gunned me down from the gun tower. It is absolutely true that I think that everything that is interesting goes on outside genre, in films certainly, or I had thought that. Of the films I have been involved with, *The Hours* was obviously in that well known phenomenon, the lesbian suicide movie. We used to joke about it. *The Reader* was the defence of the Nazi war criminal movie. That sense of getting out of genre was very, very important to me in film, but it is true that I could not resist the delicious temptations of the spy thriller, mainly because I felt that nobody was doing it. Le Carré is absolutely brilliant up to the year 2000 but he then diversified, as indeed MI5 and MI6 did, into different subjects and nobody has written about the arguments going on at the moment inside MI5, arguments about torture, about rendition, about legality, about surveillance. It is wrong to think of MI5 as an organisation that is committed to all these things. It is not and to represent those arguments seemed to me a tremendously interesting thing to be able to do.

BIGSBY One of the actors in *Page Eight* was Bill Nighy, who you have often worked with. What are the virtues, not to mention the pleasures, of working with an actor in a number of different works?

HARE Oh, loads. I personally believe it raises your game. So much time in rehearsal is spent getting to know actors and seeing how they work, understanding what their working method is. You all come from different backgrounds. Maybe somebody has been more in television, maybe they are from fringe theatre, maybe from commercial theatre. So you spend weeks trying to find a common method. I have worked with Bill Nighy ten or eleven times, Judi Dench many times, Kate Nelligan a great deal. You just go from day one. You are already at a level and I think you urge each other on. I don't think it creates complacency, or it never has in my experience. It just means that three weeks of getting to know one another, which is time wasted, is behind you.

BIGSBY Arthur Miller once said that his career would have been different if he had had a theatre, by which he meant something like The National. He never knew whether he could get a play on. You surely do have a theatre, do you not?

HARE Portable was an attempt to create our theatre and it lasted three years. Then we became totally exhausted. Apart from anything we knew that driving round Britain's motorways we would eventually have an accident, because you leave at 11 o'clock at night, exhausted, and you get home at two in the morning. It is a tough life, theatre on the road, a wearying life with one- or two-night stands so our spirit got broken by it. The actual motor accident where the van turned over one-and-a-half times was the point at which we began to feel it wasn't such fun anymore and that we were not making the lasting effect on the theatre that we wanted. I have always dreamt of a theatre that was different but I haven't been able to create it.

BIGSBY But if you were to knock on the door of the National Theatre with a new play?

HARE Yes, if you are saying to me is life better for a British playwright than for an American playwright, self-evidently. It must be simply because in this country you feel that theatre can access society at large. That essential illusion, that people are listening, does buck you up and keep you writing. I think that if you are an American playwright the sense that you are working in a very disempowered and impoverished form, especially now that regional theatres are closing all over America, makes it tough.

IAN MCEWAN

Ian McEwan was born in Aldershot in 1948. He was educated at the University of Sussex and completed a Master's degree in English literature at the University of East Anglia. His first book, a collection of short stories entitled *First Love, Last Rights*, was published in 1975 and was followed by a second, *In Between the Sheets*, in 1978. His novels include *The Comfort of Strangers* (1981), *The Child in Time* (1987), *Enduring Love* (1997), *Amsterdam* (1998), *Atonement* (2001), *Saturday* (2005), *On Chesil Beach* (2007), *Solar* (2010), *Sweet Tooth* (2012) and *The Children Act* (2014). His awards include the Booker Prize, the Shakespeare Prize and the Jerusalem Prize. He is a CBE.

This interview was recorded on October 22, 2014.

BIGSBY A year ago you wrote a piece in which you talked about occasionally losing faith in fiction because there is something rather strange about it. You invent characters who have never existed. They go through trials and tribulations which never happened and then you send your novel out into the world. Obviously in one way it expands the imaginative experience of the reader. You occupy the sensibility of others, so there is a moral dimension, but having gone through that dark night of the soul about fiction what leads you back to the computer?

MCEWAN What leads me back is reading. It won't be a whole book. Sometimes it will be half a page, a sentence, even just a trope, a metaphor that catches my attention and excites me, even if it is something I have read before. This is usually the beginning, a kind of hunger coming back, 'Oh, this is what it can do.' Even just picking up a Shakespeare play. But the falling away is not a dark night of the soul, by the way. It is just a vague sense of impatience and a feeling that as I get older I want to be informed about the world not by novelists but by historians, physicists, biographers. I have a hunger for that, for everything that is not fiction. The rightly named non-fiction is where I want to live for a while to recharge the batteries. The thought of going back in the foothills of another novel appals me, but it could be some little felicity on the page of an Updike story, it could be just anything, that leads me to sit back and think, 'Oh, that is so sweet. That it is just the perfect thing.'

BIGSBY When you do go back to the computer do you know where it's going or are you led by the words you are putting on the page?

MCEWAN In the case of *The Children Act*, this was a story told to me by a retired High Court judge, an Appeal Court judge. We were waiting at a concert for the pianist to come on and play us *The Goldberg Variations* when he started telling me about a Jehovah's Witness boy who refused a blood transfusion. There were a couple of aspects of this story, which he told in the course of about four minutes, that were so appealing to me that even before he had finished I knew he was telling me something about a short novel that I was going to write. I had just started writing *Sweet Tooth* at this point so at home I just jotted down some notes. Then, three years later, I went back to him and said, 'I am thinking of a novel. Would you be my guide through the intricacies and rituals of the law?' and he said he would love to do it. So I met him maybe five or six times during the course of writing it. I had no clear idea how to adapt it to my own ends, so in that sense the writing did dictate what happened and the characters slowly emerged. It was very different from what he had told me, but not in structure. A Jehovah's Witness boy urgently needs a transfusion of blood. The hospital goes to the courts to get permission to treat the boy against his will. Jehovah's Witnesses do not generally permit themselves blood transfusions so the Court has to make a difficult decision because the boy is so close to the age of eighteen that his wishes have to be taken very seriously into account. At the same time a hospital treating a patient against his will is common assault, so doctors need the protection of the courts. The fact that the parents wept for joy when the court decision went against them, and their boy was going to live after all, was one of the first things that snagged my attention, that paradox which seemed so human, which had such a human touch. They had done their duty by their religion and yet their son would live.

The other thing that touched me in his story was that my friend, the judge, took the boy to a football match because that is what they talked about at the bedside when the judge went to hear what his wishes were. He took him into the directors' box and the boy met all his soccer heroes. His eyes were gleaming with the joy of being alive. He had had the blood transfusion (he suffered from a fairly common, curable, form of leukaemia and the judge felt entirely vindicated). But, then, seven or eight years later, the boy had gone back into hospital in his early twenties and refused the necessary blood transfusion and died. By then he was beyond the reach of the court's jurisdiction. That was the second thing that caught my attention.

BIGSBY When they are making human organs they have a scaffold which they scatter with cells, slowly creating a kidney or an ear. In a similar way, then, you started with a scaffold, the story told to you in a matter of minutes?

MCEWAN Yes. In fact it was hard to keep my attention on what he was saying because already my thoughts were running on, which is why I went back to him three years later and said, would you tell it to me all over again to make sure that I heard it correctly? But, then, yes, it all had to change and it became quite difficult to write even though I knew the structure of it. I wanted to make the judge a woman who had always been too busy in her career to stop and have the children she wanted. She has been extremely successful, rising up through the judiciary and being elected onto the bench so it is now too late. At one point she says that where other women once became Brides of Christ she had married the law and it was too late to turn back. So I wanted her to see in this boy something of the son she never had.

BIGSBY So by making it a woman, though the story was told to you by a male judge, you have opened up a whole series of other possibilities?

MCEWAN Yes, I didn't want them in my novel sitting around talking about football, in which I only have a faint interest every four years when I watch the World Cup.

BIGSBY I seem to remember you mentioning that you had read a series of judgements and that they had impressed you though they were only writing for a very limited number of people.

MCEWAN Yes, and that leads me to the fact that the story actually goes back another two years to an event that had already predisposed me to think about writing a novel set in the law. I had been at the same judge's house for dinner and round the table were several of his colleagues, also judges. You know you are getting on in life when your mates are judges. What happened to all those revolutionary folk one used to hang out with? So it is a bit worrying, but anyway that is another matter. I liked the way that the judges seemed to know everything about each other's judgements. They were teasing each other, but they were quoting each other. They were also merciless about those judges who were foolish enough to be absent and I thought they are very like novelists, especially in this last regard. It was during that evening that I found a bound volume of judgements by our host and I started reading them and thought, fiction has basically lived off the criminal courts – malpractice, thugs, criminals, attorneys, private eyes, policemen – but judges are strangely absent even though family law is much closer to the ordinary disasters of life. We don't mostly live among guns, armed robberies and kidnappings but we do live among things like divorce, contested wills, the whole business of medical ethics, hospitals and dying, who is sane and who isn't, Powers of Attorney. It struck me that family law was a treasure trove that had not been investigated by predatory novelists to the right extent. So that was well before I heard the anecdote about the boy with leukaemia. I was already disposed to think that one day I would write a novel about a judge.

BIGSBY Does that connection between literature and the judgements as written by judges also apply to style? These are not over-elaborate, long works; they are pieces of prose that have to pertain to the immediate issue. They bleed out of them the irrelevant. Your novel is equally tightly controlled. It is not a long sprawling novel of the kind Henry James invokes.

MCEWAN What struck me about the judgements is that when, for example, a phrase like 'the child's welfare' was evoked, judges would then step back to define 'welfare' and that would take them into the realms of psychology, of asking, 'What is the nature of happiness?' or, 'What is the good life?' We are not only thinking, the judge would say, of the child as he or she is now but of the consequences of this court's decision for that child's wellbeing into the future. So on that evening I remember I was seeing Aristotle quoted and Milne. I wrote a novel called *Enduring Love* where I wanted to end with a psychiatrist's report. I allowed myself to write a judgement, or at least a sort of fairly compact form of one. I liked the prose and one of the pleasures of talking to people about their work is to learn the vocabulary of their work. Each word is a concept. It carries weight that only an insider knows fully how to unwrap. So it wasn't quite the same as a judgement.

BIGSBY In the novel, behind the fictional judges are real judges, the cases are real, as they say in *Judge Judy*. When precedents are quoted they turn out to be real ones. In other words fiction and a real world co-exist. In the past you have expressed to feeling distant from magical realism, admiring the products of modernism while feeling that they left things out. Did modernism leave out what realism can engage?

MCEWAN Modernism left out work, there is no question of that. Nobody seems to go to work in quite the same way that the rest of us do, except novelists of course. Kipling is wonderful on work and so are Conrad and Hemingway. Margaret Atwood is very, very, good on work and ranges across a whole set of disciplines in her writing. But this is oddly neglected in the modernist tradition, partly I suppose because of its leaning towards the very nature of consciousness. A lot of Henry James's characters have private incomes, the assumption being that if you have got a private income then you can really concentrate on the human condition. If you can't be happy with a private income, he seems to imply, then you are really at the soul of what is troubling about existence itself. I really disagree with that. I think we are in part made by what we do, the work that people do, the fact that it often brings into their lives, and that of their spouses and children, their sense of achievement or their feeling of utter desolation and oppression, of repetition, their very identities. These are vital to the consciousness they end up with. So I have become more and more fascinated by work itself.

BIGSBY You are fascinated, too, it seems to me, whether you are dealing with a brain surgeon, a scientist or a judge, with the procedures, the protocols, which govern what they do. I seem to remember you quoting Nabokov about the importance of detail.

MCEWAN   Fondling the detail.

BIGSBY   And surely getting the details right is what substantiates the world you are creating.

MCEWAN   Yes, although what you don't want to do is overwhelm, I mean did you ever read Arthur Hailey's *Airport*?

BIGSBY   Strangely no.

MCEWAN   If you want to know how to run an airport you are told in 800 pages. So the details have to be highly selective. What I discovered about the law is that judges, who have the power to deprive citizens of their liberty, have therefore developed a powerful sense of humour as a kind of protection and all their jokes, the ones I heard anyway, were always against the law as if to fend off any criticism of it by saying, 'We are here first.' One that one of the judges tells in the novel refers to the cross-examination of a pathologist. The barrister says, 'How could you tell that the victim was actually dead?' The pathologist says, 'Because his brain was in a jar that was sitting on my desk.' But the barrister says, 'But can you be sure that he was really dead?' And the pathologist says, 'You are right. I guess he could have been practising law somewhere.' That is an archetypical judge's joke.

BIGSBY   Is there a sense in which the fact validates the fiction and the fiction elevates the fact?

MCEWAN   Maybe it is because I always find that the artifice necessary to create realism always needs that extra boost of the real world. My first experience of this was at the age of thirteen. I was in the school library alone and was reading *The Go Between*. If you remember it was getting hotter and hotter through the novel and the little boy staying in this big country house goes out each day to check the thermometer to see if it is going to reach 100 degrees Fahrenheit. When he comes back from one of those missions the edition of *Punch* has just arrived and it has Mr Punch mopping his forehead, which had not been seen on *Punch* before. Now in that school library were the bound volumes of all the *Punches*. I remember in a kind of trance putting the book down, going across the library, getting the volume out for July 1900 – the novel is very specific when it is set – and there it was. There was Punch mopping his brow, and I felt a thrill to realise that that was how realism could work, not that I phrased it to my thirteen-year-old self in those terms, but it made a big impression that running fictional characters alongside real ones, or in real situations or real historical events, or, in this case, having real recent legal cases penetrated by imaginary beings, was compelling. Maybe it is because I do feel that there is always something a little wound down and tired about realism that needs this rooting, or maybe it is just because I have got a strong empirical bent and I like the world of the actual that is shared and brought into the world of the imaginary.

BIGSBY And that is part of what takes you back to the computer, to engage with the real world that is out there?

MCEWAN Yes, but one that you could fill with ghosts.

BIGSBY It is called *The Children Act*. What is the essence of the Children Act?

MCEWAN It is a piece of legislation dating from 1989, probably the best bit of legislation that came out of Mrs Thatcher's time, though I don't think she had any hand in it. Basically it sets out something that had been accumulating anyway in English and Welsh law: the rights of children. Its heart is in its very opening sentence, which I quote as an epigraph. It instructs that when a court has to consider the interests, or the future, of a child the child's interests must be the court's paramount consideration. It sounds rather circular, a kind of truism, for what else would you do. But in fact what it does is liberate children, in these situations, from being the possessions of their parents. There comes a time when the parents' interests are not paramount nor, for that matter, the gods those parents worship, but simply the child's interests.

That begs the question of what interests are, but judges are quite willing to pitch in and define what that is, and quite a few judgements had some ringing descriptions of what they considered the good life to be for a child.

So this rather self-evident pronouncement is actually quite helpful because in a case where Jehovah's Witness parents are refusing a blood transfusion for their ten-year-old child the Court can simply say, it is not in this child's interests to be dead and so therefore we overrule the parents, who would normally be the ones who have to give their permission for medical treatment. The child will therefore be treated against the parents' wishes. Where it gets dodgy or anxious, as the courts call it, is when that child is almost eighteen, is articulate, mentally stable and able to say, 'I don't want a blood transfusion.' But still the Children Act applies and in the case that Alan Ward described to me, he simply said, 'I don't care that he is not eighteen and the Children Act is clear. It is not in his interests to be dead and I rule for the hospital.'

BIGSBY Something strikes me about the first page of your novel. It sounds like the instructions on a film script.

MCEWAN I thought you were going to say it sounds like the opening of *Bleak House*, which is what it is meant to be. I somehow felt we couldn't enter the temple of this law, or the temple of this fiction about the law, without bowing or curtsying in Dickens's direction. It needed a hat tip, as it were.

BIGSBY There are a series of cases which involve religion, whether it be Islam, Judaism, Roman Catholicism, or other sects. In almost all cases their view is inimical to the best interests of the children. In fact in all cases they are inimical. Earlier, you mentioned your interest in science, which represents rationality in a world in which the irrational is surprisingly dominant at the moment yet in this book your judge is quite gentle in the way she deals with these people and their beliefs even though she is going to overrule them in all cases.

MCEWAN I think in all the judgements I read where the secular law was in conflict with religion, the judges bend over backwards to be extremely nice about faith then go on to ride roughshod all over it. Generally the cases that come to court represent religion flying in the face of rational compassion. In the case of the separation of two Siamese twins, which is an important case here, if they aren't separated both will die. One of them is not a viable human being, has hardly any brain or heart or lungs, but the parents are Catholics and very sincere in their belief that God gave life and only God could take it away, and they have a point in that it will require a surgeon to go into the chest cavity of the unviable child and sever the aorta. How is the Court to licence murder? And that is a very interesting point I think because we are always interested, when we read about cases in the courts and especially judge's verdicts, in the gap between what is lawful and what is moral. It is a fascinating matter and they don't always overlap. So in the case of the Siamese twins, the then supreme authority in Britain of the Catholic Church, the Archbishop of Westminster, wrote his own submission to the judge saying that the twins must be left alone to die. Well the twins were divided, followed by a massive reconstruction on the viable twin and she is – I mean in the actual case – now a very lively, extremely intelligent, young girl whose passionate wish as it happens is to study biology at university.

BIGSBY What the judge has to do is find a legal reason for right action. In other words the right action is actually painfully clear but they have to find a legal justification.

MCEWAN Any cab driver will tell you that it is better to have one child alive than two dead but that is not the point and in fact in Alan Ward's judgement – which is 14,000 words long, that he wrote in a week, and which I thought was one of the most brilliant – its opening sentence is, 'This is a court of law not of morals and our duty is to find a lawful way to what we know is right.' So in other words he had already decided what was right but needed to do it lawfully. To sanction murder is a very difficult thing and he did it by relying on what is called the doctrine of necessity, which grows out of a case well known to all law students. It refers to the occasion on which some shipwrecked sailors ate the cabin boy to survive. Religions like to claim that they are the source and fundamental spring of morality but they are often very lacking. The truth is that reasoning and compassion running together can make far better, more wholesome, and decent judgements about people's fates and their wellbeing than someone who is referring either to a supernatural entity or to a point of dogma that is in Leviticus. My conviction, although I keep my own convictions well out of this novel, is that the Archbishop of Westminster was plainly wrong in that that young girl is living a very meaningful life. I have got a photograph of the three of them standing together, the parents who wanted her dead, as it were, and are now delighted, with this very beautiful, incredibly intelligent, extremely articulate girl who lives in Malta.

> BIGSBY But sometimes things can go wrong.
> MCEWAN Oh God, they go wrong.

> BIGSBY It seems as though the judges are always siding with the hospital. As you know, just a month or two ago parents walked out of a hospital seeking treatment abroad. The hospital said this was damaging to the child and went to court. The court issued an order, an International Arrest Warrant went out, and they were in handcuffs while their five-year-old was in a hospital in a foreign country.
> MCEWAN They happened to be Jehovah's Witnesses.

> BIGSBY And they were also Jehovah's Witnesses.
> MCEWAN Which I think was part of the cause of this bureaucratic panic. Jehovah's Witnesses have got absolutely nothing against surgical procedure. It is the transfusion. The parents, I think, were perfectly reasonable in this. Their methods might have been better but the administration could have simply got social workers nearby to be in contact, in Prague, with their counterparts there and dealt with it as a welfare issue. It was never a criminal issue. To issue a European Arrest Warrant was such a nonsense. These parents just wanted to try every last damn thing. There is no worse fate for an adult than to lose a child, but I would say it was not the court that was at fault but the hospital.

> The courts make terrible errors in relation to the Children Act often by taking children away from their parents and putting them into care without the parents being able to give evidence. They have these draconian

powers and it is often working class parents, without the reach or connections to get a barrister quickly into court, who then find themselves at a disadvantage. Social workers are always over anxious not to neglect to rescue a child. I am only addressing the spirit of the law, the intention of the law, which I think is very civilised but there are daily examples of getting things wrong.

I quote the case of Sally Clark, the solicitor, whose two babies died of sudden infant death syndrome, and the jury and the judge were largely persuaded by absolutely ludicrous statistical evidence from a medical expert, a very esteemed one, Roy Meadow, who said, 'It is 8,000-to-one that a child could die of SIDS so for two to die in this way you multiply these two things out.' Now any statistician, or anyone with a smattering of probability theory, will tell you that either genes or environment are responsible for SIDS, we are not entirely sure which yet, and these children shared half their genes and all of their environment, so what you ought to be doing is asking yourself, 'What are the chances of a mother committing murder in a professional, stable, loving home?' If you do that you get to a figure even greater than 64 million-to-one. So one comes away thinking all judges and all barristers, as well as all juries, should be forced to take a little course in probability theory before they are allowed in court because in fact it is very useful. The great tragedy of the law is you have got to decide either something happened or it didn't. There is no middle place. If the court says it happened, it happened, if it didn't happen, it didn't happen, or if you don't know you had better say it didn't happen. It is a far worse thing to convict an innocent person than let a guilty one go free, and that is an important principle constantly neglected.

BIGSBY You describe another case. It involves a fight and somebody who is present but not the person who struck the blow goes to prison for the same length of time as the others simply because there is a law that permits that to happen.

MCEWAN Yes, it is a new outrage called 'joint enterprise'. You come to the scene of a scuffle and you arrest everyone and throw them all in prison. If you can't work out who did what you just say, 'Off you go, all of you.' My friend, a young friend, was on the edges of a pub brawl. The whole thing was on CCTV so we watched it in the barrister's chambers. He got a massive blow to his own face and you see him staggering off the scene. The fight went on, someone fell to the ground and got kicked. His jaw was broken so that immediately becomes GBH. Four were students from good homes. They were not arrested, but the four who were from rather dodgier backgrounds were all scooped up and got two-and-a-half years. The one who did the kicking maybe should have got two-and- a-half years but our friend got two-and-a- half years too. It seemed a fantastic miscarriage of justice to me, extraordinary, so my feeling about the law is that a lot of the time it is very good, patient, procedural, and arrives at the right conclusions. Then there is a substantial minority of cases which really fly in the face of one's sense of natural justice. By the way, the prosecution were pushing for nine years. We didn't know anything about it but hired a barrister at the last minute. All four had been found guilty already but before sentencing we managed to get a barrister to lower the sentence. So while we were fuming at two-and-a-half years, the parents behind us were sobbing with relief because they thought their child was going to get nine. This is the difference between what is lawful and what is just.

BIGSBY David Hare has written a series of plays which focus on journalism, politics, religion, in an attempt to build up a portrait of the society in which we live. You have covered similar territory, but I suspect don't have that kind of programmatic approach. Nonetheless in the background of *Saturday* is the anti-Iraq war march while in the background of this, albeit off stage, is Syria, the anarchy that is going on out there while we are talking about this very ordered world here. Is there any sense in which you are looking at different aspects of the world we inhabit?

MCEWAN I think there is still something powerful in David left over from the Portable Theatre days when plays were a very good way of righting wrong. But that is not my starting point, I am afraid. I am not trying to right wrongs, whatever I have been saying here about my own feelings.

    BIGSBY But you do have a couple of sentences about Syria.
    MCEWAN It just places it in time for me.

    BIGSBY Yes, and you do locate the action precisely, in 2012. I suppose what I am getting out is that on the one hand you have the ordered world of the courts and of law while elsewhere things are falling apart and there is also anarchy in the private life of your judge. The law becomes the place to which she can go because that is the one place there is order.
    MCEWAN Here's a starting point. A Yale psychologist I shared a platform with recently told me of an experiment which I thought was beautifully devised. He got two hundred or three hundred self-described rationalists and atheists and then he offered them a $100 if they would sign a document. The document was on parchment in heavy gothic lettering in which you were being asked to sign your soul to the Devil. Thirty per cent refused. I would sign it for free and I am sure you would. What appeals to me about that is that Fiona loves the law and all its reasoning and rational compassion, but as soon as an emotional disaster happens in her own life, what is the first thing she does? She does the very thing she told divorcing couples when she was a barrister not to do. Do not change the locks when your husband goes off to have an affair because you are instantly on the wrong side of the law; you are on the back foot even if you feel wronged. The first thing she does is change the locks of her apartment. When she is in the middle of this crisis with her husband the phone rings and it is her clerk to tell her that there is an emergency application from an Area Health Authority in the case of a Jehovah's Witness and she feels a kind of relief. Here is her own life descending into mess but here is an opportunity to go back onto what she thinks of as 'the treeless heath of other people's problems' and other people's problems are the places

where we can be very rational. But self-described rationalists, all of us, however reasoning we think we are, can be so easily unhinged and I am much more interested in the personal aspect of this than in wishing, as David does, and I think in a brilliant way, to reform institutions or to see how they are rotten. This is not a reforming book. I just take it as it is. I am much more interested in what the limits of rationality are in the face of those genuine problems that suddenly sweep chaos into your existence.

DAVID MITCHELL

David Mitchell was born in Southport in 1969 and raised in Malvern, Worcestershire. He graduated with a BA and MA from the University of Kent. His first novel, *Ghostwritten*, was published in 1999 and was followed by *number9dream*, *Cloud Atlas*, *Black Swan Green*, *The Thousand Autumns of Jacob De Zoet*, *The Bone Clocks* and *Slade House*. He is a winner of the John Llewellyn Rhys Prize and has twice been shortlisted for the Man Booker Prize.

This interview was recorded on November 18, 2015.

BIGSBY David, when you were young you were a fan of science fiction and fantasy fiction. In particular, you were drawn to Ursula Le Guin's *Earthsea* series. What was it about it that appealed to you?

MITCHELL It was human. It didn't have any hobbits, or elves, or orcs, or talking trees in it. I like those as well but there was something quite secular and human about *Earthsea*. These are just human beings like us. There is an ethnographic range, though she doesn't let you know that Ged, the protagonist, is of Native American ethnicity until halfway through the first book. I liked the human scale of it. I liked the way that it wasn't that long, so there were still large areas of the Earthsea archipelago that the narrative never went to and that – in a Dungeons and Dragons kind of way (which dates me and marks me off as someone who didn't have a girlfriend until he was eighteen) – let your imagination work on it itself without being contradicted by a *Lord of the Rings* hobbit-sized land grab.

BIGSBY But she did have a map of this world that she created.

MITCHELL She did.

BIGSBY And when you were young one of the things you did was to draw maps. Why?

MITCHELL My parents encouraged me because it was a very low maintenance, inexpensive, way of getting me through the half terms. They would mount a piece of A1 cartridge paper on a huge drawing board, with masking tape around the edge so it just looked perfect. So there it was, on a huge board that was mine, all mine, and I had my pens and what more beautiful, what more fulfilling and nourishing, what more imaginative way could there be to get through five days of rainy, muddy, early 1980s Worcestershire half-term than to fill it up with imaginary continents and draw on the trees to make the forest, one by one, and the mountains. Then, well who lives there and what's their name and where are the cities and who are they and who are they at war with and what do they believe and what is their religion etc. etc.?

BIGSBY How old were you then?
MITCHELL It was when we lived in Upton, so about ten or eleven.

BIGSBY And then at thirteen you told your mother you were going to be a writer on the basis of what exactly?
MITCHELL Absolutely nothing. Just arrogance, but that is all right.

BIGSBY Twenty-five years ago I interviewed Ursula Le Guin in Oregon and the one thing that annoyed her, and that I suspect annoys you, is that the kind of books she wrote were not considered literary.
MITCHELL That is correct, yes, though I have been lucky. You get away with it as a man. Look at Dickens, Poe, Hawthorne, its fine for them. You write *Brave New World* and that is published by a mainstream imprint and you find it in Penguin Classics or Vintage Classics. You write *1984*, a dystopian view of the future with machines that do not exist yet and that is fine if you are George Orwell. Try writing it as a woman, though…

BIGSBY So you have come up for awards because of your gender?
MITCHELL I don't know. Probably chance and the fact that my imprint is Sceptre which isn't a genre imprint. It is a mainstream literary imprint and the Booker was very generous, sprinkling its magic dust of literary imprimatur on me. I have always been in that camp, though, and things like *The Bone Clocks* and the science fictionary bit in *Cloud Atlas* is me having an excursion into genre but trying to do it another way.

BIGSBY You are playing with genre but respecting it at the same time?
MITCHELL It is eminently respect-worthy. You shouldn't be a disrespectful tourist. For one or two fantasy writers I have spoken with, it is not so much the fact that they are pigeonholed as the existence of pigeonholes. No one went up to Dickens and said, 'Tell me Mr Dickens, I notice you have made a trip into fantasy

in your recent book,' or Mikhail Bulgakov, 'So, Mr Bulgakov, you have a talking cat who fires a machine gun and the devil comes to Moscow. Where did this come from?' It is a valid perennial discussion but why are we even having it? Surely what matters is, is it any good or not, rather than the fact that it is set in the future or has a dragon in it.

BIGSBY But when Doris Lessing wrote her space fiction series she encountered resistance from science fiction writers and felt there was a coterie world which blocked her out. She was playing games with science fiction while they were doing it seriously.

MITCHELL Where there is snobbery there is also inverted snobbery. One reacts against the other, but I would like to think that these walls are becoming more porous and dissolving away. So I am grateful to the judges that with *The Bone Clocks*, longlisted for the Booker Prize, they didn't get defensive about their patch, their territory.

BIGSBY We will come onto the *The Bone Clocks* in a moment, but there is one other aspect of your youth I want to ask you about because you stammered when you were young.

MITCHELL I still do. I didn't really speak until I was five. I was a very, very late developer and I get fuzzy with dates and ages but I do have a memory of the first time I blocked on a word and couldn't get it out. It was some distance between speaking for the first time and then realising that there were words that something inside me wasn't going to let me say.

BIGSBY Oddly the people around you don't seem to have acknowledged it, even your own family.

MITCHELL That was between five and seven, so just too early. Later, friends don't mention your stammer. It becomes an elephant in the living room because they don't want to hurt your feelings. Maybe there was also the feeling that if we don't acknowledge that it is there it will quietly slip away. Given the ignorance about stammering I am not blaming anyone for it. I think most parents don't know what to do and the default mode, when you don't know what to do, is actually nothing. I went to a speech therapist for a little while but it is a particularity of some stammers that when you are in the presence of a speech therapist it improves dramatically and you block a lot less.

BIGSBY Richard Dawkins was here and he stammered when he was young and had to develop strategies to deal with it. Did you?

MITCHELL Yes, some I am using right now. The bluntest is word avoidance. Incidentally, I am one of the Honorary Presidents of the British Stammering Association, a great organisation. We meet to talk about the charity and how it is going and what we can do, but one of the people who is always there is Nicholas Parsons. I feel I'm happy to share this because he talks about it himself. His job is to chair a radio show whose point is fluency. Isn't that great? As to strategies, as I say the bluntest is word avoidance and that is perhaps why as a young stammerer you read a lot, because it is easier than talking but actually it helps because you learn new words to say the things you can't say. You also realise that that won't always work. When you are thirteen you cannot get away with using the word 'autodidactic' otherwise you get beaten up, at least in the kind of schools I went to. So you learn about register and the appropriateness of language for certain age groups, certain gender groups, certain class groups. So that is word avoidance. You autocue a sentence and you see a word you are going to block on coming up and you skirt round it. You generally stammer on two or three consonants of the alphabet at any one time.

BIGSBY But it is interesting that you see some connection between that problem and a facility with language. It gives you an alertness to alternative words, word structures, which may in some sense have fed into your work.

MITCHELL Oh, yes. It is a gift. If God had fixed my stammer – you can't know this, of course, because you can't compare yourself to another in a parallel universe –

I might not have been able to do dialogue with the facility I can, or that I hope I aspire to.

BIGSBY Your fourth novel, *Black Swan Green*, is the one in which you came out about your stammering. It is your fourth novel but it reads like a first novel.

MITCHELL It does.

BIGSBY Why did you wait so long and does it have anything to do with the kind of novels you had been writing? It is almost as though you are changing gear, a deliberate attempt not just to speak about the past but to use a different mode of writing to do that?

MITCHELL Firstly, I didn't actually think that my own life was remotely interesting. I didn't really want to write about families and the human mud that most of us live in. I wanted to do more rarefied characters in other times and places than the ones I knew personally.

BIGSBY And you did that for three novels and then you wrote that fourth one.

MITCHELL Yes. Kazuo Ishiguro is someone I really admire for a number of reasons and one of those is that he performs ninety degree changes. He started off being Mr. Japan in English Letters with *A Pale View of Hills* and *An Artist of the Floating World*, then he wrote *The Remains of the Day*, this beautiful exquisite thing about a butler more English than the English, a quintessentially English novel full of words like 'quintessentially'. Then, before he got pigeonholed, he wrote *The Unconsoled,* a hard-core seven-hundred-page pretty Germanic premodernist novel, with admirable aplomb. More recently he has turned to science fiction with *Never Let Me Go,* about a future in which people are grown to be organ donators.

BIGSBY But you do ninety degree turns within your books, not just from book to book.

MITCHELL Yes. Guilty as charged, but, just to answer the question, why *Black Swan Green*, then? There are lots of people publishing novels in their thirties. I'm interested in what happens to them when they get to their sixties? Do they forget how to write, which seems improbable. More probably they have a hit and then spend a lot of time in the next few books writing variations of the hit, but a little less good. That seemed to be a pretty normal trajectory and one to avoid because you get older and, after a career in writing novels, who else is ever going to employ me so I had better make this work or I won't have a pension. The way to do that seems to me to react against oneself, put some clear blue water between your books and consciously engage in experiences that you never had before. You need to replenish the reservoir of raw material that is pretty much drained after the first one, two or three books.

BIGSBY   Let me take you back a step or two. You went to the University of Kent where you majored in English and American literature. Then you did a Master's in post-modernism, which presumably means you were delving into Pynchon and DeLillo.

MITCHELL   DeLillo, yes; Pynchon, yes. I tried *Gravity's Rainbow* but it was like being locked inside a Picasso painting. Maybe I should go back to it. *The Crying of Lot 49* was great but also really short.

BIGSBY   Did you derive anything from your reading then that was going to be useful to you?

MITCHELL   What I think I gleaned was a fondness for levels of reality, ontology, the idea that there is a reality we live in. When you read a book you go inside a different reality. You go into Narnia. Every book is a kind of a wardrobe you go through and there is a Narnia inside. I have always done this but never really thought about the mechanics, the electronics of it. What makes this work? How come you can? With some books you are on page thirty six and suddenly it is page four hundred and twenty and how the hell did that happen? It is more realistic than the room you are reading it in. Isn't that great when that happens? How come it works with some books but not others and what is this thing, the novel? What is it made of? Plot, characters, style, ideas and structure. Which of those are propulsive, which of those are retardants, which are neither? And how about when you are inside that reality and then there is another one inside that, a wardrobe inside the wardrobe? That is what post modernism was partly about, and it could be sterile, a cul-de-sac.

BIGSBY And there are frequently conspiracies, as there are in your work.

MITCHELL Oh yes. Just because something is a cul-de-sac that doesn't mean you can't find small black iron doors out of it.

BIGSBY During the year you were writing your dissertation, you went to Sicily, to Catania. When you came back you wrote a novel, a science fiction novel set on an interstellar vessel.

MITCHELL Oh God, yes. That was rubbish. That was awful. I didn't write all of it but, yes. It was one of these space ark novels where something is launched and it will take decades or centuries to get there and of course all knowledge of earth, or wherever they were launched from, recedes into mythology.

BIGSBY Is it in a drawer or burnt?

MITCHELL God no. It was crap. It really was. If you don't do a creative writing course then your crap is your course, as it were. The early manuscripts that are indulgent and abysmal and long-winded and prolix and over-written and over-awed and precious and far too self-regarding, this is actually what you learn from. When you identify these negative qualities in it, don't be discouraged, young writers. It is a good feeling when you read next week what you thought was great last week and you think, 'Oh my God, how did I think that was ever…' That means you are improving and you can find why it wasn't working and the bits that are working and that is how you learn.

BIGSBY You then went to Japan, not because that was the thing you most wanted to do, but because you had met a woman who was Japanese.

MITCHELL There was a romantic element to my globetrotting in those days, yes.

BIGSBY And is it correct that you then wrote another novel which did not turn out to be published?
MITCHELL Yes.

BIGSBY So what was that one about?
MITCHELL Oh, hello skeleton, hello cupboard. It was a thing set in a pub. I had read a twelfth century proto novel called *The Pillow Book of Sei Shonagon*. It is a beautiful document of Heian period Japan and I thought what would a twentieth century novel look like in that form? It was still just the twentieth century back then. It was set in a pub, with a section every day, an East End pub, and the protagonist arrived there and got a job in this pub. He was basically a slave and couldn't really leave.

BIGSBY How far did you get before you dumped it?
MITCHELL I wrote the whole thing.

BIGSBY Did you send it out?
MITCHELL Yes, I did, and got a nice sheaf of rejection letters. Those are the good ones. Mostly it was ignored but two agents said, 'Not this one, but when you are next in London, come and say hello and actually let's have a look at the next thing you write.' The next thing I wrote was the first few chapters of *Ghostwritten*.

BIGSBY So we have come on to something you have actually published. *Ghostwritten* has suddenly a disturbing relevance because it starts with a terrorist assault on Tokyo.
MITCHELL Yes, unfortunately they never really go out of fashion.

BIGSBY You were writing this while you were travelling.
MITCHELL I took about eight months off my job and went from Hiroshima to Tokyo, Hong Kong, Beijing then, via the trans-Siberian express, to Moscow, St Petersburg. I finished off in Cape Clear, oddly enough just round the corner from where I live some years later. So I went to all those places and wrote impressions that

I didn't want to forget from those places, those locations and the first few coagulated into stories. They were independent stories at that point.

BIGSBY And when you were writing those stories, did you have a sense of the totality?

MITCHELL The first three or four, no. Then I noticed that they were all answers to the question, 'Why do things happen?' The first concerned the application of the will to a cult leader. The second one was about love, the third one greed, the fourth one history, the fifth one the presence of disembodied souls that move from person to person and occupy us. Then I noticed that there was this pattern and I designed the remaining stories, from the remaining locations, around that question and made something happen in each of the stories. I had to retrofit the first three or four, let one thing happen that creates a domino that topples and makes the next story happen. So it is a row of toppling dominoes that ends in the destruction of the earth.

BIGSBY It also establishes a template for what was to follow. It is the way you structure most of your books, a series of novellas, each of which can be complete and convincing in its own right. Then you start playing games expanding our notion of what is real as you introduce another element. I don't know what the right word is – magical, mysterious?

MITCHELL We live in fractured times, in times of competing narratives. Earlier, imperial, certainties are gone. In our multi-cultural times, our society consists of competing narratives about what it was, what it is and what it should be so that maybe it is inevitable that artists in the broader sense, including writers, who are saturated and infused with this multiplicity of narratives, end up with a tendency to write more polyphonic narratives.

BIGSBY You speak English and Japanese in your house so there is a polyphony built into your daily life. Incidentally, do you stutter in Japanese?

MITCHELL You don't stutter when you are singing. You don't stutter when you are talking to animals. You don't stutter talking to yourself in the shower, but, yes, you do stutter in other languages.

BIGSBY Your next book was *number9dream*, which is in nine parts, though when you reach the ninth there is nothing there. I am interested in your relationship to your reader because in this novel you play games with the reader and not just the non-existent section nine. Part of the novel turns out to have been a dream.

MITCHELL You touched on what I rather fancifully call 'the secret architecture', the reasons why things happen. The secret architecture is that each chapter is a state of the mind. The first one is fantasy, the second is memory, another is dream, another is image. They are all things the mind does. They are functions of the mind. Nightmare is another. There are so many dreams because that's the state of the mind you are moving through at that point of the book. It was my infancy as a writer and I am not altogether sure what I was doing but just occasionally I do meet someone who likes *number9dream* more than anything else I have done, and they are always really interesting people.

BIGSBY Then came *Cloud Atlas* which has sold…
MITCHELL About a million in the States and somewhat more elsewhere. It paid for the house and I am really grateful to it, so thank you for that, *Cloud Atlas*.

BIGSBY Someone once said to Arthur Miller after *Death of a Salesman*, 'You must be grateful because now you don't have to write anymore.'
MITCHELL Miles Davies said the same thing about *A Kind of Blue*, which he called, 'that damned record'.

BIGSBY This is again a novel which moves around in time and space and we go into the sensibility of some other entity. Did you find it more difficult to find a language for the future than you did when you were reaching back into the past?
MITCHELL They have their particular difficulties and their particular free passes. In the past they obviously didn't speak as we do now but if you don't get it right it

will sound like Blackadder and be unreadable. I know because with the next one I combed through Smollett to get late eighteenth century speech and I wrote the first thirty, forty pages in really good authentic eighteenth century English and it was unreadable. It just sounded like a spoof, so you have to create by calling up bygonese, the language that we think was spoken then. You know it is actually not completely authentic but you import enough that is authentic within this bygonese that we absorb from everything we read written in the present but set in the past.

BIGSBY Do you mean you are freer to create the language of the future?

MITCHELL Yes, but the reader must sense the presence of syntactical, grammatical, lexicographical rules that you are sticking to. The moment the reader thinks you are making it up for your convenience as you go along then it is as annoying as when you were a kid playing a game and someone made up the rules as they went along. That pops the shimmering bubble of fiction that we need to keep inflated and beautiful and whole. So if anyone is writing something set in the future, you need to write a dictionary and a grammar book and stick to it.

BIGSBY Do you mean that literally?

MITCHELL Yes, though it is a few pages in a notebook. I drew the language from present Hawaiian slang, the tendency of language to drift towards contractions, generally away from Latinisms towards more Anglo-Saxonisms, along with the mistakes that my Japanese students were making. That then became correct twenty-third century English. It was an amalgam of those things.

BIGSBY It was commonly thought to be unfilmable but, of course, it was filmed?

MITCHELL Yes. It is my least filmable book.

BIGSBY Most writers say that you sell your novel and then walk away and whatever they do with it has nothing to do with you. Did you feel that or did you want ownership of the film?

MITCHELL It was a very positive and, I think, an atypical experience. I got to know the directors personally. They met me. There is often a little courtship at the beginning where they say, 'we will honour the spirit of your book absolutely' while having no intention of doing so but we got on well, and my friendship with them I still value very much. They invited me on set. I actually appear in the film a couple of times. Blink and you miss me, but I am there.

BIGSBY I blinked.

MITCHELL Yes, that is appropriate given the film but I had a really positive experience of the whole thing. No one forces you to sign your work over which is why I always think that it is a little bit rich of writers who join in the dissing of an unsuccessful adaptation, though if you do it with an American studio there is a clause that you can't publicly slag the film off. American entertainment lawyers are scary people.

BIGSBY The conventional tense of books tends to be the past tense. Even science fiction books set in the far future tend to be in the past tense. You are, at times, drawn to the present tense as you are drawn to first person narratives rather than third person. Why is that?

MITCHELL Yes, it is becoming a bit of a habit. I wrote *number9dream* in the past tense, then switched it into the present and it suddenly became alive and more immediate than it had been before and, yes, that was pretty much all third person. But there are different types of third person, aren't there? There is the more authorial omniscient, looking down at the stage and describing what is on it, and then there is the helmet-cam third person where, yes, you are using the third person, you are not using I, but the perspective is limited to a helmet-cam wearing character. So if that person isn't in the room then you can't see what is going on the other side of the wall. You have to send that person through to see. That is the least third person of the third person tenses, and that is as far as I have really gone. I do it with the Luisa Rey section in *Cloud Atlas* and also in the whole of *A Thousand Autumns*, partly because there were so many different distinctive Englishes that I had to portray in it. There is the English that the Japanese people are using when they speak in Japanese to each other for male and female, educated and less educated. It is exactly the same thing with the Dutch. There are different registers in which the British speak to each other. There are about nine different dialects of English that I need to have in the book to represent the English and the Dutch and the Japanese that is being spoken. But what English are they thinking? And it's in bygonese as well. So I sorted that one in the first person. It was all right so long as nobody was thinking but the moment they were thinking 'Oh, no, I am now in the third person.'

BIGSBY One of the marks of your work, which people are familiar with, is the way characters move from novel to novel. How do you keep this in your head? How do you keep control of that? Why do you do it? Is it to do with this notion, which is not merely a strategy of the book, a technique in the book, but a philosophical conviction, that all things do connect in some way?

MITCHELL I have an antenna that twitches when it senses that someone I have written already could be good for this role. Firstly, I did it because it was cool, or I thought it was, so the links between *Ghostwritten* and *number9dream* were no more profound than that really. Secondly, I noticed that they carry things with them, as Falstaff does in *The Merry Wives of Windsor*. Thirdly, because it lets me make my life's work be that sheet of A1 paper. It allows me to be a maximalist, to make something as big as Earthsea, as big as Middle Earth, as big as wherever it is *Game of Thrones* is set. It allows me to think I would like to do something about the Dutch in Japan or I would like to do something about growing up in the early 1980s. I would like to do something about this house which is kind of a diabolical engine. So I can have my cake and eat it.

BIGSBY Within the books the different sections connect. Characters arch from one book to another connecting them so that it becomes in some sense a major novel in itself. You have referred to it as an uber novel. Different as they are, there are connecting elements. In *The Bone Clocks* there are immortals who exist outside of normal life. There are immortals who are occupy people's minds and bodies, in contention with one another so that the human beings are incidental, mere mechanisms. These are forces that act upon people and to which they submit, apparently willingly. It is tempting to think of terrorists who submit to an idea.

MITCHELL   And it is called faith.

BIGSBY   Yes, it is called faith and it is terrifying and the people who believe they have the truth are the most terrifying people.

MITCHELL   You are dead right.

BIGSBY   But in a sense you are occupying people too, though not for malicious purposes.

MITCHELL   Yes, every writer does, every playwright does, every actor does.

BIGSBY   Most recently, you have created a story for Twitter. Were your publishers surprised when you offered *Slade House*?

MITCHELL   They were less surprised than I secretly hoped they might be. They know me by now. *The Bone Clocks* grew away from, and orphaned, material that then grew into *Slade House*. Then I thought I would have a go at telling a story via Twitter. What would the constraints be and how can I wriggle my way out of these constraints?

BIGSBY   Was that like writing a sonnet, discovering what you can do within constraints?

MITCHELL   Exactly like that, even shorter than a sonnet however, micro-sonnets. Yes, it was that but yet to make a continuous narrative built of micro-sonnets. Twitter would love to hear their tweets called micro-sonnets.

BIGSBY   There is something very gothic about *Slade House* and you are you a fan of the gothic.

MITCHELL   It's there in the soup that we all imbibe

from in varying degrees of thinness or thickness, though that is a three-star metaphor I wouldn't use in a book, and, yes, a fan. I don't read read gothic novels now, though I have studied them, but as a flavour, as a conviction, as a mode, as a warehouse full of costumes and setting and lighting that you can plunder and still use in the twenty-first century, it would be a strange thing to refuse to go there.

PAUL NURSE   IAN MCEWAN

Sir Paul Nurse is a Nobel Prize-winning geneticist, former President of the Royal Society and currently Director of the Francis Crick Institute. He is a graduate of the University of Birmingham and completed his PhD at UEA before moving to the University of Edinburgh. His original research was on cell division in yeast. His work has taken him to Oxford University and Rockefeller University, New York, where he served as President. Among his many honours is the Legion d'Honneur. He is the Director and Chief Executive of the Francis Crick Institute.

Ian McEwan was born in Aldershot in 1948. He was educated at the University of Sussex and completed a Master's degree in English literature at the University of East Anglia. His first book, a collection of short stories entitled *First Love, Last Rights*, was published in 1975 and was followed by a second, *In Between the Sheets*, in 1978. His novels include *The Comfort of Strangers* (1981), *The Child in Time* (1987), *Enduring Love* (1997), *Amsterdam* (1998), *Atonement* (2001), *Saturday* (2005), *On Chesil Beach* (2007), *Solar* (2010), *Sweet Tooth* (2012) and *The Children Act* (2014). His awards include the Booker Prize, the Shakespeare Prize and the Jerusalem Prize. He is a CBE.

This interview with was recorded on November 13, 2013.

BIGSBY This is not going to be an evening in which we replay the two cultures debate of over fifty years ago when C. P. Snow and F. R. Leavis raised personal abuse to the level of an art form. It was, you will recall, an occasion on which it was proposed that there was a gulf between the arts and the sciences and a wilful gulf at that. C. P. Snow said that scientists don't read novels and arts people don't know what the second law of thermodynamics is, and are proud of that fact. What I am rather more interested in seeing is the similarities, because on some fundamental level they are both asking questions about who we are, how we relate to one another, to the world around us, what that world around us consists of and how we relate to the universe.

In 1977 the Voyager probe set off into space and thirty-six years later it left the solar system, twelve billion miles from the sun. It will take another 75,000 years to reach the next sun, the next star, and that star is only one of – there is a debate about the number – 100 billion to 400 billion stars in this galaxy. Meanwhile, according to the latest German super-computer, there are an estimated 500 billion galaxies in the universe, that is if the universe is not infinite or if there are not ten, eleven, twelve, thirteen, fourteen, alternative universes. In the face of that, the mind, at least mine, stops, but it also stops when we contemplate the temporal limits to the human lifespan. So, on the one hand we are bewildered and slightly terrified by huge numbers and on the other we are bewildered and slightly terrified by the small numbers that represent our lifespans. It was a character in Samuel Beckett's *Waiting for Godot* who said, 'We give birth astride of a grave.' How do we deal with that? We look for master stories. Originally we found those stories in myths, then in religion, but we also turn to science, the science that touches our lives every day. But, of course, we also turn to story, to fiction. We put our children to bed at night and read them stories to introduce them to aspects of our world. We sit in front of the television and watch stories. We go to sleep and our mind creates stories. If it did not, indeed, our grasp on sanity would slacken. Now that's a rather roundabout way of coming in, but Paul your attraction to science did in a sense start with the stars.

NURSE It absolutely did. It started with the stars. I was eight, maybe nine. I was living in Neasden, that very famous literary centre. I didn't come from an academic family but I read in the newspaper that Sputnik 2 was going to pass over London and Sputnik 2 had that dog Laika on it. Well, I had a dog and I felt sorry for Laika up there. It was about to be burnt as the satellite came in, though actually we learnt thirty years later that Laika was already dead. It had died on the launch. Anyway, I was in my pyjamas, because it came over at eight or nine o'clock, and I remember going out to my front garden and there was this bright star just tracking across the sky, a man-made object in the sky. I got so excited I tried to chase it down the road. I was running down the street and telling everybody, 'That's a satellite.' That was my introduction to science, not so much because I was interested in the technology of satellites but because, having looked at this man-made object, this star crossing the sky, it made me think what did all the other stars mean? What were all those other twinkling things? And what about planets? What about the moon? So my parents bought me a little one-inch diameter telescope and I could see Saturn's rings, the moons of Jupiter, the mountains and craters on the moon and that really got me into science.

BIGSBY And do you still have a telescope?
NURSE Do you know, I do. I don't do anything serious with it. I just look at things which I think are beautiful, that's all.

BIGSBY But you weren't only interested in space, you were also interested in the natural world.
NURSE I was. Looking at the stars makes you also think about looking at what's around you. That's really what happened. Once I got interested in the stars I also got interested in the flowers, the insects, the birds and everything around me and I rather rapidly got attracted to biology because you felt you could contribute something in biology. The problem with physics is that you feel you need big colliders, or big telescopes, whereas

I could go out into the back garden and just see where spiders' webs were and think about what they might mean. I didn't need big bits of kit. You could investigate biology and feel you were actually discovering something new. That is what really turned me on, curiosity-driven thinking about the world and the creativity that goes with that.

BIGSBY And when you were researching here at UEA the scale shrank yet again because now you were looking at a cell.

NURSE Yes, that is very true and I can explain why. I started with natural history, but the problem with doing that is that you got wet and cold. You had to go out in wellington boots, which was a bit miserable. The second thing was that actually it is very complicated because there are so many factors going on. Ecology is very complicated. It is very, very important, but it is very difficult to study so I gradually withdrew, still dealing with life where you could make a contribution but to a much simpler system where I could control all the variables, well not all but as many as one could. I could study, investigate and find out something fundamental in a more controlled environment which also happened to be centrally heated as well.

BIGSBY Now in a second I really want to ask you, Ian, to talk about literature but can I create a context for this by saying a word about education. In this country, as you know, at the age of sixteen we require our children to decide whether they are going into science or the humanities and indeed pupils are nervous of mixing them because they think it may prejudice their chance of getting on to university. So they specialise for those last two years and when they arrive at university they will specialise yet again. As a result, certain doors have opened, there is a greater intensity of focus, but other doors have closed. Ian, I know you ended up taking four arts subjects as a core – two languages, history and literature – but on the side you did get to do some mathematics and were quite keen on studying physics had that been possible.

MCEWAN I did a maths, I think it was an A level or half an A level, I can't remember. A very nice maths teacher came into the room and said, 'I will take ten of you ignorant bastards' – he actually said that – 'and get you through a maths exam.' I stuck my hand up with everyone else. There were only ten of us and he had a marvellous Socratic way of teaching which was on the basis that the convoy can only go as fast as its slowest ship so he would say, 'Has everyone got that?' and we were completely open about whether we had got it or not. If someone said no he would say it all over again and, even if you had got it, it was a great relief to hear it again. I did then learn a huge respect for mathematics because he taught us not only how to use calculus but how it was invented and how it was put together. It seemed to me at the time – actually I still think this – one of the most extraordinary inventions, how to plot a system through change, a dynamic system, and how to express that in functions. You only had to blink and it would be gone. A sneeze and the whole lot would go, but I thought that that was probably the highest interaction endeavour I ever attained because you can go to any university as an arts graduate and get a good degree without ever having to do anything particularly difficult.

BIGSBY A different degree of difficulty.
MCEWAN OK, a different degree of difficulty. Let's be kind to ourselves, but it is quite possible to get an English degree or a history degree and not ever have to say, 'I don't fully understand that.' When theory was rampaging through universities it was very difficult to understand but here there was actually something hard and intelligible that had to be grasped and that gave me a lifetime's respect for people who can do maths but I knew I could go no further than that, that that was about as far as I could go.

BIGSBY You went to the University of Sussex at a time when there was a wide range of subjects available for an arts student?
MCEWAN I did a course in quantum mechanics for a liberal arts know-nothing, which was all without maths

though I don't think any theoretical physicist would dream for a moment you could understand quantum mechanics without maths, but there is something to be understood about it. So, yes, it was a very polymathic course. It was Asa Briggs' new map of learning. It was a marvellous thing. I had an extremely privileged one-on-one with Peter Calvocoressi, who was a lawyer at the Nuremberg Trials, for international relations, and along with quantum mechanics I did analytical philosophy, and then Freud and Jung and Kafka and all those other things that Sussex was famous for.

BIGSBY So can I ask you both, if you were in a position of power would you change that education system? Would you stop that decision at sixteen?

NURSE I would. I remember when I left school I said, well now I have got to get educated. I remember coming to that decision because, though I went to a very good school and it prepared me for examinations, I was specialising at fourteen. I was a scientist. I had to leave school at seventeen for various reasons but then I thought I now have to educate myself because I haven't been educated. In some ways that was quite good because I have never stopped.

BIGSBY When you and I went to university we were required to have a foreign language. You failed O level French six times.

NURSE Yes, I believe it's a world record.

MCEWAN Six?

NURSE Yes.

BIGSBY And hence couldn't go to university?

NURSE Correct. So, yes, I did have a problem, though I did end up in UEA eventually and I did end up in Sussex, so we both have been to the same places. But you are right. This was deeply embarrassing. I don't know if you are trying to embarrass me in front of this distinguished audience but it is true that I managed to fail O level French six times because at that time you needed to matriculate with a foreign language, without which you couldn't go to a university. I actually had very good

A levels, a year early. I had everything else but I didn't have this qualification.

BIGSBY So if you want to change the system which requires a more general syllabus in A level, aren't you putting a trip wire in for other people who, because they fail in the subject they are not going to specialise in, can't go on?

NURSE I think that is a risk. I think we need to be generally educated but we have to be rather careful about the assessment and the examination of it, and I think we also have to be rather careful about quite what we demand because clearly some of us have blocks. Ian was obviously very good at maths but some people have blocks on maths and when the government says everybody has to have maths to the age of eighteen there are some people who just don't get it. I think you have got to be more subtle about it, which perhaps doesn't map on very well with present education policy.

BIGSBY Would you change it, Ian?

MCEWAN I think Paul is right. Somehow you have got to get everyone into university who wants to go and is reasonably clever, and people are clever at different things, but at the same time we do want some basics. The great thinkers we admire of the Age of Enlightenment, like Descartes etc., wanted to discuss the human condition and the nature of the mind in a philosophical way, but they were natural philosophers, rooted in what was available in science at the time. I think we should be able, in our modern equivalents, to look for the same kind of synthesis. So I would say that the humanities have rather cut themselves off even as your description of the size of the universe could only come to us through science which informs our sense of who we are, where humans came from, how societies are formed. It's not drawn from the revelations of faith or authority but from available science, and I feel that the humanities could embrace this more than they do. There is extraordinary work going on in so many branches of science that impact upon the humanities and on our studies of literature and philosophy. We should be embracing it a little more hungrily. There is a golden age of discovery, especially in the biological sciences.

BIGSBY It is surely also a golden age when it comes to those who write about science in an available way in a way that wasn't true fifty years ago?

MCEWAN Yes, we have been very lucky in having all sorts of people write for us and inform us in that way, so I think if it was possible for Descartes and Spinoza and Adam Smith to use the science of their time and yet to be addressing the things that concern the humanities the most, it ought to be possible to run these cultures a little more together. I think the scientists are 'reaching out', to use that very dodgy American term, but the humanities are a little defensive because they feel their patch is being invaded. Neuroscience and cognitive psychology are looking at things that we writers always thought were ours. I have been to a neuroscience lab to hear a lecture on revenge done through game theory. Paul Bloom at Yale, for example, is doing work which will really fascinate us all asking, how much morality does a six month old baby have? Quite a lot, it turns out. They have a sense of what is just. You can study morality also in another way by looking at what holds across cultures. There is an extraordinary amount going on and I think the humanities should be opening their hearts.

NURSE I think you might be being a bit hard on the humanities because I think part of the problem is that when you look back to the seventeenth century, to those polymaths, they could embrace so much. I am a scientist but truthfully I can only work at the very edge, in quite a restricted area, and one of the great troubles to me is in fact how even within the sciences we become so specialised. So I think it is partly to do with the fact of trying to embrace the complexity of knowledge. The second thing I would say about the humanities is that although we often separate science and humanities, the intellectual processes involved are much more similar than perhaps we think. The outcome is different but there are really commonalities. One thing that does interest me greatly is creativity and how that is common to the arts and to science. There are real similarities. If you are an historian you will use many of the processes that we would use in science. You are pursuing truth. You test ideas. Where science has the advantage is that we can often devise very precise experiments to test an idea, which isn't so easy in the humanities where you may only have accessibility to a certain limited data set.

BIGSBY Can I pick up this idea of the imagination? Einstein said that the imagination is more important than knowledge, which he glossed to mean that knowledge is about the known and the imagination is about the possible, all that can be known, and surely the imagination, which we associate with the writer, is equally powerful and necessary in science. You have to imagine the possible. You have to ask what if, which is also what the novelist asks.

NURSE I can describe how I think about this in science, and then it might be interesting to see how Ian works, because there is a period of time in a scientific enquiry when you really have no idea where things are going. You make some observations, you get some data, you get a bit of experimental evidence, and you have some sort of idea. Then you start walking in fog. People think this is a very defined process, the scientific method, as if we could lay it out, but actually what you are doing is trying to imagine what would actually work. This is the creative bit. You have to imagine this or you imagine that, and to get that to work you have to put different things together. You have to stop running on rails. You have to jump around, which is one reason why I like reading widely. I have often found that when you have an idea to explain something, for months it can be the only idea you have because everything you do directs towards that idea. Creativity in science requires you to jump out of that and then suddenly you will have another idea which works just as well and you would never have got it except for that creative dimension. You have this hypothesis, this imaginative leap, but then have to crawl your way back, proposing experiments and observations that will test that idea. That is a bit different from the humanities I would suggest but I think that creative jump may have some similarities?

MCEWAN Yes. Last night I had the great honour to be with Peter Higgs at the Science Museum. It is extraordinary to think that he had posited something that must exist, if his theory was correct, forty odd years ago and that mathematics explains the world, whereas a novelist comes at it in a very different way. For the novelist the world isn't intelligible, or we don't have that suspicion, because what we are generally interested in, in literature, is everything that goes wrong. Lyric poetry can celebrate everything going right, the adoration of the lover, but novels track human fates through time and generally human fates through time come unstuck in some interesting way. We have always been interested in conflict, misunderstandings, the misreading of each other, sometimes leading to reconciliations but sometimes not. More not in the twentieth century. Our business is not necessarily with a sense that the world is out there waiting to be explained, which is a highly contested idea in the humanities. That would be described as naive realism, I think. V. S. Pritchett used a term which I can never put out of my mind. He was putting down Ford Madox Ford and he said that Ford Madox Ford was not a great writer because he didn't have the capacity that a great writer had for determined stupor. I love the phrase 'determined stupor' and in fact I think we all need it and have it and it should be a great privilege of civilisation. Determined stupor is when you sit around looking very un-busy to everyone else, thinking or gazing or daydreaming. That moment is maybe what we do have in common, that and the impulse to draw things together that you thought did not belong together, that moment of surprise when you think 'oh that actually belongs here with this' and as soon as it comes together several other moments of freedom are realised.

NURSE Koestler had this idea that creativity is putting together things that were different and he made that very nice analogy to humour because so much of humour is actually putting things together that spark something off.

BIGSBY That is also the basis of metaphor.
MCEWAN Eliot's famous yoking together of the

heterogeneous was in a sense a celebration of the breakthrough moment in poetry.

BIGSBY Maybe another connection is an aesthetic one because not only you but a lot of scientists will say that when they arrive at a theory or a formula they know it is right because it is beautiful. In this context, what do you mean by beautiful?

NURSE Yes, but I think sometimes this can be overstated.

BIGSBY You stated it.

NURSE I have said it. Actually it is often said by physicists who are very attracted by the mathematical, by a reduction of something in terms of mathematics. So you have Schrodinger's equation and physicists are very attracted to Ockham's Razor, which says that the simplest solution is usually the best one. If you can do something with two variables that is better than doing it with four. My subjects are rather messier. We evolve by natural selection from something that was before. We are not intelligently created which means that we have all sorts of redundant things going on. We can't explain it with two or three variables. We might need ten. It is a rather different area from mathematics. So for me beauty, aesthetics, are not to do with that mathematical simplicity. It is to do with a putting together of things that you haven't seen before and there is an aesthetic buzz about that which I can't quite explain.

BIGSBY You have also said that data trumps beauty.

NURSE What I actually said was that data trumps even the most beautiful idea. The point I was making is that we shouldn't be so seduced by the beautiful idea unless there is data and testing to show that it still stands up. I think that is important because we are weak vain creatures and can be seduced by our own ideas. That I think is one of the weaknesses that scientists have.

MCEWAN Paul, you are in a descriptive world of biology and maybe there is a connection at least with the realist novel. Societies and humans are messy, just as biological processes are not perfectly designed. Why do we eat through the same tube we breathe through? That is such a mess, and we have an s shaped spine.

BIGSBY And give birth the way we do.
NURSE And let alone birth.
MCEWAN Yes, birth, between pissing and shitting and all that.

BIGSBY Ian, if we are talking about beauty, a sense of rightness, below the level of plot, below the level of character, writers are interested in the sentence, the word. When you are writing do you have this sense of beauty that derives from the conviction that you have got something right, like sounding an octave on a piano. You hear it is right.
MCEWAN There is an inner ear. Sometimes there are those blessed mornings when things fall out in a certain way and those are the slightly hotter passages in the novel. But sometimes in novels you have to get characters across the room and into a taxi and there doesn't seem much room for beauty. You have just got to get them somewhere else in the space of a paragraph. I think poets have a much more direct line with this. It is not an issue in contemporary music and I think it remains an issue in poetry but I am not sure that if you ran a course called Beauty in Literature on what grounds it would stand.

BIGSBY You would probably be back in the nineteenth century which leads me to ask another question which is whether the idea of the sublime can survive scientific analysis. We all know what a rainbow consists of and how it is generated. We know how it works, and yet don't we all stop when we see a rainbow? Does a scientist stop when he sees a rainbow?
NURSE I think science is sublime, too. Of course we all stop at the sight of a rainbow but what science tells you is sublime, that there are, as you said, billions of stars. A recent calculation has worked out that there are probably up to forty billion earth-like planets orbiting stars. It is almost inconceivable that there hasn't been life elsewhere.

BIGSBY Ian, you have also talked about the beauty of scientific language.

MCEWAN I am an outsider to this but an admirer of it. I like it when scientists talk to each other. They have to break out of their specialisms and talk in the language of ordinary mortals and they often have great need of each other. Neuroscience now needs mathematicians. There are all kinds of collisions taking place in that world and they do have to break out. In fact everyone seems to be needing mathematicians at the moment. It is really cool, a good thing to be doing, which is why I admire John Brockman's Edge.org which I think is a wonderful talking place with computer scientists talking to biologists talking to physicists, mathematicians, psychologists. It is my favourite website. I love going there. It is all perfectly comprehensible, sometimes furiously debated. All kinds of hatred are included but it is no different from an English department. Let's not idealise these guys. Scientists are dogged by this terrible issue of originality and priority which we don't have in quite the same way. One thinks of Einstein racing to get to his general relativity with David Hilbert at his back or Darwin on that awful day when he received that twenty-page letter from Wallace.

BIGSBY And yet scientists will tell you that the individual doesn't matter in terms of science.

NURSE I have got a view about this. I think a problem we sometimes have in conveying science is that we rush to the conclusion while what is interesting in science is the journey to that conclusion. What we don't tend to do in science is tell the stories of how you get there, which actually gets you into a much more human frame of mind. If you just focus on the outcome the individual never matters. We just don't tell those stories well enough.

BIGSBY Right, but if Crick and Watson had not been there, someone was behind them. Penicillin would surely have been fortuitously discovered.

NURSE That is absolutely right. What I am trying to say is that we shouldn't just focus on the conclusion, we should focus on the journey to that conclusion. You could describe a novel in terms of reaching a conclusion but that is not the reason you would take that journey to read it. Could I just go back to something else, because whilst Ian was talking about explanation and understanding and quantum mechanics and maths, and so on, one thing that has struck me is that there is some science that is really quite difficult to communicate in a common sense sort of way, science that is often at the extremes of human experience: the very small quantum mechanics, the very big relativity. If you read a book about relativity what I find is that when you close it, it starts to drift away. Now if you have that difficulty with relativity, which I personally do, if you come to quantum mechanics you are in *Alice in Wonderland*. There you have cats that are both dead and alive at the same time. It probably only makes sense in terms of the mathematics. My daughter is a high energy physicist. She works on the Hadron Collider and bangs protons together. That's her job and it was really illuminating to me when I realised that she doesn't understand it either, because what she understands she understands in terms of the mathematics, but she can't understand it in a common sense world. Many of the books will be on string theory, or whatever, and they are full of metaphors not the real thing.

MCEWAN But, Paul, the mathematics is also a metaphor. It is not the thing itself. It is a way of describing a thing. One of the great issues is whether quantum mechanics describes the world or whether it is simply an efficient way of predicting it and some of it is fantastically inelegant, gloriously so. The M-theory suggests that there are eleven dimensions. String theory started with ten then someone said no there would have to be eleven. And for those of us who like to absorb this unfolding story – because here is a story that has happened in our lifetime, how to unite relativity theory with quantum mechanics is the great quest, probably the greatest intellectual quest of our time for which the Higgs boson is just one tiny part – the fascination is to see how that story unfolds and changes. So when Stephen Hawkins talks of multiple universes, and others pose an almost infinite number, all of mathematics breaks down because in quantum mechanics you can no longer have probability in an infinite number of universes. You can say something has a 10% chance of happening but in an infinite world 10% is infinite and that tenth is endlessly repeated so there are versions of us in every conceivable possibility.

NURSE So it gets absurd and that absurdity is what raises a little ghost of scepticism in me because sooner or later, and I hope it is in our life time, someone is going to say no there is actually an underlying simpler theory that describes the world in terms of gravity and quantum mechanics.

MCEWAN But of course some people think string theory isn't even science. It is taking us into a place which is so hypothetical that it is like a novel.

NURSE A really bad novel, I think.

BIGSBY Surely another difference between science and a novel is that the novel can deal in ambiguity. In fact that is one of its weapons, while science surely can't, or can it?

NURSE Oh, no, ambiguities are really important at the creative stage. You are right we search for certainty but if you are trying to search for certainty too early you will not find it.

BIGSBY But can you end with an ambiguity?

NURSE If you begin in doubt you are more likely to end in certainties. You have to keep uncertainties going because otherwise you will end up going in the wrong direction. In creative literature I think quite often there is an emphasis on uncertainties and what I am saying is that there are stages in science when you need to recognise you are uncertain and even savour uncertainty but the objective, you are quite right, is to reach certainty.

MCEWAN But quantum mechanics has dissolved this into probability and of course Heisenberg has given us an apparently beautiful theorem as to why we can't know the momentum and position of the same particle. What is the equivalent of that in a novel? Well, I suppose, actually to think of a play. Frayn's *Copenhagen* has a wonderful enactment of a parallel set of possibilities through a conversation between Niels Bohr and Heisenberg.

BIGSBY I think it was Karl Marx who said that if the appearance and essence of things were the same science would be superfluous, and that is surely equally true of literature. There is a profundity in surface but on the whole the energy of a novel comes from getting beneath the surface, from a tension between the seen and the hidden. Science too is concerned less with how things appear. After all, Paul, you worked on the yeast cell.

MCEWAN We live in middle earth, don't we? Between the very large and the very small. I notice that a theoretical physicist is now proposing that time is the most real thing in the universe and it is space that is illusionary. That would be a relief for novelists because time is of the essence in the structure of a novel.

JANE SMILEY

Jane Smiley was born in Los Angeles in 1949 but grew up in Webster Groves, Missouri. She graduated from Vassar College and has an MS, MFA and PhD from the University of Iowa. For fifteen years from 1981 she was a professor of English at Iowa State University. She published her first novel, *Barn Blind*, in 1980. Among her many novels are *The Greelanders*, *A Thousand Acres* (winner of the Pulitzer Prize), *Horse Heaven*, *Ten Days in the Hills*, *Private Life* and a trilogy: *Some Luck*, *Early Warning* and *Golden Age*. She is also the author of short stories and novels for young adults. She is a member of the American Academy of Arts and Letters.

This interview was recorded on November 5, 2014.

BIGSBY You were born in California.
SMILEY I was born in Los Angeles but the family only lived there for about a year and then I grew up in St Louis.

BIGSBY You moved to Webster Groves, which is on the outskirts of St Louis. Was that a fairly upmarket community?
SMILEY Webster is a very interesting town because it varies from fairly downmarket to fairly upmarket.

BIGSBY Which bit were you?
SMILEY Both.

BIGSBY At different times or simultaneously?
SMILEY Yes, because my grandparents lived in a very, very middle class neighbourhood and my mother lived in a very working class neighbourhood. She rented the house and would take me to school and then I would walk home to my grandmother's house which was your basic wooden three bedroom house in the neighbourhood. So I knew all kinds of people. The neighbourhood where I grew up, where my mother's house was, was a mixed neighbourhood. In second grade I remember standing outside the door of the school when the first black students showed up. It was an interesting town to grow up in. Then my mother re-married and we moved to a very upscale area of town and I started going to a private school. So I lived in a lot of places and I had relatives in a lot of places.

BIGSBY You went to a private school and when you went to university you went east?
SMILEY To Vassar College, yes.

BIGSBY Why did you go east?
SMILEY Because that is what everybody in my high school did. You were expected to apply to the Seven Sisters, or if you were a guy to the Ivy League, or you might apply to Stanford. Nobody stayed in Missouri and I was glad. I really loved getting away. I loved getting out of town. I enjoyed Vassar a lot and met a whole new group of people that were quite interesting.

BIGSBY Was it a women's college when you arrived, or did it go co-ed while you there?

SMILEY It went co-ed while I was there but one of the allurements of Vassar while I was contemplating where to go was that they were playing footsie with Yale. So there was the chance that you could end up as a Yaley if you went to Vassar. But when I got there I ceased caring about that and met my own set of Yaleys. I liked the change. I liked spending the week at Vassar and then the weekend at Yale. I thought that was very nice.

BIGSBY You had been writing a bit as a teenager but did you write while you were at Vassar?

SMILEY Absolutely. I immediately took creative writing. That was my freshman class, and I kept taking creative writing and a combination of various English literature courses. I took Anglo-Saxon for four years. I took medieval literature. I took eighteenth century literature, but I kept taking creative writing. So when we had to write a big senior thesis I said that I wanted mine to be a novel.

BIGSBY What happened to the novel you wrote at Vassar?

SMILEY It's under my bed. It was about the tormented lives of college students. It was never going to go anywhere but it was a good practice novel and when I graduated from college John Whiston and I (he was a six feet ten basketball player who I would later marry) decided to go to Europe. He was a Marxist medieval historian from Casper, Wyoming, and so was unique in many ways. Anyway, we came to Europe and worked on a dig at Winchester before hitchhiking all around England. Then we went over to the continent and hitchhiked around there. We went to Greece for the winter and we looked at many cathedrals. He was a wonderful practice boyfriend and practice husband because he was really smart and told me all kinds of things.

BIGSBY You both then went to Iowa, but in your

case not immediately onto the famous creative writing programme there.

SMILEY No, we were in Crete and decided we were going to apply to only two places, Virginia and Iowa. So we sent off our applications and he got into both places and I didn't get into either one. He wanted to be able to get quick access to Wyoming. He loved the landscape there and so we decided we would go to Iowa rather than Virginia because it was on Route 80. When we got there he immediately started his class work in the history department and I got myself a job. They had this teddy bear factory, a very small factory in the living room of somebody's house. My job was after one of the other women stuffed the teddy bears I would sew the back seam and listen to all the women talking gossip. Then, about six weeks into the semester, there was a big party in the history department and John McGalliard, who was teaching Old Norse, was there and I sucked up to him and asked if I could get into his class. He said I could so I bought the book. I caught up within a week because I had had all that Anglo-Saxon and that is how I got into the University of Iowa.

BIGSBY And you eventually did your PhD on that subject.
SMILEY Yes.

BIGSBY I don't know why it strikes me as odd but there you are in Iowa doing Old English and Old Norse. What was the attraction to you of Beowulf and the sagas?
SMILEY I think it was because I had read Ole Edvart Rølvaag's *Giants in the Earth*. That was one of the central texts of my early life. It is a story of Norwegian emigrants to the Dakota Territories and it is truly in the Scandinavian tradition. Nothing funny ever happens and it starts out frightening and becomes terrifying. I thought it was really good. Why they would ever give it to fourteen-year-olds I have no idea but I really loved it and I also loved English language for whatever reason. So to read about the Angles and the Saxons and Wessex and East Anglia was really fascinating to me.

BIGSBY And you later went on a Fulbright to Iceland?
SMILEY Yes, nobody else wanted to go.

BIGSBY But out of that came a book.
SMILEY Yes. I was fascinated by the sagas and by the style of the sagas, their brutal simplicity. And while I was there a friend said to me, 'You know if you fell out of your boat in Greenland you would freeze to death in five minutes.' I said 'Wow, that's interesting.' That was the source of *The Greenlanders*. I knew that the end of the Greenland colony would be a quite interesting subject and that it would fit into the history of the Icelandic sagas so I waited for a while until I knew I could organise that bit of the subject and then I started on *The Greenlanders*.

BIGSBY Going back a bit, you did eventually get onto the Iowa Writer's Programme?
SMILEY Yes, I did get in.

BIGSBY When you were there was there a prevailing mode of writing?
SMILEY No. There was no prevailing mode of writing. We all were different and still are different. It's a fiction that writers all come out the same. The main support that most of us got, and that I got, was from my fellow students. We loved the workshop. We loved to talk about our work. We would do extra workshops just to talk more about it. Those of us who were lucky didn't pay any attention to our teachers because who cares about the teachers. We didn't want to impress the teachers. We wanted to impress each other because those were our peers. I was really lucky because my best friend the whole time I was there eventually became an editor so when I had my book ready she decided she wasn't going to be a writer but was going into publishing and was in a position to read it and purchase it. That was the benefit for me. The first book got pretty immediately published and then the second book got pretty immediately published. The problems were around the murder mystery *Duplicate Keys* because her boss didn't want to publish it.

BIGSBY You said earlier that the novel you wrote at Vassar was practice, but you have also said that your first three novels were practice.
SMILEY They were.

BIGSBY In what sense?
SMILEY They didn't seem like it at the time but when you are in your twenties, and maybe early thirties, you are trying stuff out. If you are like me you are not telling your life story, not telling your own experience, but are casting about because something interests you or you are curious about something and you are just trying to learn how to write a novel. Then what you really need is to get a little pat on your head and remain obscure because you don't want the publisher to put too much weight on your book. That makes you too nervous so you want to have the freedom to try this or try that, so Barbara, my editor, gave me the freedom to try a family book and then to try a different type of family book and then to try a murder mystery. I wrote the murder mystery specifically because I wanted to know how to write a plot. I knew that was the most highly plotted form and I was intending to write *The Greenlanders* so I knew I had to learn how to do a plot. Since I had grown up reading Agatha Christie I figured I would try that type of plot. I never felt a moment's pressure because I was just allowed to do what I wanted.

BIGSBY Is it true that you had a list of the different kinds of books you were going to write and that you wished to try different genres, different models for your books?
SMILEY Yes, I grew up reading Shakespeare. We read starting in the seventh grade and read a Shakespeare play every year and then all through high school. Then, in college, because my English classes were all medieval and renaissance, we read a lot of Shakespeare, too. I read *King Lear* lots and lots and I was always taken by how ready he was to try this or that so I wasn't intimidated. I said, well, if he can do it, I can do it too. My favourites weren't the tragedies. Probably my favourite is *Measure for Measure*.

BIGSBY There is one thing you wrote that really surprised me because you wrote an episode of the television series *Homicide: Life on the Street*.

SMILEY One of my teachers, when I was in the workshop, was a young man who was two years older than me. His name was Henry Bromell and he had just published his first book of short stories. They invited him to come and teach and then a year later he published more short stories and went out to Hollywood. He got involved in the movie and TV industry. He was the mover and shaker behind *Homeland* but also *Homicide* and somehow he talked me into writing an episode. So I wrote the episode but then of course they changed everything about it, which is what they do in Hollywood, but they have kept my name on it. That is just the way they are.

BIGSBY To come up to date, you are now engaged in a three volume novel.

SMILEY Yes. I came up with the idea of the trilogy and the title – *The Last Hundred Years*. As soon as I came up with the title I knew it was going to progress year by year. I knew that each year was going to be relatively substantial, that all the years were going to be equal and I knew that it was going to add up to way more than four hundred pages per volume. So it was going to add up to thirteen or fourteen hundred pages. It was only in the interests of the joint health of readers that I decided it had to be a trilogy rather than a single volume. I want my readers to be able to lift the thing. The alternative was to use tiny print that nobody could read so I said, 'A trilogy is the way to go,' and they said, 'Ah, OK.'

BIGSBY Each book will be a third of the story, while each year has a chapter. In other words there is a programmatic approach. What is the virtue to you of that?

SMILEY Because I am a nerd. No, when I wrote *Ten Days in the Hills* I wanted it to be four hundred and forty four pages and every day to be exactly the same and every half day to be exactly the same. That is just how my mind works. There has to be a structure of some kind in any book.

BIGSBY But that is quite a strict structure isn't it?

SMILEY Yes, it is. It started out as an idea that made the book make sense to me, so in subsequent drafts, once you have used your idea through the first draft, you can fiddle with your idea. But you do that with a plot too. Every novel, every book, needs an organisational principle. The logic of a plot is essentially an organisational principle in the way that in a memoir you go back to your memories as the organisational principle. If your story is quite loose then your organisational principle can be just numbers. All it is, is something to discipline you. So in this sense knowing that each year was of essentially equal length disciplined me to pay attention to how time was passing, what we were doing in that year, how much time we were spending on any given episode. There are some years in which there are only one or two episodes but there are other years where there are five episodes. So I really had to pay attention to how time was passing, what the season was, what would be the likely things that they were doing in that season, even if it wasn't about farming, what are the likely things that these different characters of different ages would be doing in that year. So that was my organisational principle and what it did was it made me pay attention to the progress of their lives and how old they were and what was plausible that they were like in that particular year. It also helped me not lose sight of the characters too much.

BIGSBY It strikes me that time is relevant in another way because quite a lot of it is set on an Iowa farm. Time on the farm is different from urban time so that time matters in a different sense. Sometimes a chapter is set in the Second World War when major public events are under way, sometimes a chapter focuses on a discussion about the price of wheat or buying a bicycle . You switch between them. Was that another organisational structure?

SMILEY Yes. I wanted to go back to the farm because there were still people I cared about back on the farm. I didn't want to lose sight of them. What happens if you move away from your family is that sometimes you are attentive to your family and sometimes you are attentive to your own course of action. So there was that juggling as the characters proliferate. Who was I going to pay attention to? Where is he? What is he or she doing? How are they relating to one another? In volumes two and three there is some essential pruning that has to be done. You can't kill off all the unimportant characters so you have to just push them aside a little bit and stop focusing on them because we are principally following the main characters and I didn't know exactly how I was going to do that. But that is what subsequent drafts are for. You scratch your head through volume one, through draft one, and then you re-read it and you say, 'OK, I can fiddle with this, can cut this. I can add to this.'

BIGSBY We ought to say something about Iowa, not least because you lived there for more than twenty years.
SMILEY Twenty-four years.

BIGSBY And this novel is set largely on an Iowa farm. I am always struck by the fact that when they talk of American values mentally they are out there in the mid-west.
SMILEY That's true.

BIGSBY Yet those on the east and west coasts have a tendency to condescend to what they call the fly-over states. Can you explain that?
SMILEY No. Partly the paradox is that many people leave the mid-west and so they have a nostalgic view of what is going on there but they left and you couldn't drag them back with a rope. I think that accounts for some of the nostalgia but also some of the condescension. The other thing is that one of the qualities of mid-westerners is that they don't complain, so whether they are jerks or not you hardly know because they hardly ever complain. You could have a wonderful kind, sweet, loving, darling person from New York City or Philadelphia and they complain constantly and you just think why doesn't this guy shut up but that is just the way the culture works in those towns. In St Louis, when St Louis's famous Cardinals get on the field, we all cheer. It doesn't matter

whether they are losing. In Philadelphia, the Phillies get on the field and we all boo, and it doesn't matter if they are winning. We boo anyway. That's just the culture of that town.

BIGSBY I think people also misread Iowa. Historically, it has had radical settlements, including Davenport where Germans who left in the 1848 revolution settled down, and you have your characters speaking German occasionally?
SMILEY A little bit, yes.

BIGSBY And you introduce your characters to radical politics. You also had something of a radical past.
SMILEY I was a radical politician-in-law because my six-foot-ten-inch Marxist basketball playing boyfriend from Casper, Wyoming, got to New Haven and became a Marxist. He was won over by his economics professor who was a Marxist and you know, gosh, he was six foot ten and good looking. What did I care what his political beliefs were, but it was also enlightening to me because I grew up in a family that flirted with the John Birch Society. Well, only one person flirted with the John Birch Society. Before my step-father came along, my family was pretty apolitical but my step-father flirted with right-wing politics and always voted Republican though he was a wonderful, wonderful man, so there's a conundrum for you. So, when I met my first Marxist, I said, 'Ooh,' but I have to say he was the only cute one.

They would have these arguments about the weirdest things in the commune. There was one guy in the commune who came from a very wealthy family and his last name was Parks and so one night we had a discussion, a serious discussion, about whether he should change the spelling of his name to Parx in honour of Karl Marx. Meanwhile, I, the novelist, am sitting there going, 'What in the world are they talking about?' But they were dead serious. Then another guy turned out to be sleeping with his girlfriend in our house and another girl in one of the other houses and we had a discussion about whether it was good for the commune or not that he was sleeping with two girls. Nobody ever said what

I wanted to say which was, 'What did the girls think?' So I had my issues with members of the commune but from a novelist's perspective they were absolute gold.

BIGSBY   One thing that seems to interest you in the three volumes is the interplay between the development of private lives and the public world in the background, though of course you had already done that in a way in *Private Life*, which starts in the late nineteenth century and goes through to the Second World War.

SMILEY   *Private Life* is about one of our very own familial crackpots. One of my grandfather's older sisters married this local crackpot, not thinking, not realising, what an eccentric he was. His problem was that he was born too soon and so he had already made up his mind about the nature of the universe before Albert Einstein came along. He couldn't buy into Einstein's theory. He thought it was a conspiracy. He thought it was absolutely ridiculous. He would pick up his glass and drop it and say, 'See, that's what gravity is. Don't give me any bullshit.' In our family he was viewed as just this weird eccentric that my great-aunt managed to put up with but in the larger scientific community he was viewed as an actual destructive crackpot because he had a column in the *San Francisco Examiner* where the headlines would be things like, 'The universe is filled with…' something I can't remember anymore. He didn't know what he was talking about and so I decided to investigate that guy because I was interested in a particularly American phenomenon which is that you have a population of decent well-meaning normal people and the crackpot seizes the process and drives everybody crazy but changes the discussion so that it is now a crackpot discussion, as witnessed in our most recent election. So *Private Life* is my tale of American crackpotism.

BIGSBY   Yes, but that's not all it is, because it includes the San Francisco earthquake and the influenza epidemic. There is a panoramic element to the book and the three volume novel is going to have that social panorama, is it not?
SMILEY   Yes, yes, yes.

BIGSBY And for that reason they have to leave Iowa?
SMILEY They do.

BIGSBY For one thing, Iowa is pretty solidly white so when you start engaging with race they are going to have to have left there.
SMILEY That's right. They have to leave Iowa. But I couldn't talk about every single American problem so I had to pick and choose. So race comes in volumes two and three but what interests me most is the distribution of power, the control of the food system, the destruction of the landscape and whether it is changing. Race is addressed by many other people and so I address it as best I can but it is not one hundred percent central in the way that farming is. If it were I would have set it in Ferguson.

BIGSBY And if we are talking about capturing the spirit of the age that would be equally true of *Good Faith* and *Ten Days in the Hills*, which is very funny.
SMILEY It is supposed to be funny.

BIGSBY And very sexual. I might say, extremely.
SMILEY One third graphic sex. Everybody has got to do it sometime. When I gave readings of it I would say that it was one third graphic sex and usually at the signings it would be men lined up all the way back.

BIGSBY *Some Luck* is dedicated to all your husbands, that is to say four. So, husbands past, husbands present, actually not husbands future – why is it dedicated to all of your husbands?
SMILEY Well I am on good terms with all of them and they were all –

BIGSBY Not that good or they wouldn't be former husbands?
SMILEY Yes, they would.

BIGSBY Oh, really? You left them because you were on good terms?
SMILEY I didn't leave all of them, some of them

left me. But I am on quite good terms with them and they were extremely helpful. One of them is a lawyer and he has helped me with legal issues. One of them is a pop culture person and he helped me with music and pop culture issues. One of them has an incredibly good memory so I would call him up and say 'Do you remember… ?' and he would reply and I would say hallelujah. My current husband was also an extremely bad boy and had very various episodes to recount of a bad boyhood but he is also my mentor in writing because I read to him and he tells me it needs a little of this or it is really good or whatever. So they didn't mind having it dedicated to them and the kids know we get along.

BIGSBY When I was reading the book the analogy that was in my mind was as if the book were a long narrative poem into which sonnets had been dropped. You have the master story and then you have the deliberate constraints of the chapters themselves. It seems to me that you like these challenges you set yourself?

SMILEY I do. I think what the real motivation is, is at the end of every novel, whatever the form, I say 'Oh, you know something is missing.' So, for example, at the end of *A Thousand Acres*, which I spent a lot of time and focused on quite strongly, I finished it and said, 'that was depressing.' It wasn't funny and so immediately I wanted to do *Moo*. I wanted the change. I wanted to do something funny and then I finished *Moo*, which I truly loved writing, but I said, 'Oh, not that deep; broad, but not deep,' so then I went on to *Lidie Newton* which is deep and also broad because it is a romance and she moves around from place to place. So I guess, because I am a lover of reading and a lover of literature, I understand that no form can encompass everything, no form can be all things. Some novels come close, some plays come close, but I just like to move on to other stuff. I am curious. Also new ideas demand different tones and different forms, so I knew that when I wrote *Horse Heaven* I didn't want to focus on one horse. I didn't want it to be about the fabulous winning career of one horse. I wanted there to be lots of horses which meant there were going to be lots of trainers, which meant there were going to be lots of stories. So that is just the way my mind works. I get tired of stuff.

BIGSBY We have been talking about the first volume of the trilogy but you have already written the second volume.
SMILEY And the third.

BIGSBY Which will take you up to 2019. What happens if there is another 9/11 before that?
SMILEY Well, I might have foreseen it and I might not have. We will just have to see.

ROSE TREMAIN

Rose Tremain was born in 1943 and educated at the Sorbonne and the then newly established University of East Anglia. Her first novel, *Sadler's Birthday*, appeared in 1976. She is the author of 14 novels, the latest being *The Gustav Sonata* (2016). She is also the author of short story collections and plays for radio. She is the winner of the Orange Prize, for *The Road Home*, the Whitbread Award, for *Music and Silence*, The Prix Femina Étranger and the James Tait Black Memorial Prize for *Sacred Country*, the Sunday Express Book of the Year for *Restoration* and the Giles Cooper Award for her play *Temporary Shelter*. In 2013 she was appointed Chancellor of the University of East Anglia.

This interview was recorded on October 2, 2013.

BIGSBY What brought you to UEA?

TREMAIN There is one very simple reason. I applied to UEA because I read that Angus Wilson was going to be teaching here. When you are not yet the thing you imagine yourself to be, it was as if I said to myself perhaps the proximity of a living writer would in an osmotic way transfer some genius to me. That was my main reason. Also I had the feeling that it would be fun to go somewhere that was small and new and where there was everything to be done. I remember I was involved in starting the university magazine, which was called *Decanter* for some reason. Nobody could remember why. I asked some of the 1963 lot if they could remember why and nobody could. So I was involved in that and in the foundation of the Drama Society. So, the idea of a place where you are starting from ground zero was quite enthralling.

BIGSBY Did you gain anything from your years at UEA that would lead into your career as a writer?

TREMAIN I gained the friendship and support of Angus Wilson. I didn't really get to know Malcolm Bradbury until a bit later on in my writing life. There was no formal teaching of writing then, but I remember giving Angus some probably very bad pieces of fiction and him reading them and being in his adorable way very encouraging about it. So it wasn't a time when I was really writing much in the way of fiction apart from these few small stories, but just to have that feeling that there was somebody in the literary world who knew who I was, who knew that I was passionate about this, was wonderful. It took me an awful long time, though, for me to get started. I left here in 1967 and my first novel wasn't published until 1976, so nine years went by doing bits of journalistic writing and some teaching, all the kinds of things that writers have to do when they can't make a living from writing. Then, in 1976, I published my first novel which was very generously endorsed by Angus. I think that was fantastically helpful because first novels back then were ignored and I think this helped it to be noticed.

BIGSBY You mentioned the Drama Society. Earlier this year an honorary degree was presented to the actor John Rhys-Davies, who was in the first year as an undergraduate at UEA, and was also involved in founding the Drama Society. He was in a play with you and there was a nice moment in the graduation ceremony where he walked across and, instead of the formal handshake, you hugged one another because this was the first and the second year of UEA meeting. You played the Countess, he played the Count.

TREMAIN Yes, we had been married for three days in this play.

BIGSBY Was there ever a moment in which acting attracted you, other than just at that student moment?

TREMAIN Not seriously as a profession, no. I think as a little girl I was a bit of a show off. My sister, who was older than me, was always very shy and I had to be the one who went in to see the grownups and do my party piece but not seriously, no. It was enormous fun doing student drama. I remember that John Rhys-Davies and I were really badly behaved. We were always corpsing at the wrong moment and annoying the director terribly but I could see the thrill of acting, the lure of it. It is a collaborative thing and, whatever else one might say about writing fiction, it is a very lonely exercise and in the times in my life when I have been involved in more collaborative kinds of writing, for screen and radio and so on, I have enjoyed working with other people and then, eventually, with actors. That is fantastic but I never thought of myself as an actor.

BIGSBY The reason it crossed my mind is that anyone who has heard you read will I think hear something of an actress in you. There is, though, a connection between a writer and an actor in that you both have to inhabit the sensibility of somebody else and at the same time be standing apart in some way, conscious of what you are doing. As a writer can you do that simultaneously or does the one follow the other?

TREMAIN I think there are moments where they are separate and moments where they are conjoined.

What I do know is that the voice in which one tells a story – whether it is the distant third person authorial all-knowing all-seeing voice, or whether it is internal, the first person narration, which I do favour quite a lot – is central. I suppose you could argue sometimes that this first person narrative is a cheap ventriloquism, and that has on occasion been levelled at my work, but it is a wonderful way of finding the shorthand of characters, to be able to inhabit not just the way they think, which of course you can do as the third person narrator, but the way their thoughts lead on directly to speech. So I think it is like a kind of friendship which is deeper than the friendship you have when you are writing in a third person mode. You are snuggled up closer to this person which enables you to get to know them faster, and this thing of getting to know a character I do think is really very interesting.

I like to plan in a skeletal way but leave quite a lot to chance which means that the process of getting to know a central character can be quite long, just as the process of getting to know real people is sometimes quite long. You meet them a few times and think, 'I like that person. I want to talk to that person,' and then you don't see them for a bit. Then you have to start all over again. It is a little bit like that getting to know a fictional character and I do think that one of those old ideas about characters sometimes taking over, though a terrible cliché, has an element of truth in it. Once you have got to know a character, it isn't that he or she takes over but that they have an integrity about them which they don't have when you start because you are not actually certain who they are. That integrity, which may be by about, say, page fifty, has to be respected. So it might be that down the line things you planned for them to do or say or think aren't any longer relevant, or they don't feel earned or right.

BIGSBY You are the author, you have the authority, you are creating these figures but there is, then, a kind of freedom for those characters and, anyway, writing surely generates writing. Things surprise you. The next sentence sometimes surprises you, doesn't it?

TREMAIN Yes. I sometimes liken the writing of

a novel to going on a journey, and I think this is appropriate especially since some of my novels are indeed about journeys. *The Colour*, for instance, is about an enormously long journey and the novel is a wonderful form for the voyage, the quest. But, yes, I think that that way of not absolutely knowing what is going to come next, getting on some form of conveyance and then stopping at certain stations or discovering new landscapes and having only a notional idea of where the thing will end up rather than an absolute idea is important. Absolutes, I think, have a way of crushing the imaginative invention. This is the fuel of the novel, the imaginative part. I think in my case, even with something as tiny as a short story, if I haven't left myself enough journeying room then the imagination is in some way curtailed and crushed.

BIGSBY You came back to UEA to teach creative writing and you said once that for the first few years that fed into your work. Then that ceased to be true and eventually you left. In what sense did teaching creative writing feed into your work?

TREMAIN I think it did. I taught here for seven years and I think that for the first four or five years it has to be said that I was very lucky to have excellent groups of people and quite small groups at that, so I could get to know these people really very, very, well and give them lots of attention and time. The power of a creative writing workshop, when you have got very clever people in it, is really quite potent and as the tutor of the group I learned as much from my students as I was able to tell them. In the discussions it is definitely a two way thing. I learned a lot about what they were trying to do but I would also sometimes hear myself saying theoretical things about the practice of writing which I didn't know I knew and I thought actually that is quite astute. I must write that down. So that process of analysis and having young people feed their ideas back to me was very, very good.

The reason why I began to worry about the act of teaching was what you were referring to earlier. Writing is an amalgam of the two parts of a mind, the

imaginative, unknowing, dreaming ideas which are
a product of one bit of your mind, and the other bit of
your mind which, in a long career you have honed and
cultivated. You know the actual nuts and bolts of how it
is done, the technique if you like, and what the students
wanted from me was where in their own stories they
were going wrong and certain techniques might be
brought in to save them. So the technical side of my
mind was very engaged with all of this and the technical
side of a writer's mind is very bossy and quite cross
with the dreaming side. So I began to worry that this
fragile, dreaming side of my mind would be completely
crushed by all this technique and all this knowing. This
question of knowing and unknowing is very important
in a writer's life, so that is why I decided eventually that
I had to stop teaching because the dreaming side of
my mind was throwing up ideas and the bossy side of
my mind was saying no, they are not good enough, not
funny enough, not strong enough, not this, not that. So I
thought I would wind up not being able to write anything
because it would be too censored as I went along.

BIGSBY Among other people in your group was Tracy
Chevalier. How far could you spot a real writer at the
time and how far did they flourish later?

TREMAIN In the year that I had Tracy in my group
I will say straight away that she was wonderful . She
was very generous to other people and her criticisms
were constructive, funny and very enabling. She was
working on a novel set partly in contemporary life and
partly in the seventeenth century in France and what
I quickly determined was that the seventeenth century
sections in France were very powerful. She had done her
research very well. She understood the landscape. She
understood the language. They had enormous power.
The contemporary sections were OK – she is, after all,
a writer who understands technique and can more or less
do anything – but they were much weaker. I remember
saying to her at the end of the year, and here comes the
boast, 'You know, I think I have understood what you
are really good at, Tracy, which is that you love to work
with historical time. In some way it just inspires you.

You do the research in a proper way and it allows your imagination great scope but if I was you I would put aside the contemporary material and find another idea which is purely historical.' Then she wrote *Girl with the Pearl Earring*.

BIGSBY But it is not only her that was interested in the past. Every one of the fourteen writers in this series has set novels in the past and I get the impression that, for the last twenty-five years or so, the past has been a favourite place for British writers to turn to.

TREMAIN Why does one write in the past? I think that one of the reasons is that the contemporary is so swiftly passing. Before coming up with *Restoration*, which was written in 1988, what I wanted to comment on was the materialism of the Thatcher age that we were all living through but as soon as I came up with ideas they were superseded by what was happening in the news. The contemporary is viciously hard to get hold of in something as slow in arriving as a novel. It is great for TV and film, which are made fairly rapidly. But the past doesn't move. You can say new things about it but it doesn't move around. It doesn't suddenly change. Think what happened to Ian McEwan when he was writing about East Berlin and West Berlin. The wall came down. I think another reason for turning to the past is that it is this extraordinary wonderful larder from which you can select and with which you can play. Even if it is some small thing it can transform into something quite powerful for the book. I think some people see history as a receding road. I don't see it like that. If I have to find an image for it I see it more like a great lighted mansion and I can go into any one of all these wonderful rooms and find extraordinary things. I think this question of surprise is important. If we say that history is an accumulation of knowledge, of what is known, I think what the so called historical novelist has to do is to come up with the things that are much less well known, to come up with inventions, to come up with surprise.

BIGSBY You referred to the so-called historical novelist.

TREMAIN That's because it isn't a term I like, but I have never been able to find a better one. I think it is tainted with a mediocrity and with the idea that if one is writing about the past then the work one is producing is not serious, that it is in some way escapist, that we don't have to take this seriously because, although it is set in the eighteenth century instead of the seventeenth century, it is all safely in the past so we don't all worry about it. It doesn't go to the core of the things that worry us. Some historical fictions simply tell a lovely bejewelled story which doesn't engage with our deeper sense of purpose and worry.

BIGSBY You jump around in time in your books but you also jump around in place, setting them in Denmark, New Zealand, France, America. When you set something in another country, how far is it an imagined country and how much an actual researched object?

TREMAIN When I wrote *The Colour*, which was set in the South Island of New Zealand, the idea was gifted to me. It hardly ever happens in a writer's life that an idea comes fully fashioned into my head, and I think it has probably only happened that one time, but Richard [Holmes] and I were in the South Island of New Zealand and on a rather grey afternoon we went to this little museum which was dedicated to the New Zealand gold rush. It was a small place but it had a very good display of all the artefacts, tools and clothing that were worn by the New Zealand gold diggers in the 1860s. I knew nothing about the New Zealand gold rush. I didn't know there had even been a gold rush there. I knew about the forty-niners but not about New Zealand.

There was one picture I remember in this little museum which was mainly of a group of men with their moleskin trousers and their hats and the things in which you sieve the gold back and forth. Because gold is heavier than earth it falls down, at least that is the theory. I think these things didn't work terribly well but anyway they were using very amateur tools and in this photograph there was a young woman sitting on a hard chair slightly to one side of this group of gold miners who were working incidentally in terrible conditions. I remember looking at this woman and thinking, I wonder what she is doing there? What is she doing on the goldfields? Is she prospecting for gold? Is she just supporting somebody? Why is she there? And into my mind, in that very same afternoon, came this idea about a young couple who came out from England. They had to come from England because, I said to myself, this is actually a New Zealander's story and I am not a New Zealander so I have no right to it. So they come out from England and think they are in it for the long game. They think they are going to put down roots and be farmers and eventually perhaps be the owners of a very profitable sheep ranch. Then they start their farming enterprise and are surprised, caught on the hop, by almost everything, including the weather. Then comes the news that gold has been discovered on the other side of the island. So it is a story about people who go with one idea and have to change direction. I think this is very pertinent to many lives. You go with one idea, a determination to achieve one thing which is going to take you a long time, and then, sometimes fatally, you are turned aside by something which promises something faster, success, whatever it may be. You are turned aside and then all kinds of calamities follow.

Anyway, this idea came to me in that afternoon but we were very near to leaving New Zealand at that time and when I started making notes for the novel I thought I must go back, because we hadn't been able to see very much in the time. I must take photographs. I must rediscover what this place really is. But then I started writing and couldn't fit in the time to go back to New Zealand, and the further I wrote myself into the book, the more terrified I became of going back. I thought I am just going to have the courage to do this imaginary thing and then when the book is finished I will send it to various experts. I have a couple of New Zealand friends. That was a very good illustration of how the jewel that gave me this idea was only briefly glimpsed, ridiculously briefly glimpsed, and there was this voice in me which said I must go back, I must research more, but in the end the imagination trumped that voice and said no because what you have inhabited here is this landscape which now belongs to you. It is your landscape. It is the landscape where these people are going to have their lives and you can see every inch of it, so it mustn't be disturbed.

BIGSBY I want to talk about *Restoration* and *Merivel* but it is worth remembering that you have, of course, written contemporary works and I remember when I was reading *The Road Home,* about an East European migrant coming to this country, that it felt to me that there was some kind of moral imperative behind it. Is that true?

TREMAIN It is but I hope there is a moral imperative behind all the books, some little moral nugget there.

BIGSBY But in the case of migrants, who tend to be treated with suspicion, inhabiting the sensibility of one is potentially a public gesture isn't it?

TREMAIN It is a public gesture and a dangerous one and I was aware how dangerous it was. Novelists are endlessly asking themselves if they have a right to certain stories. That book absolutely arose out of seeing a television programme about a migrant from Poland, though my character is never located in a particular country. I was very moved by the fact that he had nowhere to sleep but had made himself this shelter in a little basement area. I lived in London as a child and I remember these little basement areas. They used to have coal in them. There were holes in the pavement and the coalmen used to come, pour the coal down and it would arrive in one's little coal basement. I remember my sister and I were not allowed to go in the coal basement because my parents thought we would get filthy, which was probably true. But here was this man making his tiny living space in this thing. I was moved by that on two accounts. This space that he had for his whole existence was so small and of course it brought back memories of my own childhood and the strangeness of London in the nineteen-fifties. I thought it would be lovely to bring something like that to life but the question was whether I dare to do it. I think I probably wouldn't be able to write that novel now because the real stories are being told by immigrants themselves who are writing novels about their real experience. I did go and talk to a lot of people. In East Anglia there are a lot of Eastern European immigrants working on farms and I talked to a lot of them. I kept reassuring them that I was not a journalist, I was not going to sort of steal their stories, that I just wanted to get a flavour of it.

BIGSBY   Did you find the voice for Merivel immediately?

TREMAIN   Yes. Occasionally pieces of work have a false start, perhaps born out of the fact that this decision about what voice in which to write is such a crucial one. Yes, I wrote about thirty or forty pages in the third person. I thought this would be interesting because the story is quite fast paced but it is essentially boring. I thought I would write it all in this heightened language of Merivel himself but then chickened out and thought that I wouldn't be able to master this for four hundred pages. It was like getting into a wonderful flamboyant new suit of clothes. He is sartorially chaotic and putting these clothes on, in my mind, was an amusing and wonderful moment so I thought I am just going to go for it, and I got very, very fond of him.

BIGSBY   You said that one way into the novel was reading Pepys. What did you get from Pepys, the social world, the voice?

TREMAIN   I think a lot of things. I think that without having a very good knowledge of Pepys' diaries I couldn't have written *Merivel*. I think he has a lot of Pepys' characteristics. Pepys is always making resolutions about the things that he is going to do. He makes a resolution that he is going to pay greater attention to the Sunday sermon and then finds his mind is wondering about the colours he is going to paint his dining room or the clothes he is going to buy himself. He buys far more clothes for himself than he does for his wife. So this kind of self-delusion is how Pepys gets through his life. But he was also very clever and was interested in every facet of society. He takes you from the court to the Navy Office, to the river, to the theatre, to the coffee houses, everywhere. He is the most enthusiastic, imaginative guide you ever had through that century so, yes, I think I owe him a huge debt. When I came to read the John Evelyn diaries, which I thought I had better read, there was much less there for me.

BIGSBY Merivel is a marginal figure. He accidentally stumbles into a relationship with the King. He is ambitious. He wants everything he can get and that derives from the King, but there is a curious real relationship between him and the King who had himself been marginal for a long time, been waiting. Is that in your mind what brings the two together, that there is a point of contact outside of their roles?

TREMAIN I think there is a point of contact because he has known what it is like to be in exile and of course the irony is that in the middle of the Restoration Merivel himself is sent into what is virtual exile. The real Charles II never forgot those years of exile and the sacrifices various people made to help him. He never forgot it and that it made him strong in all kinds of ways. But, yes, the point about Merivel is that Charles II was not to be the protagonist because I think that sets up in the mind of a reader a biographical unease. Is this fiction or what? Wouldn't I be better off reading a history or a biography? So my way in is to have an invented person and to see the real people only through his eyes. To Merivel he is a kind of a god, a father figure. He is a depressive, a friend, lots of different things. He is, of course, a construct really.

That is not to say that I didn't research the life of Charles II almost exhaustively in order to write these two books because I think you really have to do that research in a scholarly way. Then you have to forget it. Kipling said that research is like riddling a fire. You build up this great white mass of data, this fine flame of data, and then what you, the fiction writer, have to do is to riddle it down until you have got this red hot nuggetty coal which is your imagination at work on that data. Graham Greene went on a visit to Vietnam with a journalist and on the way back the journalist said to Greene, 'So, you have seen some terrible things. What are you going to do with this?' And Greene said 'It's yours to remember and mine to forget.' What he meant was that it wasn't necessarily the real things he had seen that he was going to write about. He was going to transform it. It would undergo this Kiplingesque riddle. It would be transformed by his imagination to something as potent as the real thing.

BIGSBY You finished *Restoration*, the years went by, and you made some uncourteous remarks about the lack of wisdom of having a sequel. Then three years ago, when you were asked what you were writing about, you said that you were bringing Merivel back, and it was clear that you were pleased to be re-entering that world and re-introducing that character. Why did you decide to bring him back?

TREMAIN I think because he is such a vibrant character. He is so irrepressible. The adoration of life is so intense that that is quite a seductive character to have lurking in your soul somewhere and I think that he amuses people a lot. People find bits of themselves in him and I find lots of myself in him. I put a lot of myself in him, I think, in a very displaced way. So I think he called for me over the years. It is a very sentimental thing to say but I think he had this, 'Come on, Mistress Rose. Get me back.' He loves the limelight. He wished to come back. When I wrote this, nearly three years ago, just when we were hitting an extremely difficult time in our own society, I thought this was a great moment to bring him back. He is ageing. He is broke. The country is broke. The King has no parliament. It is all going a bit pear-shaped and I thought, let's see what we can make of him. He is in his fifties, which we don't think of as being old, though it would have been quite old at the time. His beloved servant Will is seventy-five, which was one foot in the grave. That was one of the ideas I started with, this idea about Will, the servant, who can no longer fulfil his servant role because he is so bent over and so decrepit that he can't carry the soup tureens. He can't wait at table, he can't do the things for which he is paid and yet Merivel's affection for Will is such that he can't sack him so he is in a terrible bind. All these ideas came in and I eventually went to see my publishers and said,

'I have got this mad idea to do the sequel.' I expected them to say 'Don't touch it. *Restoration* was a successful book so don't spoil it, but to my surprise they didn't. They said, 'Yes, it is a good time to do it. It is the credit crunch's *Restoration*, so do it now.'

BIGSBY   Merivel has reached the stage when he wants to make sense of his life.

TREMAIN   You could say that once you pass the age of sixty that is the only subject because this is when you start to measure your own life against those of your peers, against what you might have done, what you might still do, the life of your children. When we are young we are just driven by the purpose for each day and we don't think about what things mean, and what is important. This idea of finding meaning in one's existence and questioning the whole damn thing starts, I think, around sixty and that is a subject worthy of exploration. What amused me about writing the Merivel bits is that you wouldn't choose him if you wanted a life lesson. This would not be the man you would go to for wisdom, but he is struggling towards it in the only way he can, by experimentation and folly, really.

BIGSBY   He is capable of loyalty and compassion, even, in one case, towards a bear and I gather there really was a bear.

TREMAIN   There was a bear in the Jardin des Plantes in Paris and this same bear figures in a contemporary novel of mine called *The Way I Found Her*, which is set in Paris. There is something about bears, isn't there? They have tremendously sad faces, like certain species of dogs. I think they talk to us in a way that some animals don't. I found this bear entrapped literally underground. The spectators would peer down into this rather awful concrete compound and this lonely bear walked round and round gazing upwards. Children would laugh and throw things and it was a deeply terrible existence. One of the questions Merivel is endlessly asking himself is what distinguishes him, who is quite a bestial kind of person, not very good at curbing his appetites of all kinds, from an animal. He finds that he has a tremendous affiliation with animals of all kinds and that he almost feels as if they are talking to him and that he understands them. Towards the end of this book he embarks on what he thinks is going to be a serious piece of work, which is this question about 'Do animals have souls' and of course the question that he should really ask is 'Does he have a soul and where is his soul?' He has lost his faith quite early on, in *Restoration*, when his beloved and very devoted parents are killed in a fire. He thinks that a God that can take away these dutiful parents cannot be worthy of his love anymore. He has lost his faith and so has to keep asking himself these metaphysical questions.

DAVID VANN   LAWRENCE NORFOLK

David Vann was born in Alaska in 1966. He has degrees from Stanford and Cornell. His first book, *A Mile Down: The Story of a Disastrous Career at Sea*, appeared in 2005 and his first novel, *Legend of a Suicide*, three years later. Subsequent novels were *Caribou Island*, *Dirt*, *Goat Mountain* and *Aquarium*. Among his awards are the Grace Paley Prize in Short Fiction, the California Book Award, the Prix Médicis étranger and the Premi Llibreter. His work is translated into twenty-one languages.

Lawrence Norfolk, novelist and journalist, was born in London in 1963. He is a graduate of King's College, London. His first novel, *Lemprière's Dictionary*, was published in 1991 and was followed by *The Pope's Rhinoceros*, *In the Shape of a Boar* and *John Saturnall's Feast*. He is the winner of the Somerset Maugham Award and the Budapest Festival Prize for Literature. In 1993 he was listed as one of Granta Magazine's Twenty Best Young English Writers.

This interview was recorded on November 18, 2014.

BIGSBY David, you were born in a rather remote place, in Alaska but not in one of the main cities.

VANN I was born on Adak Island in the Aleutians. You could almost see Russia. That was a stupid line from Sarah Palin but it was almost true from where I was born. My father was a dentist in the Navy for two years. It was a naval base and not a place you would want to visit or live. It was for sale recently. You could buy it. There was a port, a little navy town and the forest, which was about six trees this high. There were a hundred mile an hour winds almost every day.

BIGSBY You left at the age of six, when you parents divorced. Was that a traumatic moment?

VANN Yes. In the first story in *Legend of a Suicide,* "Ichthyology," the four year old boy goes to the neighbours across the street and puts pickles in their fish tank. That was the time my parents were fighting, and those first three stories are very autobiographical. My parents were fighting a lot, especially at night. My mother would end up on the couch in the living room so I went and trashed the neighbour's house. It was my form of therapy, and it wasn't just pickles in the fish tank. It was also ketchup and mustard on the couch and yoghurt down the hallway. So it was very disturbing. I think if you are a little kid and your parents are getting divorced it can feel like the end of the world. All the rules are falling apart, but it was fine afterwards, better for both of them in some ways, and we moved on.

BIGSBY People in this country have a hard time understanding American attitudes towards guns. At the age of seven you were given a rifle. When you were nine you were given a carbine and at the age of eleven you were killing deer. If there was an element of trauma attached to the divorce of your parents was there none involved in killing animals.

VANN Yes, there was, absolutely. I killed, we killed, every kind of animal that was available in Alaska and California. We hunted and fished and basically killed things every day. It was just part of how we bonded as a family, that and playing cards. It seemed natural to me.

I have a line in the book that a child born into brutality will find it natural and it did all seem natural. It seemed good and I enjoyed it. It is fun to shoot things. The power is great and I was good at it. I shot and killed a lot of things but it was also disturbing. There were various disturbing moments. My father shot two deer with a shot in the stomach, which is very painful, and they rolled down the hill at us, screaming the whole way. I wounded a squirrel once, shot it three times up in the trees, and it just kept screaming as it was going along. The worst part about the screaming of the deer is that it sounded just like human screams. It really didn't sound different. In the book (*Goat Mountain*) I recount a real weekend from when I was eleven years old and killed my first two deer as a coming-of-age ritual to become a man. I had to kill a buck and then eat its heart and liver.

BIGSBY You actually did that?

VANN Yes, I did, and it was really a stand-in for killing a man as a ritual of coming of age. We kill large animals, I think, as proxies for the feeling and experience of killing another person, at least that is the way it felt to me, my coming-of-age as a man. And it was disturbing because the first one I shot I hit in the neck. It died right away, but when I came up to it, it looked like Bambi with its eyes open so I wasn't as excited as the men in my family at what I had just done. But the second one I hit in the spine so I paralysed it and it wasn't dead. When I came up to it, it was still alive and could look around and see me. I could sense its fear and my father made me go up behind it and put my rifle at the back of its head and execute it, essentially. At eleven years old that was really disturbing. I could never kill anything after that. I made up imaginary deer and just took wild shots and my dad would come and try to track these things that didn't exist. With real deer I would just flinch and turn away and not shoot them.

BIGSBY But that wasn't your only source of trauma, because your father shot himself?

VANN Yes.

BIGSBY And messily. I don't know how you can do it un-messily, but…

VANN But it is more messy than others. A .44 magnum pistol to the head is actually messier than others. My family thought it would be a great idea to give me all his guns after that. So I was thirteen years old and I had his .300 magnum rifle for killing bears and a 30-30 Carbine for deer and a 12 gauge shotgun, which the police use, and a 28 gauge shotgun. So of course I shot things. I shot out all the street lamps in our neighbourhood. I aimed at people in their living room windows with a shell in the chamber, so one little tap of the trigger and they would be dead. My father had had me aim at people when they would come onto the ranch. There would be hunters hunting illegally on the land and he would have me look through the scope of his .300 magnum rifle at these guys sitting on the rocks up there and with a shell in the chamber, the safety off, almost willing me to kill them. So in the very first chapter of *Goat Mountain* that is what happens. The boy pulls the trigger and that creates a very big problem for the men in the family.

BIGSBY Lawrence, you must be sitting there wondering how you could match that.

NORFOLK I gave up on sentence two actually.

BIGSBY But you did have a little trouble. You and your family were in Iraq at the time of the Six Day War and therefore were forced out of the country.

NORFOLK Yes, we were. My family moved to Iraq when I was, I suppose, two and so my earliest memories are of living in Baghdad. It was idyllic, a wonderful place to live as a child. You were completely safe. My father once accidentally left $17,000 in the back of a taxi and went into the police station to retrieve it. He was sent away. They said, 'You have to come back at teatime.' So he said, 'Why?' 'Because the taxi driver hasn't gone off shift yet so he hasn't had time to bring $17,000 back.' It was that sort of a place. There was no crime whatsoever. I think it was because they were so vicious if you were caught. Then the 1967 Six Day War happened and all the Europeans were kicked out, including us. My father was simply told to leave. He tried to drive back, unsuccessfully, and in the end the rest of us, women and children, were put on a coach and aimed at Iran, I think.

We went into the desert and when we got to Kurdistan we got surrounded by Kurdish tribesmen as if they were going to hold us up, but when they saw it was all women and children they loaded us up with food and gave us an armed guard for some of the journey. Then we went up into the mountains. I only know this because my mother told me about it, but at this stage she would always stop the anecdote and say, 'I actually can't tell you anymore' and she would get very emotional. She died a couple of years ago so now I am never going to know what actually happened. I think she feared for my brother's life. He was very young, a baby, at the time and I think it got very, very cold on the coach and she thought he was going to die, but I don't know and now I never will. So I haven't got an ending to my story, but it is a happier one, I think. I know we got through Iran.

BIGSBY   But if I flash forward a few decades, you were in danger in Bosnia, were you not?

NORFOLK   Yes. I was in Vienna at a wine festival and you wouldn't think you could get into so much trouble but I bumped into a journalist there who had read my first book, some of which is set in Bosnia in the eighteenth century, and he said, 'I read your book and I was there three weeks ago and exactly the same things were happening, the same sorts of atrocities.' The war hadn't really got going by this point and he said, 'Would you like to come and have a look and write an article for our magazine?' So it was eleven o'clock at night and you have had a few, so you say yes because you can always say no later, but of course you don't ever say no later. So off we went to Bosnia in a white VW Golf, trying to pretend to be the UN, I suppose. We drove through Serbia and then to Sarajevo and spent a little bit of time there before driving on again. I wrote about it but it was, yes, a salutary experience. It was an interesting experience, being in a war. I hadn't done anything like that before and I hated it. I hated every minute of it, and I am not going to go again, but it was interesting.

What was interesting about it was not all the things you would think. It was that you were in an environment in which you had no idea what was going to happen next. It is a radically anti-novelistic environment. The key to it was that there wasn't any logic. We used to do this thing called 'car counting'. You would be on the road and cars would come the other way so you knew that the road ahead was relatively safe because cars could come down it. So you would start to count the intervals between the cars. The longer the intervals, the more dangerous it was. Of course it was a negative knowledge. You never actually stopped the car thinking that it had been so long between cars that you had to stop, because what would you do? Go home again because you haven't seen a car? So actually you just keep going and in the end realise there are no cars coming the other way, but you still keep going, having no idea what's around the next corner. You don't know what is around the next bend. I mean it might be nothing. Often it was nothing, but then, sometimes dramatically, it is something. So that was the most interesting and disturbing thing, not knowing.

BIGSBY Lawrence, is it right that at seven you wrote your uncle's biography?

NORFOLK Yes, I did, and I sold it to him too. My uncle is a knight and a painter, so I knew he was famous and so I wrote his biography and at the end I put a list of questions for him. It was quite a post-modern production. I know that one was, 'How high is the sky?' and another was, 'What are seeds made of?' There were about twelve questions. He never answered them but he paid me ten shillings for it, which back in the day was quite good. It was only an afternoon's work, and it was self-published.

BIGSBY You went to university in London where you read English and American Literature and, surely, discovered Thomas Pynchon because his influence seems to be there in your work?

NORFOLK Yes, I did. At a certain point I realised – and this sounds obvious at this stage of anyone's life – that you are allowed to read any book you want, but for a long time when you are at school, when you are seven, eight, nine, you think, 'Oh, I can't read any book I like because I have to read Reader Level Seven,' or something like that and I can't get onto Level Eight before I have read Seven and I certainly can't do Level Nine. The idea that I could read Thomas Pynchon was a proposition from the planet Jupiter. So at a certain age I realised that you could read anything you liked and the school that I went to did have a library and I started reading . I would just pick someone and then read everything they had written. Some of them were unlikely, André Gide for example. I read everything that André Gide had written, and he only wrote two good books, *The Immoralist* and *The Counterfeiters*. All the rest are awful, but nevertheless I ploughed my way through them. I was a completest. I approached Thomas Pynchon in the same sort of spirit. Once I had started I was going to finish.

BIGSBY There was an element of happenstance about your first novel, *Lemprière's Dictionary*.

NORFOLK I went to college and you were given a list of books you had to buy for the course and amongst them was a classical dictionary. I wasn't well off at the time, though you did at least get a grant in those days even if it wasn't a huge amount of money. So I went to a remainder bookshop to try and pick up anything I could because it was much cheaper than anywhere else and I found that the cheapest classical dictionary I could find was one called *Lemprière's Classical Dictionary* which was fifty pence, or something like that. It had five stickers on it. They had started it off at a fiver and there had been no takers and down it had come until there it was at fifty pence so I bought it and got it home only to realise why it was so cheap. It had last been updated in 1788 so it was really out of date. Its utility was limited but as a work to read it was fascinating. The entries are wonderful. He was an eccentric but he did know all this stuff. In fact he had one of the most boring lives of anyone you could possibly imagine, so eventually I decided to give him the life he should have had if he had been as interesting as his dictionary. *Lemprière's Dictionary*, incidentally, was, of course, the worst title you could ever come up with. Most people can't pronounce the first word while 'dictionary' gets it put in the wrong parts of bookshops.

BIGSBY Bernard Cornwell, a different kind of writer of historical works, has said that he looks for the gaps in history, and there is a sense in which you do that too, isn't there? The facts are there but then you fill all the spaces between.

NORFOLK Yes, there has to be somewhere for you to be. This is true of David's work as well. At a very literal level you can insert a fictitious king into the pantheon of English kings and queens but you have to have a very elaborate apparatus to account for it. It is better to find a gap and then fill it. There are plenty of gaps. It is worth remembering that 99.999% of everything that happens is not recorded. It falls out of history. What we call history is a bit like drifting through space behind the Kuiper belt and every hundred thousand years you go, 'Oh, here's an atom. Brilliant. And there's another one.' That is what we have recorded from history. Every time you breathe the air curls in a particular way, the atoms change. Everything has an effect and most of it is not recorded, so there is plenty of room for artists and that is room that can't be colonised by anyone else. Historians will never get to this. It is not within their purview. Scientists might have theories to explain it but they can't describe it.

BIGSBY One thing you do in your work is to pick events that are distant from one another and bring them together. Did that raise problems?

NORFOLK With the first one. I was twenty-four, twenty-five when I started. I hadn't written anything else apart from the aforementioned biography of Uncle Pete, so I just set off. I invented things. I invented characters and stories and off I went. It was great. I enjoyed it. It was a wonderful six, seven or eight months and at a certain point I woke up to the fact that it was a novel and the realisation that all this stuff would at some point have to come together and form a conclusion. So I thought, no problem, I will take a couple of days off and figure all that out. Anyway three weeks later, three weeks in which

I thought that I would just have to start again, I had this chart which I made. It was too big for single sheets of paper so I made it out of different sheets of A4 which I blu-tacked together. There were at least sixteen, it might have been twenty. The trouble with that was that when you were one side of it you couldn't see the far side. So I would lay it out on the floor and put a stool on it. Then if I stood on the stool I could see the whole thing. I would then get down and go on with the rest of the book. It didn't follow that plan exactly but I more or less followed that outline. So the book goes off in this very chaotic way at the beginning but then works like a Swiss clock after that. Everything does come back together because I got very worried about that. I thought it would fail.

BIGSBY David, you beat Lawrence in one way because you started writing the book that became *Legend of a Suicide* at the age of nineteen.

VANN Yes, but I didn't finish it until I was twenty-nine or thirty and it got published when I was forty-two. It is not like I have won any races there.

BIGSBY So, a slow burn but a good deal happened to you in that period. You went to Stanford and Cornell universities. You wanted to be a writer but to make money you ran a business on the side. In fact you had a boat in which you taught creative writing. But life still had a surprise or two in store. You had a boat made for you and it sank when you were on your honeymoon?

VANN Right.

BIGSBY And at thirty-five you were bankrupt?

VANN Yes, my life doesn't skimp on disaster.

BIGSBY So the first book to be published wasn't the one you started writing when you were nineteen but one called *A Mile Down*, which is an account of the disasters.

VANN Right. It was supposed to be about how everything worked out. We were living the dream in the Caribbean but after the boat sank it suddenly became a publishable story.

BIGSBY Then, finally, came *Legend of a Suicide* which you can tell from the title has its roots in your own experience and was surely part of your attempt to come to terms with what your father had done. Nonetheless, it is a fiction in which you come at that central event from different directions. How did you arrive at that as a structure for the book?

VANN Well, at first it was just a big mess for a long time. I didn't know what I was doing there. I was learning to write. It consists of a novella, framed by three stories before and two stories afterwards. Each of the stories is written in a different style. The novella is influenced by Cormac McCarthy and the last story is not realistic and was influenced by Donald Barthelme. The second story "Rhoda" is minimalist from reading Raymond Carver but the third story, called "The Legend of Good Men," came from reading Chaucer's *The Legend of Good Women* and seeing the different literary structures that were possible, a series of portraits from the hagiographic tradition, writing about saints lives. I saw that you could structure a story that way, so in that story we learn about all the men the mother dates after the father had gone and the fact that the boy wants a new father. But then I saw that that could be the structure for the whole book.

Legend of a Suicide means a series of portraits of a suicide and that made sense to me because in my family we didn't have one story about my father. Because of our shame and guilt and anger we each had a very different version of who he was, what happened and what it meant. So there is a debate in style and content, stories that disagree with each other, as in *The Canterbury Tales*. That seemed to give a more full picture of what the whole experience was like. The novella within it was a huge surprise I didn't see coming but that also provides a frame for everything. It reverses and changes everything, so it is a story that un-writes itself as it writes itself. That was the only way that the whole thing made sense to me.

BIGSBY You followed it with *Caribou Island*, which is still about your family, particularly about the relationship between your father and mother.

VANN My first four books of fiction all have family stories in the background but they vary in strange ways as in *Legend of a Suicide* and the central novella in it, 'Sukkwan Island'. My father asked me to spend a year in Alaska with him and I said no. Then, a couple of weeks later, he killed himself. So I felt that if I had said yes maybe my father would still be alive and I do actually still think that is true. He might have still killed himself but not then probably. So I felt very guilty and that novella is an account of a boy and his father going homesteading for a year in Alaska. It is a second chance for me to go back and say yes to spending that year but with all the nervousness I had about my father's despair and his heading towards suicide.

In *Caribou Island* there is the murder-suicide of my stepmother's parents. I am very lucky in that I come from a family with five suicides and a murder, in very beautiful locations in Alaska and California, so I couldn't help but use it across the four books, but the stories have really transformed quite a bit. I don't remember my stepmother's parents so the characters aren't them at all and the role that my father has is just as a minor character in kind of a comedic role. The two main characters really reflected on my own marriage and were both me in a way. They were two different ways of thinking about my marriage. So the question was how could a woman get to the point of wanting to kill her husband? And I have been reassured now in many countries that it is not hard to imagine, so apparently it wasn't a difficult question but it seemed to me a question to explore.

BIGSBY One of the deaths that we haven't mentioned is of a person who when young came in and found her mother hanged.

VANN Yes, that is my grandmother's story. Her mother committed suicide when my grandmother was about ten. It is nice to have it on both sides of the family, but I don't know the true story of how her mum died because of course she didn't talk about it, no one ever told the truth about anything related to suicide. So it might have been when she was fifteen in California but it could have been when she was ten years old in Canada.

It could have been a hanging. It might not have been, who knows.

BIGSBY This is another book which takes an unexpected direction. How far are you aware when you are writing of where it is going?

VANN Not at all. I really do write with no plan, no outline, no idea what the book will be about. I didn't know there would be seven points of view in this book with four couples reflecting on marriage. I started it, restarted it. I had written fifty pages of it twelve years before and failed. Then I was on this frozen lake in Alaska in the winter and as I was walking across the ice I thought I should check how thick it was because I imagined I would be the first jerk to fall through and die on the ice after all my disasters at sea. But when I burst the snow it was just black. It is a six hundred foot deep lake and you can't tell if the ice is a couple of inches thick or ten feet thick. There is no way of telling and I realised that this could be Irene looking into her marriage. Thirty years of marriage have just become nothing and I realised how terrifying that would be and so I scampered back to the hotel, didn't get out to the island, and wrote a scene which is on page two hundred and fifty three now. It's a winter vision of going across the ice and I could see that the book would come from a character and a landscape. All my books have been generated in that way. There is a landscape which is evocative and has been important in my life. It acts like a Rorschach test, like an ink blot drying. In other words I can't describe it in a neutral way. If I start describing the forest or the water it will take shape and pattern and indicate the inside life of the characters and the themes of the book. That is where all the books come from. There is an incredible amount of pattern and structure to the unconscious or subconscious mind.

Goat Mountain as published is the same as the first draft. Not a single paragraph has been added, cut or moved. It is only line edits and is the result of just six months of writing every day and having no idea what will happen each day. But it turns out it is very structured. The Holy Trinity shows up in strange forms and in

Caribou Island there are these four couples all thinking of marriage. That to me is what is amazing about writing, that our minds are essentially pattern makers, that we don't have to have a conscious plan or outline and that our ideas and conscious plans are small and limited. I now think an idea is the worst thing that can happen to a writer and that landscape and a character with a problem are the places that I go constantly. It is then that I find out what the book is going to be about. *Goat Mountain* I was sure was about nothing and then in the last fifty pages I started to understand.

BIGSBY Lawrence, David's work is deeply embedded in personal experience, which is then refracted and transformed. Your interest in history would seem to take you a long way away from the personal. How far is that true?

NORFOLK This anecdote could be told about any of my novels, but I will stick with the first one. When I started writing *Lemprière's Dictionary* there was a thing around called 'the Hampstead Novel' which was about how a young man would come from the countryside, usually to London, and there he would have an unfortunate experience usually involving a girl, and this would take an awfully long time. Happily the unfortunate experience would be somehow solved through an unexpected twist and then the resolution of the unfortunate experience would be a final scene in which he was seen, usually in Hampstead, tap tap tapping on a typewriter, writing the book which you have disconsolately just finished reading. I was determined, above all, not to write that book and so I thought, OK, I will write a book about a dead dictionary writer in the eighteenth century accidentally starting the French Revolution and with no sex in it. That way it would leave no room for me in it. So I wrote the book and I did get almost to the end before it was pointed out to me by, I think my then girlfriend, that I, like my hero, had come from the countryside to London where I had studied and while my hero had written dictionary entries I had financed myself through the latter stages of college by writing encyclopaedia and dictionary entries. My hero had had an unfortunate botched affair with a girl, which was something that had actually happened to me. So it went on. This patterning of my life was catching up with me in the book. It was as if I was running away as fast as I could but then as fast as I wrote or ran the damn thing would still come and grab me. I then started off with the next book. I got all the way through before seeing the obvious parallels with my own life again. So it goes on. With my latest book I did know, I think about halfway through, that this was an autobiographical book. I have generally written to escape autobiography and I have failed.

BIGSBY Your first book was about an unlikely subject nonetheless with roots in the real. Your second one was equally unlikely: *The Pope's Rhinoceros*. And again, part of it was real.

NORFOLK Yes. The first book, worst title in the world, second book, brilliant title even if I say so myself. It does exactly what it says on the box. In *The Pope's Rhinoceros* Pope, rhinoceros, slowly come together. In the sixteenth century the Pope was dividing the world between the Portuguese and the Spanish. Exactly where he put the line was an occasion of great debate. Everyone wanted a little bit this way, a little bit that way, so there was a great deal of bribery going on. Leo the Tenth was the Pope, a pleasure-loving Pope, a Medici, and he had a great hankering for exotic animals so I think it was the Spanish who got him an elephant called Hanno, which gambled around in the Vatican gardens for several years. I am not making this up. It is true. Then the Portuguese, not to be outdone, imported a rhinoceros and the story that I tell is about the events surrounding the importation of the said rhinoceros.

BIGSBY It is a big book. You write big.
VANN It's a big animal.

BIGSBY How far do you write big books because you feel the need for elbow room, for a large cast of characters? Earlier you explained how you charted things out for *Lemprière's Dictionary*. This must have been one of the main challenges in this book.

NORFOLK Yes, logistics. You shouldn't get that wrong, though, because it is a mechanical skill and you can just work at it until it works. You shouldn't have people being fifty-seven in one scene and thirty-two in the next. It should work at that level. But, yes, I am a proliferator and particularly in that book I had to cut it down. I started off with the idea of five interlocking novellas and by the time I got to the end of the second one, which is the Rome section, it was already 300 pages long so I think binding technology at that time wouldn't have coped with the results. So I sliced the other ones down to size. They are just thirty or forty pages.

BIGSBY You followed that novel with another featuring an animal, *In the Shape of a Boar*. But it offers an interesting contrast in methodology. When you thought you had finished you sat down with your editor, not for an hour or two in a café but for eight hours a day for several days on end. Even when you got the proofs back you were still working on it at that stage. That would seem to be very different from the way you normally work.

NORFOLK It was necessary. It is a very complicated book. There were a number of technical challenges in the writing of it and indeed in the reading of it.

BIGSBY It has quite a few pages of footnotes for a start.

NORFOLK Yes, and they are all genuine and they are in Latin. I thought they were going to love it in Germany but I remember having an interview with a woman in Germany and she said, 'Why did you put all these footnotes in? Did you want to just make us think you were clever or something?' I said, 'Don't you already think that? Haven't I already proved that point, for Christ's sake. Just look at these frigging books.' The answer was 'No.' That was a very difficult book to write. It touches on the Holocaust, only touches. I couldn't get any closer than that, and the footnotes are intrinsic to it. It is the book I am proudest of. It is also my least popular book. It is the book that sold the least and I knew that when I published it. I knew that when I set out to write it but if I had to choose, if I had to pull one book out of the burning building, I would pull that one out.

BIGSBY David, there is another of your books which also reflects aspects of your life, albeit very different aspects than your earlier novels. It is called *Dirt* and features a particular lifestyle, California New Age. It includes fire walking, which is something you actually did.

VANN Yes, I was a true believer. I taught meditation and relaxation workshops at high school and helped with the fire walking workshops, crunching my feet across the coals. I also tried to walk on water over and over, small mountain lakes and hot tubs.

BIGSBY There is only one person I am aware of that has succeeded in that.

VANN For me, it did not work. I had faith each time that it would. I was a true believer. One of the most unfortunate parts of New Age philosophy is that it tries to incorporate quantum physics without much understanding of scale and speed so my friends and I tried to walk through walls and it was considered a cheat to put your hands up. You were supposed to have faith and just walk.

BIGSBY How did your family react to all these books in which you are engaging with your family history and your own life?

VANN I think a writer is the worst thing that can happen to a family. I mean all the shame. All the family stories are exposed for everyone to read in twenty languages. And, of course, I am a liar. It is all fiction. It has been changed, so I actually do feel bad for them. It is traumatic for them but if they didn't want to be written about they could have behaved better. I feel that it was my life I get to write about. I tell my students that they just have to put the family on the altar and swing the axe. You can't think about what they are going to feel like, but I got worried about *Dirt* at the end. I actually got really depressed for the last three weeks of writing it because I thought my mother would never speak to me again. I believed that I would never hear her voice again. So I thought about that and then went ahead and finished it. I realised that I care enough about the books that I am willing to lose all shame in myself, give up my family, give up my marriage. I don't care about me as much as I care about the books, so I went ahead and did it and when I was writing it I had these wonderful moments of guilty pleasure where I knew I was being so bad and enjoyed it, really enjoyed it. I loved writing this. It was fun writing about my family and creating a bonfire out of all their experiences. My mother really surprised me. She responded so generously and has always been like that in every way. So it turns out my family tend to be beyond my estimation of them, which is great. I feel very lucky in that way because this exposed the bad relationship that she and I have had at various times, and all of her family history with her father, being a mother and the favouritism and fights over money. It is set right in her childhood home. It is all fiction. None of this stuff happened, but it would be very recognisable for her.

BIGSBY Lawrence, there was a gap between the novel we were just talking about and *John Saturnall's Feast*, which is the most recently published, a gap of twelve years. The reason for that was that you were writing a novel called *The Levels*, a reference to the Somerset Levels, and you ditched it after how many years?

NORFOLK Eight. I worked on it for eight years, yes. It is interesting who you tell this story to. I have got a lot of friends, not writers, and they do things which come to nothing. They work on a project for a couple of weeks and present it and it just gets shot down. They have lost two weeks work. I would tell this story to them and they would get it. I have got a lot of other friends, who live in West London, and they are all bankers and lawyers. You tell them that story and they say, 'that is terrible' because they don't do that. If you are a doctor there is a patient in front of you when you come to work. If you are coalminer there is coal in front of you. If you are an artist what there is in front of you is nothing. You do something and you make something and at the end of the day you have done that, and that's that, then the next day you come and there is again nothing. There is always nothing. So I did that for eight years to try and write this book and I couldn't get it to work. There is a lot of it. I have written six hundred or seven hundred pages and I have got huge amounts of research, but we were in the middle of an auction for the book when I realised that it was all going wrong and I remember having this conversation with my agent. I said, thinking that she would contradict me, 'I think in the circumstances, Carol, the only thing I can do is ditch the book.' And she said, 'In the circumstances, Lawrence, I think that is right.' That was an interesting moment because we had both agreed and it was like holding a stone over a well and you only have to let go for an instant and it is gone. It just takes an instant. You know it is not the time it takes to drop or anything, you just have to do that for one micro second and it is gone and I felt it go. It was the feeling of eight years of my life being dropped down a hole. Then I had to go home and tell my wife. I am a writer, I am a professional writer and my income looks like a heart attack. I had to tell my wife and I said, 'I am fucking useless. I can't even pay the bills.' And I just cried. I can just about tell the story now. I was actually on the floor and the floor was wet from my crying. She was great. She picked me up and said, 'You tart. Get on with it,' and I did, but that sense of loss, those eight years, that was a lot of work, a long time.

BIGSBY The book that you wrote instead was *John Saturnall's Feast*, set during the English Civil War. Its central character is a cook.

NORFOLK Yes, it's about a cook in the seventeenth century. This is the only bit of the novel I researched really thoroughly. I would research it every night.

BIGSBY He is a cook but there is an artistry to his cooking and there is surely a parallel between his artistry as a cook, which he uses to entertain and to seduce, and the writer who is doing somewhat similar things with his art?

NORFOLK Yes. I have realised again that it is autobiography because halfway through the book he loses everything and after I had finished the book I realised that I cared because this had happened to me. I think everything gets filtered through 'I' at some point.

BIGSBY David, one thing I forgot to say about you is that you you explain at the beginning of *Goat Mountain* that have a Cherokee background, and it is dedicated to some of your relatives, who are Cherokee?

VANN Yes. There is a Chief David Vann, believe it or not. The reason I mention it at the front of the book is that it is essentially a crazy book unless you take that heritage into account, because Jesus shows up as a poacher hunting illegally on the land and has to be killed off, which makes sense from a Native American perspective. Religion as you know, has involved violence and invasion, the taking away of culture. I can only understand why I wrote the book if I think about that background because otherwise how does it make sense really and also where does my anti-Americanism come from? I have three Chiefs in my family and they were all accommodationists, which of course failed for Native Americans, so maybe through my grandfather I somehow got their resentment. It is amazing to me that you can be shaped by a heritage that you knew nothing about because I didn't know we were Cherokee all the time I was growing up. The grandfather becomes a kind of terrible Old Testament God in this book and he is the one who is Cherokee Indian.

BIGSBY The central event in the novel is the young boy seeing a poacher and looking through a telescopic sight, as you, when you were young, and given your father's guns, would look through the telescopic sight at people who were inside their houses. You didn't pull the trigger. In this book he does pull the trigger and as a matter of fact you have also written a book about a high school shooting which raises the question of American violence and how you can account for it. As far as I can see from your books, you still don't know.

VANN No, it is still a mystery why we can kill and not feel anything. How is it that we can kill and not feel bad. All stories in the Bible seem to come from the story of Cain and Abel, but we don't finish off questions in books.

VENDELA VIDA   EMMA HEALEY

Vendela Vida was born in San Francisco in 1971. She is a graduate of Middlebury College, in Vermont, and has a Master's degree from Columbia University. She is the author of *Girls on the Verge* and of four novels: *And Now You Can Go*, *Let the Northern Lights Erase Your Name*, *The Lovers* and *The Divers Clothes Lie Empty*. She is also the co-founder of 826 Valencia, an organisation that teaches creative writing to young people.

Emma Healey was born in 1985 and grew up in London. After a foundation year at Central St. Martins she completed a degree in bookbinding from the London College of Communication, subsequently receiving an MA in Creative Writing from UEA. Her first novel, *Elizabeth is Missing*, won both the Costa Book Award for First Novel and a Betty Trask Award.

This interview was recorded on September 3, 2015.

BIGSBY Vendela, can I begin by asking you about the origin of your name, which sounds like a South American dance craze but actually is European.

VIDA My mother is Swedish and Vendela is a very old-fashioned Swedish name. It was my grandmother's name, actually. My real name is Ingeborg, so put that in there and it is even stranger – Vendela Ingeborg Vida. My father is Hungarian and Vida is a Hungarian last name. Put them together and you just have mass confusion.

BIGSBY Your father was born in San Francisco, but what brought his family over originally?

VIDA My father's family migrated from Hungary at a time when lots of Hungarians were coming to California, and San Francisco in particular. My mother came to San Francisco when she was in her early twenties. She was working as a nurse and first went to Hawaii. There was a doctor there with five children and he and his wife wanted to sponsor her to come to the States so that she could be a help with them. So he sponsored her to come to California and then my parents met at a dance on Vann Ness Street in San Francisco, so my sister's name is Vanessa because that is where they met.

BIGSBY There is a reason I am asking about this because the notion of there being another place was going to be quite important in your writing and the strategy of a number of your novels. You once said, jokingly but interestingly, that you had a good beginning as a writer because you were an inveterate liar as a child.

VIDA I was a terrible liar. I was a really good liar. I would lie about everything and I was the kind of kid who was always getting in trouble in my neighbourhood. I remember one time I had a friend come over and decided to tell the whole neighbourhood that my family was adopting her and that she was going to be living with us. So that night my parents started getting dinners delivered to the door and notes saying, 'Oh how nice. We would love to help out' and they were very confused. Then, when they found out what I had said, I had to go around to every single house and apologise to every neighbour. I distinctly remember that the following week in school I was asked to write a short story, to just make something up, and the teacher said, 'great job' and I thought this is so interesting. I made something up but in one situation I call it fiction and get rewarded and in the other situation I didn't call it fiction and was punished. So there you have it.

BIGSBY You were eight or nine when you tried your hand at writing. As you grew up were you thinking of becoming a writer?
VIDA I was one of those teenagers – and I know this is going to sound very, very, unusual – who thought that they were alone in the world. I was so unusual in that way. I felt like everyone else was not as alienated as I was and I turned a lot to the Czech writers, to Vaclav Havel and to Milan Kundera.

BIGSBY How old were you then?
VIDA I was fourteen. I would do all my reports on the Czech Republic and on Havel and I would tell people I was Czech because I just felt a deep infinity.

BIGSBY You were still lying?
VIDA Yes, I was still lying and so I think I knew at that point that I wanted to be a writer as well. I had great admiration for what they were doing and felt a camaraderie in my own head. It was not reciprocated.

BIGSBY When you went to university you chose to go to the other side of the country.
VIDA I went to Middlebury in Vermont because I knew they had a really great creative writing programme and I knew there were some teachers I wanted to study with, namely Julia Alvarez, who wrote *How the Garcia Girls Lost Their Accents*. I really admired her work but my parents hadn't gone to college – I was the first in my family to go – so I had to tell everyone that I was going to study international politics and economics because that sounded very impressive. My grandmother, who was Hungarian, was so proud of me, though at first she was suspicious. She said, 'Do we have to pay twice, once for

the international politics and once for the economics?' I said 'No' and she said 'So you are getting a deal if they don't know you are pulling one over on them.' She was so proud of me and then I realised I had no talent in any of those subjects, international things maybe but nothing in economics or politics. So I came out with an English degree.

BIGSBY There is a tendency in creative writing programmes to encourage short stories because they are something containable that you can present. Were you writing short stories?

VIDA I was writing some short stories but I was never a very good short story writer. I think part of the reason there are so many short story collections in America, and so many short story writers, is because of the prevalence of creative writing programmes. When you are submitting work to a workshop to have people comment on it, it is much easier to submit short stories rather than a novel. I think professors much prefer people to work on short stories because there is something that they can perfect during that time period. So I have written short stories but it is not my strength as a writer.

BIGSBY You went on to do a MFA in creative writing at Columbia. The fees for Middlebury are currently $47,000, the fees at Columbia for the MFA are $56,000. Did you have a colossal student debt or rich parents?

VIDA Remember that part where I said I wasn't good at economics? That's how that came in. I graduated early from college because I ran out of money. I didn't even have credit so I went to work for the *Paris Review*, a literary magazine that George Plimpton edited and was based in New York. I worked there before going to Columbia and didn't really realise at the time about student loans. Because I am not good at economics it all just seemed imaginary to me, all the numbers. Going to an MFA programme was obviously not like going to law school or medical school where several years after graduation you can probably start to pay back your loans but now, when I talk to young students or people who are considering going to creative writing programmes,

my number one rule for them is, 'Unless you have a trust
fund do not pay. Get a scholarship or go to a work
study programme and choose one of the universities
that has some substantial funds to help financially,
because it is hard.'

BIGSBY How important was that time you had with
the *Paris Review*?

VIDA It was incredibly formative. I don't think
I even realised at the time how important it was to me
and my job was just to go to the office every day, which
was above George Plimpton's apartment, a very nice
apartment, and just read manuscripts and write down
what I thought. In a way that was terrible because it
spoiled me for the rest of my life. I thought that was what
life was like. You just go to work in a nice apartment and
you read and get paid for it. Then fast forward three years
because by then I was waitressing in restaurants and
was thinking, remember that time when I had a different
kind of life?

BIGSBY And is it right that you started a novel and
then threw away a lot of it?

VIDA I threw away a whole novel.

BIGSBY Was that different from the novels that you
subsequently published?

VIDA It was different and, yes, there was one novel
I worked on after I went to Columbia and got lots of
feedback on the point of view, how to annotate it and
after three years of getting this constant feedback on my
work I made a decision that I wanted to write a book and
not get any feedback. I just wanted to write it and get to
the end and it would be perfect, right, because no one
had intervened or interfered with it. So I got to the end
of the book, printed it out and stacked it up on my desk.
It was all nice and really thick, too. It was 400 pages. And
I started reading it and I kept falling asleep, it was so
boring. Then I thought, if I can't even stay awake through
this novel there is no hope for me. So I showed it to some
friends just to see what they thought. My analogy would
be if you are standing on a bridge should I jump? and

people go, 'Er, I don't know.' The same thing happened to me. I said to my friend, 'Should I throw this novel away I have worked on for years?' and my friend said 'ah' so out it went.

BIGSBY   Did you destroy it or is it in a box somewhere?
VIDA   You know, it might be in a box somewhere. I can't even look at it. I did get one sentence from it that I used in a later book and somebody, at a reading, came up to me and said, 'You know, I really love that one sentence, that description of the moon.' I said, 'You don't even know how much that means to me because it took four hundred pages to get that one sentence and I am not even kidding.'

BIGSBY   And then your first book wasn't a novel at all?
VIDA   My first book was non-fiction. It was about female initiation rituals in America and the lengths that young women go to in order to belong and whether they are going through rituals that their parents want them to go through in order to show they belong to society in some way. An example in the first part of the book would be Debutante Balls, parent-sanctioned initiation rituals. The second part of the book was about female initiation rituals that young women opt to go through on their own, gang initiation, initiations into witchcraft or young marriages.

BIGSBY   And you actually threw yourself into some of these situations?
VIDA   Yes, I did throw myself into some.

BIGSBY   It sounds a bit scary.
VIDA   Not into the gang situation, although I did get the chance to interview a lot of gang members which was easier than I thought because a lot of them were very anxious to share their stories. But with the sorority chapter – I never belonged to one and I don't think my college even had sororities – no one would answer my questions, and I was very desperate because I had a book advance, I had all these student loans and was afraid that my publisher would take back the money, so I went under

cover and pretended I was joining a sorority. That was my undercover work.

BIGSBY Can I pause you there and turn to Emma and ask about your beginnings as a writer. You have said that you thought the fact that you were the single child to a single parent had implications for you as a writer?

HEALEY Yes. I think I was more involved in the world of adults. If my cousins went to visit family members as part of a sibling group they would all be pushed to play with each other. They would have their world. But if you are a child on your own there is this expectation that you will just sit there and wait. They don't like you wandering off because you might get up to something whereas a couple of children together is somehow safer. I felt that my cousins were allowed to go off but when I visited my grandparents, or other older family members, there was just this sitting in a room listening to conversations and sometimes imagining things. There were a couple of times when I had been to see some friends of my dad's and we had all had dinner and then there was this bit where I was supposed to sit there. I remember thinking about smashing everything in their room because I was so bored, because they were talking about their university days or something. So it was definitely useful for my imagination, but I also think it was useful to be listening to how people talk, especially the older generation. I really got their voices into my head, so, yes, I thought that was useful.

BIGSBY And like Vendela it did occur to you to do writing when you were really quite young?

HEALEY Yes, I always wanted to be a writer and in fact when I was applying to do the MA here at UEA I wrote one of those covering letters you have to send in and mine was really boring. In fact I showed it to a friend to ask her what I should do. I couldn't think of a reason that I should be here and I was quite worried because my academic record is pretty poor. I felt I had to have a good hook so I went through some old exercise books from primary school and in one of them, dating from when I was eight, I had written, 'The first thing when I grow up I want to be a writer,' and I thought 'Thank God. Here's the thing I can put in my letter and say this is true.' That made me feel a lot better.

BIGSBY When you were fifteen something happened, something really quite dramatic, because you suffered from depression, a real full-blown depression.

HEALEY Yes, I had a breakdown. I was in a great school. I really loved my school, and I don't blame them at all. I just wasn't in a position to do those kinds of exams. I still feel that when we are teenagers is the worst time to make people have all this pressure. It was quite an academic school and I was fine. I wasn't a particularly un-academic child, but I just found the idea of exams absolutely appalling. I wanted out and I tried to kill myself. It is a really weird thing. I can feel it but it also feels like something that happened to someone else. It was as though I was acting in a play and when I look back it feels very distant but it meant that I had to leave school. My psychiatrist said that I should just do a couple of exams and then go. I had a year after that when I was more or less on my own the whole time, and I read a lot. I also spent the year trying to write a Mills and Boon novel because I thought that would be a way out of the world.

BIGSBY So you wanted to be a writer but the first book you wrote was a Mills and Boon, Harlequin romance?

HEALEY Yes. Even at that point it wasn't the kind of writing I would have immediately gone for but I thought if I could make it as a romance writer this would be a way of never having to engage with the world again. I could just stay in one room and write. I could just make something up over and over and over, but I wrote about 40,000 words and it was so bad, the worst Mills and Boon ever written. This was about 2011 when there was an emphasis on subverting things so in case you haven't read a Mills and Boon the main idea is that it is glamorous. The characters go to exciting locations and I thought, OK, this is great, I will subvert this and set it all in a supermarket, which, of course, was missing the

point, missing what readers actually read them for.
I was thinking, 'This is genius' and obviously it just
fizzled out.

BIGSBY   One of the founder professors of UEA was
Angus Wilson. He was a librarian in the British Library
and suffered from depression and his psychiatrist said
that he should try writing his way out of it. That is when
he became a novelist. I talked to Kurt Vonnegut who had
depression, and attempted suicide. He, too, wrote his
way out of it and was part of a survey carried out by a
university into writers, an astonishing number of whom
had suffered from depression. Retrospectively, would
you just have wished that away or does it have something
to do with who you became?

HEALEY   Oh God, that is so difficult. If I remember
the time properly I might wish it away but I probably
would have had a much more usual path. I might have
finished my GSCEs properly and done A levels and gone
to university rather than do a kind of weird roundabout
thing of doing a few GCSEs and then doing a Foundation
in Art and Design and then doing book binding, getting
further and further away from what I actually wanted
to do.

BIGSBY   You went to art college and that was in your
family. Your parents went to art college but, as you say,
you didn't go there to be an artist but to do bookbinding,
which seems incredibly unlikely?

HEALEY   Yes. It is totally useless.

BIGSBY   Well, not totally useless.

HEALEY   There are a few people who can make a
living out of it but not many and also I was really bad at
it. The whole idea of book binding is how neat you are.
At the end of every session you are judged on how clean
your paper is and how perfect your book is and I would
have bits stuck to my hair and grubby bits on the book
where the glue had dribbled and I had had tried to rub it
of. It was always just this big mess. I could do the sewing,
because you can just unpick that like any sewing, but
as soon as glue was involved, or even if you had to pare

down leather so that it was really thin, I couldn't do it. So it was never going to be a career.

Then I worked in a book shop for a long time and that made me realise things about books. It helps you to see what people are reading, what people are enthusiastic about, and it makes you become more realistic about what kinds of books are out there. I think it wasn't until I got a proper job that I really started to write because that is when you are you suddenly think, 'Am I going to do this forever? No, I am going to write something and not do this office job,' even though I have never had a bad job.

BIGSBY So you were writing in the gaps between doing other things, as, Vendela, presumably you were doing the same thing when you were bussing tables as a waitress.

VIDA I worked in publishing in New York after graduating from Columbia and I realised that that wasn't a good way to get writing done. I had a friend who was also working in publishing and she and I would call each other at five in the morning to wake each other up and say, 'OK, it is time to write. Let's write before we go to work.' It was only years later – she is also a published writer, now – that we both admitted that, after these five am phone calls, we would both promptly go back to sleep but we had to keep up the act for each other. I think it is very hard to have a full time job and focus on your own work and so I chose waitressing as a way to get my writing done because I could pick my own hours. It certainly wasn't a job I took home with me. I could leave the restaurant and leave my work behind.

BIGSBY We had a writer here, W. G. Sebald, who for years wrote academic books and then began to get frustrated because he wasn't allowed to make things up, this being the basis of academic books. Then he began to write his fictions which are a blend of historical, biographical, fictional material. You began with a non-fiction book. Were you feeling a similar frustration?

VIDA I switched from non-fiction to fiction because I think I did experience that frustration. I had interviewed all these women, all these young girls across America, and had thousands of interviews all transcribed and tape-recorded in the little room I rented in New York. I built a bed in a loft so I could have my office downstairs in this one little tiny room in the East Village. I had files and files of interviews and sometimes I would read through them and think, 'Oh gosh, if that girl had just put it this way, her quote would be so much better.' Couldn't she just have said it this way?' And it was really frustrating because, of course, I couldn't change it. So I thought, next time I am just going to make the whole thing up, then I can make it sound how I want it to sound.

BIGSBY And then your first novel, *And Now You Can Go*, was published and it has a rather startling first line: 'It was 2:15 in the afternoon of December 2 when a man holding a gun approached me in Riverside Park.' Was that always the starting point?

VIDA That was always the starting point of that book. Actually, no, now that you have said it, I am remembering there was an addition to the one sentence and there are about four pages in that book that I threw away that were about a hold-up in Riverside Park. I had a Professor at Columbia who always said that if you ever get stuck when you are writing try and think about what it would look like in a different medium and I really took that to heart. I really admire the way that plays start at the very last minute. Somebody walks into a room and something has happened, so I just wanted to start this book the way a play would start. It doesn't matter what happened before if somebody has a gun.

BIGSBY So here was somebody who suffers a trauma, a gun placed to her head right at the beginning. Later she leaves the country for a while and although your books are very different they have certain similarities and one is that notion of a trauma and the other is leaving the country. The characters are displaced. I suppose it comes back to me asking the question about your parents and being immigrants because when you leave a country you don't only see that country differently, you see yourself differently. That seems to be true of a number of your novels. People discover places but more importantly discover something about themselves.

VIDA I have always been interested in the fact that there are two kinds of novels exemplified by *The Odyssey,* a story about the person who goes away and the story about the person who stays home. I have always been interested in the story of the person who goes away. I have always loved stories that start with someone travelling to another country. I love Bohumil Hrabal's short stories. I love stories about people coming to America. I love Colm Toibin's *Brooklyn,* a novel I very much admire. I think there is something so interesting about starting with someone coming to a new country because, as you say, it is not just that they are discovering a new country, they are seeing themselves without any of the factors that made them who they were back at home. At home they might have been a postal employee or a mother or a daughter and then they arrive in this new country and they can be anything. No one knows who they were. No one knows what their title is.

BIGSBY Your second novel, *Let the Northern Lights Erase Your Name,* is embedded in some way in your family history, isn't it?

VIDA Yes, it is set in Northern Scandinavia where Finland, Sweden and Norway all come together in Lapland. I don't know about you, Emma, but there are things I heard about when I was about eight or nine that tripped my imagination. It sounds like that was the case for you, too, in some ways. I remember my mom talking about the Sami people, the indigenous people of Northern Scandinavia, who have suffered a lot of the same issues and troubles and plights that indigenous populations have all over the world. My mother had a pair of little Sami reindeer boots that she gave me and I just knew that one day I would write a novel set there. In fact I still have those Sami reindeer boots on my desk. They are very small and they can fit in the corner. They are quite beautiful.

BIGSBY Your character suffers real trauma. Her mother has walked out on the family. Her father has died, although he turns out not to have been her father. So, underlying this, and even more strongly in your most recent novel, is this question of identity. If you don't know who your father was, if you don't know the circumstances in which you were conceived, even where you were conceived and your mother walks out on you there is this sense of problematic identity?

VIDA She goes in search of her father and manages to find out the answer to her past and that is very much a quest. You know I have always been interested in identity. Even the first non-fiction book was about girls trying to find their identity. This recent book, *The Diver's Clothes Lie Empty*, is about someone losing their identity so it is just a subject that I have been interested in forever, and I think I will continue to be interested in.

BIGSBY Is it true that Ian McEwan has had some influence on your work?

VIDA Yes, there is a novel I haven't written yet but have started. I interviewed McEwan on stage in San Francisco in a situation very much like this. It was a great honour because I always admired his work and he, his wife and my husband Rick, all went out for dinner afterwards and I was telling him a story and I don't know if this ever happens to you but when you are telling someone a story that you have always been interested in it suddenly it occurs to you that there is a reason I am interested in this. I haven't written that story yet. It is set in New Zealand, so now I have to go to New Zealand because of that.

BIGSBY Is that going to be the next novel?
VIDA Maybe it will be. You have just rekindled my interest in that.

BIGSBY Emma, I left you before you had arrived at UEA and you were writing a book. Did you have readers then? Were you part of a group?

HEALEY Yes, I think I wouldn't have kept going otherwise. I had a writing group that I came to slightly by accident. I remember the first session where I gave them about five hundred words. I was so nervous I didn't want to give them very much and I can remember going home on the tube afterwards. Basically what we did was just read it out and mark as we went, so I had all these scripts where they had written their comments and I promised myself I wouldn't read them until I got home. So there was a support network of people I could call and say, 'God, they were so mean to me,' or whatever, but I couldn't resist so I started reading them on the Tube and they were all so complimentary and sweet and kind it made me feel as if I had written something that was going somewhere. I then couldn't wait to get off the Tube to call people and say, 'Oh, it went really well.' If it hadn't been for them…

BIGSBY Why did you come to UEA if you already had that support group?

HEALEY I guess it is the next level. I had been working full time and had been enjoying it but it felt as though there were these two separate parts of my life and it was getting harder as well because as you get further into a job it takes up more of your mind. I also thought, if I am serious about this shouldn't l prove it to myself? Is it going to be a hobby where I just like to get the feedback of ten people who are nice to me or am I actually going to try and see if it is something more? I also had the feeling that I didn't want to be on my deathbed and think, 'I wish I had tried going to UEA.' So I thought, OK, this is a good moment. I had dinner with my dad and I said to him, 'I think I have to do something new. I have to maybe go to Argentina or something,' and my dad said 'No. You hate travelling. This isn't something you actually mean, but how about an MA?' So I applied and I didn't expect to get in because my academic record was terrible, but I spoke to one of the tutors who did my interview and he said he hadn't noticed until I mentioned it. So he went back and looked at my recent records and said, 'Oh, yes. You really were not qualified. We shouldn't have let you in.'

BIGSBY *Elizabeth is Missing*, which is the book you did eventually finish, took you about five years to write. It is a book which owes something to your family.

HEALEY Yes, it really is based on both my grandmothers, one of whom has dementia. She was the spark for the plot idea. She was in the car with me and my dad and she said, 'My friend is missing.' It turned out that her friend wasn't missing. She was just staying with her daughter in another town, but it made me think very clearly about her position. Just for that moment it made me feel as if I had a better handle on what she was going through. Then, of course, that dissolved and I had to work hard to get back into it but it made me think, what if her friend was missing? What if she couldn't remember her friend was staying with someone else? What would she do? Also, I could feel that difference in our positions because I was in my early twenties and I thought if one of my friends went missing people would take me fairly seriously or I could go places. I could talk to the police. I could Google them. Also I had a better network of friends than she did with her friends at that time. So it just made me think about her position and I began to write the book, though I really wasn't sure about it because I was twenty-two when I started thinking about the idea and I was writing about an eighty-two year old. I thought it was incredibly arrogant and ridiculous and the worst first novel idea ever. So I tried to write a book that was about a young woman in her twenties and her jobs and her boyfriends and what living in London is like when you are young and, as you were saying about your novel, Vendela, it was so tedious. Even writing it was so tedious, let alone reading it back to myself. There is also the embarrassing thought that you are writing a diary, or at least people might think it is a diary. So they would judge you for anything that was happening. I just felt like I couldn't let go of those inhibitions.

So I went back to Maude and then, just at that moment, my mum's mum, who I was incredibly close to, died. I knew she was dying and we went to the hospital. I had a horrible two hour train journey on which I didn't really know what to do with myself. So I wrote down all the stories I could remember her telling me about her early life and when we got to the hospital I went through them with her, partly as something nice to do, because she loved reminiscing and was a very good story teller, but also to prove to her that I had been listening to all those stories. I wanted to say like, 'Look, I have them and they mean something,' and I could check names and stuff that I had forgotten. Then, when she had died, I had all these stories although I didn't really use many of them. The only one that went straight into the book was that she really was chased by a mad woman who hit her with an umbrella as she ran across the road. That was too good not to put straight in the book, but other than that it really just gave me the confidence to depict someone else's time, another voice, and made me think about her. So some of the turns of phrases and things are more her than anyone so, yes, it really is the two grandmothers.

BIGSBY Did you find it easy to find that voice and how much of a vocabulary would a person have who is suffering from dementia?

HEALEY I found the voice surprisingly and slightly worryingly easy. I think I am quite old inside and maybe it was this thing about being in the room with older relatives and feeling that that was the conversation I always felt more natural than being at school. Yes, there were things like vocabulary that were more interesting, especially when it came to dementia and how certain things just go out of your head. When I did a lot of the research into dementia you expect there to be a logic to the words you might forget but there quite often doesn't seem to be. So it was a kind of going round the houses as they try to describe something when they haven't got their tools for it. I found that really fascinating. I did originally have an idea that in the last chapter her language would have whittled down to a hundred words but it was just too hard. It was almost impossible to make it even the slightest bit interesting so I felt that was too much of a test for myself rather than something which would actually be interesting to read.

BIGSBY Vendela, your new novel, *The Diver's Clothes Lie Empty*, is once again concerned with identity because it is about someone who goes abroad and suffers a theft. Her belongings are stolen and she goes to the police. She is offered the belongings of someone else and accepts them and therefore assumes another person's identity, becoming an actress whose job it is to assume yet other identities.

VIDA   In *The Diver's Clothes Lie Empty*, as you were saying, the protagonist comes to Morocco and her things are stolen and she becomes the person whose identity she steals. There is a film set at her hotel with a famous American actress starring in it. She recognises the famous American actress and through a series of events the producers on the film set ask her if she can be a stand in for the famous American actress so she becomes one.

BIGSBY   Emma, when you are writing do you do so in bits and pieces which you then assemble or are do you work logically through a text?

HEALEY   In bits and pieces. I tend to keep a novel plan because I have to know where the bits and pieces are going to go but I can't write A to B. I had a workshop group in Norwich and a couple of times people would say, ' I don't really know how to do the next scene,' and I just said, 'Jump ahead and just do another scene.' One of my friends actually said, 'What sorcery is this you speak of?' but I couldn't write A to B.

BIGSBY   Is it right that you colour code your text at its various stages?

HEALEY   Yes, I colour code and put different things in different fonts. So, if I have written something that needs to be changed that might be yellow and if I have shown it to someone that might be pink or if it is halfway written or if it has not been written then it is another colour. So I spend a lot of time changing the colours, which is great procrastination.

BIGSBY   This is not the end of your weirdness, though. As I understand it when you are writing about someone who is in an enclosed space you go in a cupboard. Is that right?

HEALEY   There is a scene in the book where Maude is nearly pushed over a staircase. I did ask my boyfriend to…

BIGSBY Push you over a staircase?

HEALEY Push me over a staircase. He did refuse, but I did actually fall down the stairs accidentally and that definitely changed the way I then wrote a scene.

BIGSBY Vendela, do you always know where you are going when you are writing?

VIDA No, in fact I don't like to know too far in advance what is going to happen to a character. I want to be surprised by where the characters go and the choices they make, so I try not to think too far ahead.

WRITERS IN CONVERSATION
WITH CHRISTOPHER BIGSBY
VOLUME VI

Boiler House Press, 2017, in association
with The Arthur Miller Centre for
American Studies

All interviews took place as part of the Arthur
Miller Centre for American Studies International
Literary Festival at the University of East Anglia

International © 2017
retained by individual authors
Selection and arrangement copyright
© Christopher Bigsby as editor

This book is sold subject to the condition
that it shall not, by way of trade or otherwise,
be lent, resold, hired out, stored in a retrieval
system, or otherwise circulated without
the publisher's prior consent in any form
of binding or cover other than that in which
it is published and without a similar condition
including this condition being imposed on
the subsequent purchaser

A CIP record for this book is available
from the British Library

Design by Thomas Swann
Printed and bound in the UK by Imprint Digital
Proofread by Imogen Lees

Distributed by NBN International,
10 Thornbury Road Plymouth PL6 7PP
t. +44 (0)1752 2023102
e. cservs@nbninternational.com

ISBN: 978-1-911343-13-4

BOILER HOUSE PRESS

978-1-911343-13-4 £15.99